本书中文部分由赵若辉博士和熊海燕博士译自英文原作。
作者在此表示深深的感谢！

刘建宏 著

# 犯罪功能论

## Functions of Crime

人民出版社

刘建宏，国际犯罪学领域著名学者。1993 年获美国纽约州立大学博士学位，之后在美国任教多年，于 2002 年获终身正教授。2007 年起，任澳门大学教授。现任亚洲犯罪学学会会长，西南政法大学法学院院长、讲席教授、博士生导师、博士后导师，重庆市特聘专家。

曾在《司法季刊》、《英国犯罪学》、《犯罪学》等国际顶级学术刊物及多种主要国际杂志和书籍上发表大量著述，并应邀担任多种国际著名杂志的编委，包括国际顶级的社会科学引文索引期刊《定量犯罪学》(SSCI)编委，《犯罪、法律与社会变迁》(SSCI)、《国际罪犯矫治与比较犯罪学》(SSCI)专刊特邀编辑及副编辑，《澳大利亚与新西兰犯罪学杂志》(SSCI)专刊特邀编辑。目前任《亚洲犯罪学》主编。

曾获国际犯罪学会青年学者奖。曾与美国犯罪学学会会长麦斯纳教授及张乐宁教授共获美国国家科学研究基金奖，在中国进行犯罪学研究。2006 年获美国国务院福布来特学者奖。自 2009 年起，当选为世界著名学术组织"康拜尔合作组织刑事司法领导委员会"委员。2011 年应邀在"犯罪学斯德哥尔摩奖"（又称"犯罪学诺贝尔奖"）颁奖学术会议上作主题发言。在学术活动中为消除西方社会对中国的偏颇认识、促进中外学者的合作交流做出了有益的贡献。

Professor Jianhong Liu, is one of our great Asian criminologists, a towering leader and President of the Asian Criminological Society. In this book he adds a signal contribution to Durkheimian criminology. It is about the idea that disapproval of crime builds social solidarity, while fear of crime has more mixed and divisive effects. These central questions of criminology are addressed with a freshness of empirical rigor.

——John Braithwaite, Professor, Australian National University, the winner of First Stockholm Prize in Criminology, Known as "the Father of Restorative Justice"

刘建宏教授是一位优秀的亚洲犯罪学家，一位领袖学者，同时也是亚洲犯罪学会会长。在本书中，刘建宏教授对传统迪尔凯姆犯罪学理论做出了标志性的贡献。其观点论证了社会通过对犯罪的否定营造社会团结，而对犯罪的恐惧感则产生混合和分化的效果。作者以严谨的经验分析对这些犯罪学的中心问题作出了新颖的回答。

——约翰·布莱斯怀特，澳大利亚国立大学教授，犯罪学斯德哥尔摩奖首位获奖者，被尊称为"恢复性司法之父"

This is an insightful book that examines the subtle and complex ways that crime affects the social order by in some cases promoting fear and in other cases cultivating social solidarity.The author skillfully integrates diverse literatures to formulate an intriguing theoretical model and assesses this model with sophisticated statistical techniques.The careful and thorough analyses shed new light on a core topic of sociological criminology.

——Steven F. Messner，Professor,State University of New York at Albany, President of American Society of Criminology

这是一本充满见地的著作。它研究犯罪对社会秩序的微妙复杂的影响方式。在某些情况下，犯罪增加恐惧感；但在另外一些情况下，犯罪会培养社会团结。作者富于技巧地综合了多种领域的不同文献，制定出一个富于启迪的理论模型，并采用前沿的统计方法来验证这一理论模型。这些细致而透彻的分析对这些社会犯罪学的核心论题作出了重要的新贡献。

——斯蒂文·F.麦斯纳，美国纽约州立大学教授，美国犯罪学学会会长

A provocative study of the consequences of crime for society.

Professor Liu's analyses of the relationships of crime and social solidarity have important implications for China today.

——Peter Grabosky, Professor, Australian National University, Past President of Australian and New Zealand Society of Criminology

一项富于冲击力的关于犯罪对社会影响的研究。

刘教授对犯罪与社会团结关系的分析对于当今中国有着重要的意义。

——彼得·格拉波斯基，澳大利亚国立大学教授，澳大利亚和新西兰犯罪学学会前会长

Criminologists typically study specific criminal activities and individuals and do not pay much attention to crime as a larger social phenomenon in its own right. Concentrating on its negative effects is only part of the issue. A better understanding requires a scientific lens that has a much broader focus and that considers its relationship to social cohesion and institutions. In this important and refreshing work, leading criminologist Jianhong Liu draws upon the classic work of sociologist Emile Durkheim in reformulating old questions using more contemporary ideas to provide enlightening new ways to consider the broader impacts of crime in society. In doing so, the theoretical framework that Liu develops regarding the functions of crime will undoubtedly be of great interest to sociologists, criminologists, and students alike.

——Henry N. Pontell, Professor, University of California at Irvin,

Past Vice President of American Society of Criminology

犯罪学家通常研究具体的犯罪活动和犯罪个人，却很少注重把犯罪本身作为一个更大范围的社会现象来研究。集中研究犯罪的负面影响仅仅是这一问题的一部分，而一个深入的理解需要采用一个具有更广泛视角的科学的透镜来研究犯罪与社会凝聚力，犯罪与社会建制之间的关系。在这本令人感觉耳目一新的重要著作中，犯罪学的领导人物刘建宏教授从社会学家爱米尔·迪尔凯姆的经典著作出发，采用现代犯罪学的概念，重新审视并重新建构迪尔凯姆提出的古老问题，提出了研究犯罪对社会产生广泛影响的富于启迪的崭新框架。将犯罪在社会中的影响这一老问题用更加现代的启蒙新思想展示给读者更多广阔的思考方向。这本书提出的关于犯罪功能的理论框架将毫无疑问地对社会学者、犯罪学者及学生们具有很重要的借鉴作用。

——亨利·N.庞特尔，加利福尼亚大学教授，美国犯罪学学会前副会长

# 目 录

1

# TABLE OF CONTENTS

# 避免历史的遗憾

## ——发展犯罪功能研究的视角
## （代序）

犯罪和社会秩序都是刑事法学中亘古不变的话题。刑事法学家们研究犯罪,究其根本原因之一是犯罪对社会造成危害,威胁社会秩序的稳定。传统的刑事法学研究,尤其是在国内,一个重要的关注点是个人和案件层次上社会危害性的大小。学者们通常根据刑事案例及犯罪人的具体特点进行理论探讨和逻辑思维,达到对其社会危害性的准确认定。这类研究构成了刑事法学研究的重要基础。这些研究及其理论和逻辑方法对刑事法学建设和发展的重要性是不言而喻的。

但是,从犯罪学家的角度来研究犯罪,视野还需要进一步拓宽。谈到社会以及犯罪对社会造成的后果,一个必要的视角是从整体上来观察和思考犯罪与社会的关系。这至少应包括两层意思:一是全面考察犯罪对社会的后果;二是这种考察应当在宏观及微观等不同层次上全面进行。就犯罪的社会后果而言,犯罪危害社会是显然的;而从另一方面看,犯罪对社会的功能恐怕不是一个简单的议题。早期的社会科学大师迪尔凯姆(Durkheim)在他的第一部重要著作,即他的博士论文——《社会劳动分工》(1893)中首次提出:"犯罪是正常的,因为任何社会都不可能完全没有犯罪而存在"(1982,p. 99)。犯罪"在社会生活中扮演了正常的角色"(1982,p. 102)。迪尔凯姆(Durkheim)指出了一个与常人不同的观察犯罪的视角,他进一步提出一个的命题:犯罪有促进社会整合的"正"功能。他解释说,犯罪聚集正义感;这种强化的社交促进社会团结。犯罪产生的义愤使人们聚集在一起,促进社交,提醒人们什么是他们所共有的,从而促进社会团结。

迪尔凯姆(Durkheim)的观点提出迄今已一百余年过去了,而关于这个问题的专门研究在主流犯罪学文献中几乎屈指可数。他的关于犯罪正功能的论题可以说被主流犯罪学完全地冷落了。但笔者认为迪尔凯姆(Durkheim)的观点是十分深刻的,有着十分重大的发展潜力。基于这样的认识,笔者选择了发展迪尔凯姆(Durkheim)的犯罪功能论作为博士论文的课题。博士论文完成至今又有十余年过去了,犯罪功能这一视野仍然没有得到主流犯罪学家们的重视,涉及这一议题的研究仍然十分鲜见。笔者认为这是一个历史的遗憾。这种状况也许与人们对迪尔凯姆(Durkheim)的犯罪功能命题有重要的误解有关。有人甚至批评提出犯罪的"正"功能是标新立异,并没有任何理论上的重要性。所以,先对这样的误解作些解释是十分必要的。

批评犯罪功能论的主流学者往往犯了一个错误。他们和迪尔凯姆(Durkheim)考虑问题的视角并不相同,他们忽略了观察对象和层次的重要区别。批评者通常的研究视角是个人或者案例,他们的重点在于关注自己身边的人和事。故所观察到的是犯罪案件和受害者,犯罪的社会危害性即负面功能在这个层次上自然是显而易见的。这种观察的层面相对而言是一种微观的层面。而迪尔凯姆(Durkheim)在论述犯罪功能时并不是着眼于犯罪事件和与犯罪有关的个人方面,而是着眼于社会以及犯罪如何影响社会整体。这是一种宏观的观察视角。迪尔凯姆(Durkheim)的犯罪功能论是一个宏观层次上的理论。社会是他的研究对象,他将社会视为一个整体、一个社会体系来研究。他考察犯罪与社会在宏观层次上的关系,犯罪是一种社会现象,而不是一个具体的个人或案例中的行为。在社会这个宏观层次上,迪尔凯姆(Durkheim)可以观察到在个人及个案这样的微观层次上所不能观察到的犯罪的"正"功能这一现象。在这个层次上,迪尔凯姆(Durkheim)的犯罪功能命题考察社会秩序、社会整合这些高度抽象的概念,直接触及社会科学中最抽象的议题。迪尔凯姆(Durkheim)作为一名社会科学家,是从一个拓宽了的视角上来研究犯罪和社会的关系,这一视角有着独特的价值。

另外,迪尔凯姆(Durkheim)的犯罪功能论的视角有助于全面地研究犯罪对社会体系造成的全部后果。近百年来,刑事法学的传统主流观点天然假定犯罪是恶,是需要加以打击、威慑和控制的社会现象。仅从这方面看问题不利于从理论上对犯罪在不同层次上的全部后果采取一个更加中性从而冷静的观察,排除了犯罪在任何层次上可能体现出的即使是间接的"正"功能。而迪尔凯姆(Durkheim)的功能论有将犯罪的全部正负功能统一在一个理论框架中加以共同研究的潜力。

尽管如此,迪尔凯姆(Durkheim)的犯罪功能论在今天看来毕竟存在着许多不足之处,需要发展。

首先,其理论的相关概念存有不足。

第一,他的功能概念太过简单。在迪尔凯姆(Durkheim)的犯罪功能论中只有正功能这一个概念,这显然是有所欠缺的。即使是从宏观层次上观察犯罪与社会的关系,关注犯罪的正功能,也并不代表要忽视其负面的后果,即借用另外一位社会科学大师罗伯特·金·莫顿(Robert King Merton)在《论理论社会学》(1967)一书中的"负功能"的概念。犯罪功能论应该是包括犯罪的正功能及负功能,并成为一个综合的全面的理论。

第二,他的犯罪概念也过于简单。在现代生活中,犯罪具有多样性或"异质性",不同犯罪的主要后果应该有所不同,至少暴力犯罪的主要后果和非暴力犯罪的主要后果应该是不同的。从迪尔凯姆(Durkheim)对犯罪功能的论述中可以看到他所指的犯罪不是大量反复存在的暴力犯罪,至少它们不足以驱散和分离人民,相反倒使他们聚集在一起,从而达到社会整合的功能。这样的犯罪概念不能揭示出犯罪的"异质性"和不同性质的犯罪产生不同后果的复杂性。

第三,他的命题未包含其他反映现代社会生活的标志性概念。例如,与犯罪功能概念关系最为密切的当代犯罪学文献是关于犯罪恐惧感的研究。这些研究发现现代大都市内的暴力犯罪造成的恐惧感有分化社会的功能。都市中心地区的严重犯罪将有条件搬走的中产阶级驱离市中心区域,后果是造成城市人口分布的结构性改变。因此,恐惧感在犯罪功能的研究中应具有中心地位。而迪尔凯姆(Durkheim)的传统理论不包括这样的重要概念。

其次,迪尔凯姆(Durkheim)理论的逻辑关系也过于简单。

第一,理论中只有犯罪和社会整合两个概念,只有犯罪增加社会整合这一条单一的逻辑命题,未包括其他也一定存在的更为复杂的逻辑命题。例如,犯罪的直接效果的命题、犯罪的间接效果的命题及概念之间相互作用的命题。一个较完整的理论必须包含较全面反映社会生活的重要概念和逻辑命题。

第二,迪尔凯姆(Durkheim)的理论未反映犯罪功能的多样性。他只提到犯罪增加社会整合这一功能,而功能的内容应具有多样性,包括正功能、负功能等。只是"社会整合"这一功能远远不能代表人们社会生活的全部,也就无法准确地表明犯罪与社会的关系,以及犯罪给社会带来的影响。

本书继承迪尔凯姆(Durkheim)的犯罪功能命题,对其进行概念和逻辑上的扩充和发展,以产生一个较为完整的新的框架,一个新的犯罪功能论。除犯罪的社会整合功能外,笔者进一步提出四项功能,涵盖现代社会生活中的四个重要方面。这些包括:(一)犯罪对社会结构的影响;(二)犯罪对司法执法状况的影响;(三)犯罪对社会生活综合满意度的影响;(四)犯罪对人们未来社会生活预期的影响。增加的四个功能中的前三个功能反映犯罪的主要后果,而最后一个功能动态地反映了犯罪的期待效应。这样的发展在逻辑上具有相对的完整性,体现了犯罪功能本身应具有的多样性,基本抓住了社会生活的本质方面,能够比较全面地反映犯罪的社会后果。

笔者的犯罪功能论对迪尔凯姆(Durkheim)理论的逻辑架构进行了发展,提出社会整合的决定作用。新的犯罪功能论指出犯罪并不直接影响上述增加的四个社会功能,仅直接影响社会整合,通过对社会整合的影响去影响其余的四个功能。如果犯罪对社会整合功能的这一影响得到了控制,犯罪就不会再造成其他的负面后果。

新的犯罪功能论的一个重要特点就是把迪尔凯姆(Durkheim)的犯罪功能论现代化,增加"恐惧感"作为与社会整合同等重要的新功能。而恐惧感与社会整合共同影响其他四个社会功能。新的犯罪功能论明确提出犯罪对其他四个功能的影响也需通过对恐惧感的影响来实现。如果犯罪的恐惧感得到了控制,犯罪就不会再造成其他的负面后果。

新的犯罪功能论中提出了社会整合与恐惧感的相互作用的命题,指出恐惧感减少社会整合,而社会整合也减少恐惧感。这些命题反映了犯罪及其功能之间的复杂关系。新的犯罪功能论从概念上和逻辑命题上对迪尔凯姆(Durkheim)的原始命题作出了诸多发展,构成了一个更能反映犯罪及其各种功能间复杂关系的命题体系和逻辑框架。

新的犯罪功能论是许多思考的结果,但一个理论的真正价值并不在于它思考的精妙,而在于事实是否的确如此。现代犯罪学强调的是对理论的经验证明而不是理论本身概念和逻辑上的高明。研究工作的最大特点就是强调小心、精细地处理数量分析过程中的困难,采用先进的方法来更加准确地估计理论模型中的结构系数。这些结构系数告诉我们这一理论在多大程度上为真。在国内犯罪学领域中,我们已看到各种各样的理论,这种情况在国外早期的犯罪学研究中也不鲜见。但是,在现代犯罪学学术研究中,天才猜测的能力固然可贵,但还不是犯罪学家"功夫"之真正所在。思想的结论、逻辑推理的结论在经验层次上是否的确证明为真,命题可否证伪才是犯罪学家们关注的焦点。典型的犯罪学研究花在"小心求证"上面的功夫通常远大于花在"大胆假设"上面。上乘之作中花在小心仔细地克服从度量到分析、验证过程中各种各样的困难上的篇幅往往大大多于假设的提出和理论证明的部分。

在本书的写作中,前半部提出的新的犯罪功能论从理论方面发展了迪尔凯姆(Durkheim)的命题,而后半部的篇幅则是在"小心求证"上面,例如犯罪功能论命题的中心概念,如"社会整合"、"恐惧感"等都是高度抽象的概念,所涉及的相关命题也是以社会体系为研究对象的。这种抽象性和一般性决定了度量上的较大困难,度量误差不可避免如何解决?

笔者采用构造度量模型的方法解决这一问题,这种度量模型可以有效地描述度量误差。在统计分析过程中,通过对度量模型的估计来反映度量误差的影响。进一步在结构模型的估计中考虑了这些误差的影响,从而达到对结构系数较为准确的估计。又如,在笔者提出的犯罪功能论模型中存在社会整合与恐惧感相互影响的命题。这样的相互影响在统计估计中是较为复杂的。这些系数估计的复杂性也在统计分析中得到了充分的考虑和较为恰当的处理。

这项研究是十余年前所作的,一些学生读后大力推荐在国内出版。赵若辉和熊海燕将英文原著译为中文,在此我表示十分的感谢。研究所用的数据资料取自于美国多年前的社区调查。大概会有人有误解,担心资料是否会

"过时"。这又牵扯到方法论上的一个认识。笔者同意这样的观点:理论研究不同于政策研究。政策研究关注的是研究的及时性,对时间和空间的敏感性。一个再好的政策换了空间和时间就有可能"过时"。而理论研究追求的是抽象性、一般性和相对普适性。一个理论观点要有价值首先要有清晰的理论论证,然后更重要的是要有经验的支撑。不同时空条件下,不同资料来源的重复验证是最理想的状态。但研究人员比较现实的期望是发现一套可获得的资料,包含着严格验证其理论所必需的各种主要元素。例如资料包括所有必需的理论变量,资料的收集有较高的质量保证等。在这样的条件下,研究的结果将能提供一组较为可靠的经验证据,对理论包含的经验命题作出较可靠的证实和证伪。不同时空条件下新的数据的再次证实和证伪将会增加或减少我们对理论的信心。在抽象理论的研究中,这实际上不太多见。应当看到,"一套"数据和分析提供"一套"证据,"另一套"数据和分析提供"另一套"证据。在抽象命题的研究中,数据是否"过时"不是一个真正重要的问题。

　　国内犯罪学研究尽管已经取得了很多的成绩,但在很多方面尚未得到充分的发展。目前尤为突出的不足之处在于方法论方面,与现代犯罪学发展的水平尚存在较大的差距。在国内出版这本《犯罪功能论》,除了希望能将"犯罪功能论"的研究视角在国内传承下去,另外也希望与国内同仁在方法论方面增加交流,相得裨益。

　　是为序。

刘建宏

**参考文献**

Durkheim, Emile. 1984. *The Division of Labor in Society*. Translated by W. D. Halls, with an introduction by Lewis A. Coser. Mcmillan Pulisher Ltd.

Durkheim, Emile. 1982. *The Rules of Sociological Method*. Edited with and introduction by Steven Lukes. Translated by W. D. Halls. Mcmillan Press Ltd.

Merton, Robert, K. 1967. *On Theoretical Sociolog*. Mcmillan Publishing Co. Inc.

# 第一章 导 言

　　犯罪的功能性是长期存在于社会理论中的经典问题。这个问题最初由迪尔凯姆(Durkheim)在其有关社会秩序和社会组织的理论概念中阐述。跟许多犯罪学家不同,迪尔凯姆(Durkheim)并没有将犯罪看做社会的异常现象,他将犯罪看做是融合于社会体系中的一个社会现实。与犯罪学主流不一样的是,迪尔凯姆(Durkheim)在论述犯罪时并不是着眼于犯罪事件和与犯罪有关的个人方面,而是更多地着眼于社会以及犯罪如何影响社会等宏观层面的问题。但是,尽管现代犯罪学理论研究从迪尔凯姆(Durkheim)处借鉴甚多,他的著作中所蕴涵的这层意思仍被忽视了。

　　综观迪尔凯姆(Durkheim)有关犯罪功能的论述,笔者认为,迪尔凯姆(Durkheim)针对犯罪提出了两个问题:(一)犯罪在社会体系中扮演了什么角色?(二)犯罪是如何扮演它的角色的? 很显然,这两个问题着眼于社会而不是着眼于犯罪事实和与犯罪有关的个体。

　　对于第一个问题,迪尔凯姆(Durkheim)认为,犯罪"在社会生活中扮演了正常的角色"(1982,p.102)、"犯罪是必要的"(1982,p.101)。他提出,犯罪对于维持社会秩序发挥了重要功能。从这个角度来看,犯罪和偏差行为是经常的、综合的与正常的。犯罪有增强社会团结的功能。

　　为了解释犯罪如何实现其增强社会团结的功能,迪尔凯姆(Durkheim)指出,"犯罪汇集人们的正直良心并将它们集中起来。当出现丑闻时,我们不得不注意到将会发生什么。这种情形在小镇上表现得尤为明显。人们在街道上互相拦住对方，相互拜访，一起谈论发生的丑闻，引起的公愤越来越大"（1933，p. 102）。犯罪的功能假说来自于迪尔凯姆（Durkheim）运用一般功能的观点对社会体系的分析。它是迪尔凯姆（Durkheim）关于社会秩序和社会组织的一般理论的重要的不可分割的部分。不过，迄今为止，犯罪学的理论和研究并没有真正注意到这一主题的重要性。

## 一、选题意义

尽管已有若干先例（例如，埃里克森（Erikson），1966；因韦拉里提（Inverarity），1976；劳德代尔堡（Lauderdale），1976；布鲁姆斯坦（Blumstein）等，1976 等），对犯罪的功能的研究总体上并没有得到应有的重视。跟社会科学尤其是犯罪学的飞速发展相比，最近几年几乎没有相关研究成果发表。虽然近年来定量分析方法获得蓬勃发展，却很少有采用严格的定量分析方法作出的相关研究成果。该论题在犯罪研究领域中少有问津。对迪尔凯姆（Durkheim）有关犯罪功能论述的研究未获得发展的原因之一大概是因为其理论与实际政策上的意义并不直观。这一课题受限于几个方面的情况：该题目孤立于犯罪的其他理论研究；功能论点未能很好地融入宏大的犯罪学理论和研究主体中从而未得到很好的发展；研究者缺乏广阔的理论识别能力来揭示该论题的理论重要性，且没有同犯罪学的其他现代研究领域联系起来。因此有关犯罪功能的理论既没有得到过系统的发展，也没有一个系统的研究计划使之发展壮大。显然，笔者首当其冲须讨论该论题的重要性。

首先，犯罪的功能从理论上来讲是非常重要的。犯罪发生在社会中，因此对犯罪的研究从逻辑上来讲有两个出发点：一是犯罪，一是社会。大多数犯罪学理论研究着眼于犯罪事实和与犯罪有关的个体的层面，而鲜有从社会这个研究层面进行研究的。

笔者认为，迪尔凯姆（Durkheim）关于犯罪的论著很大程度上代表了这种导向，但是它却被大多数人忽视了。犯罪的功能涉及许多重要的宏观社会进程，这些进程对理解社会和犯罪而言是至关重要的，其著作堪称经典。他告诉我们,理解犯罪的功能对理解社会秩序和社会组织而言是极其重要的。如果我们没有很好地理解犯罪的功能,我们就不能说自己理解了犯罪;同样,我们也不能说自己理解了社会。

迪尔凯姆(Durkheim)探讨了犯罪的主要功能:犯罪促进团结。社会呈现出许多新面貌,犯罪的功能也在发生变化。可以毫不夸张地说,犯罪改变了许多社会进程并对社会的许多方面产生重要影响。如果不明白犯罪在这些重要的社会进程中扮演的角色以及如何扮演这一角色,我们就不能对这些社会进程有全面的理解。对犯罪功能的研究将使对社会体系和社会进程的理解置于犯罪学背景之下,同时也是在广泛的社会研究基础之上对犯罪进行研究。这对发展社会理论和研究犯罪而言都是十分重要的。

其次,犯罪既有原因也有后果。大部分犯罪学理论研究针对的是犯罪的原因。犯罪学家们致力于解释是什么因素促使个人犯罪,为什么有些人犯罪而其他人不犯罪。学者们提出了许多理论并对之进行检验。理论和研究已经证实有许多社会的、文化的、经济的、心理的和生物学上的因素能够引起犯罪。沿此方向的理论与研究一直以来发展迅速,以致我们关于有关犯罪原因的知识也得到了系统性发展。在犯罪学的这个研究方向上,犯罪是犯罪学的逻辑出发点与焦点。

然而,犯罪还会产生后果。人们关心犯罪是因为它的后果。我们研究犯罪的原因很大程度上是因为我们觉察到并且认为犯罪会对社会生活造成严重后果。基本上可以说是犯罪的后果,特别是负面后果,使得犯罪学研究变得重要。其次,犯罪的后果迫使人们去研究犯罪的原因。因此,了解犯罪的原因固然重要,对犯罪的功能或者后果的研究亦不可小觑。充分发展的犯罪学不光要研究犯罪的原因,同样也要研究犯罪对社会造成的作用或后果。研究重点应是犯罪作为一个正常的社会现象对社会的作用或影响,而不应是人们为什么犯罪。

再次,从实用角度来讲,研究犯罪的功能或后果对社会控制而言是十分重要的。许多犯罪学理论认为,犯罪原因根植于社会结构和社会文化构造。例如,莫顿(Merton,1938)认为,美国文化对目的与手段的重视程度不一,它强调物质利益而轻视达成这一利益的合法手段。美国的社会结构具有的一个明显特征,就是经济和社会机会的不平等分配。通过合法行为不能达到的目的与能力所及的手段之间存在的矛盾,使得弱势群体采取非正常行为以适应这种矛盾所带来的压力。研究证明,经济不平等、贫穷、种族不平等都与犯罪有关。应当承认,我们很难通过控制这些结构性原因来控制犯罪。但对犯罪功能或后果的研究提示着另一种可行的犯罪控制方法,即减少犯罪的后果。笔者认为,犯罪后果和犯罪严重程度之间并不是简单的一对一线性联系;相同犯罪率在不同社区会引起不同后果。犯罪率和犯罪社会后果的严重性之间不必然成比例,其他社会因素在这个过程中起重要作用。

以犯罪的一个社会后果——恐惧感为例,研究表明,社区的高犯罪率并不必然与高犯罪恐惧感成正比(唐纳利(Nonnelly),1989)。居民对社区特定的犯罪问题的评价以及他们被害的个人风险并非与官方统计的犯罪率高低相对应。这说明我们能够运用有关犯罪后果的知识来改变与犯罪有关的社会过程以控制犯罪后果的危害程度。

在研究犯罪功能时,笔者建议分析两种犯罪后果之间的差异。一是犯罪对受害人造成的直接后果,可将之称作犯罪的个体后果;一是犯罪的社会后果,其事实上对社会的危害更大。具体而言,犯罪的发生不但影响了受害人的个人生活,也深刻地影响了社区这一团体的生活。迪尔凯姆(Durkheim)指出,"毫无疑问,谋杀是一种罪恶,但不能说谋杀就是最大的罪恶。什么会减少个人对社会的负担,或者使社会机体的细胞减少? 如果犯罪行为一直得不到惩罚,公众安全将受到威胁"(1984,p.33)。因此,犯罪的社会后果更为重要和深刻,使得犯罪学研究成为一个重要的学术领域,也使得对犯罪功能的研究变得重要。本书将从社会整体水平出发研究犯罪的社会后果。

# 二、研究计划

确定某一研究领域的中心问题是在该研究领域取得实质性进展的前提。通过下一章对该领域著作的回顾,我们将看到,由于缺乏系统性指导,对犯罪功能研究的关注显得十分松散。过去有关此论题的研究局限于迪尔凯姆(Durkheim)的犯罪功能说,它孤立于犯罪学的其他研究领域。此种研究多是为了阐述和发展迪尔凯姆(Durkheim)有关犯罪促进社会团结的犯罪功能理论,论题范围十分狭窄。事实上,迪尔凯姆(Durkheim)关于犯罪功能的论著回答了两个问题:(一)犯罪的作用是什么? (二)犯罪在社会中如何发挥它的作用? 这样概括后,我们发现这两个问题蕴涵着犯罪学研究的新方向。考虑到除了促进团结外,犯罪还有其他功能或效应,我们将这两个问题扩展为两个相似的问题:(一)犯罪具有哪些作用? (二)犯罪是怎样实现它的作用或后果的?

第一个问题要求我们在社会进程的各个阶段和不同的社会体系中系统地考察犯罪的功能。也就是说,我们要考察犯罪引起、改变或者影响了什么社会进程? 特别是犯罪对人们的社会生活、对社会的经济资源、对社会文化、对人们的政治态度以及社会发展造成了什么后果? 哪些社会制度受犯罪影响? 这些受犯罪影响的社会制度发生了怎样的变化?

第二个问题是关于犯罪对社会过程与社会组织产生的各种主要后果。它要求我们首先要找到影响社会过程和社会主旨的重要变量,犯罪在其中发挥作用;然后解答这些变量之间的因果关系,亦即提出关于犯罪功能的理论。现代社会中犯罪的许多功能都没有得到系统的考察和论证,自然也缺乏关于犯罪和其他变量怎样影响犯罪的后果以及这些变量在影响犯罪后果的过程中是怎样相互作用的系统理论。最后我们应当问:这个理论对政策蕴涵什么样的启发?

这些主要问题实际上重新定义了关于犯罪功能的研究范围,并使我们能在新的系统框架下进行经验研究与理论探索。这个新框架可以方便地包容过去相关的犯罪功能经验研究。本书提出的问题也为这一领域规划出了新的研究任务。这些任务要求我们在广阔的背景下考察这个论题和相关研究领域,而不再局限于迪尔凯姆(Durkheim)的较初步的传统理论。

# 第二章　文献回顾

## 一、迪尔凯姆(Durkheim)的理论

对犯罪功能的研究与发展是独立于犯罪学其他领域的研究的。有关犯罪功能的研究大多围绕迪尔凯姆(Durkheim)的论述,非常有限,仅仅涉及了少数有限的问题。大多数相关研究是历史性的,并具有实地观察性质(埃里克森(Erikson),1966;斯科特(Scott),1976;康纳(Connor),1972;本耶胡达(Ben-Yehuda),1980;登特勒(Dentler)和埃里克森(Erikson),1959)。少数具有理论检验性质(劳德代尔堡(Lauderdale),1976;劳德代尔堡(Lauderdale)等,1984)。相关研究可以大致划分为四个密切相关的证题:社会团结、压制性司法、界限维持以及刑罚的稳定性。

首先,以往研究的重心在于证明犯罪在加强社会团结方面的功能。传统的犯罪功能说假定社会结构功能是保持社会的价值、目的和需要。迪尔凯姆(Durkheim)在分析常态与病态的区别时(1982, pp. 85 - 107)指出(1982, p. 98),犯罪"……是公共健康的一个因素,是任何健康社会不可或缺的要素"。他谈到(1982, p. 99):"犯罪是正常的,因为任何社会都不可能完全没有犯罪而存在。"对他而言,违法和犯罪起到促进社会团结的功能。只有当违法率超过特定社会类型的标准时,才是不正常的。

为了论述犯罪的正常性,迪尔凯姆(Durkheim)说道:"假设有一个由居住

在模范的、完美的修道院的圣人们组成的团体。在这个团体中没有犯罪,那么小错就会上升为丑闻,就像犯罪与一般道德的关系是一样的。因此,如果这个团体有权审判和处罚,它也会判定这些小错为罪行并采取相应的处罚措施。出于同样原因,极度高尚的人将自己最轻微的道德过失看得跟大部分人眼中真正的罪行一样严重。"(1982,p. 100)迪尔凯姆(Durkheim)还指出:"这就可以解释为什么一些行为虽然对社会并无危害,但经常会被认为是有罪的并按照有罪来处罚。"(1984,p. 61)

对犯罪功能的研究大部分是历史回溯性(埃里克森(Erikson),1966;科瑞(Currie),1968;康纳(Connor),1972;本耶胡达(Ben-Yehuda),1980)并具有观察性质(登特勒(Dentler)和埃里克森(Erikson),1959;斯科特(Scott),1976)。这些研究力图阐明犯罪是如何促进团结的(埃里克森(Erikson),1966),或者是如何不能促进团结的(本耶胡达(Ben-Yehuda),1980)。例如,埃里克森(Erikson)在其名著《放任的清教徒》(*Wayward Puritans*)中谈到,偏差行为通常来讲是有价值的,它提供了对整个社会生活都必不可少的范围和尺度。埃里克森(Erikson)详细阐述了违法和犯罪怎样促进社会团结,而这种社会进程是迪尔凯姆(Durkheim)不曾清楚表述的。埃里克森(Erikson)指出:"偏差行为人违反被社会上其他人极其尊崇的行为准则;当其他人共同表达他们对施害者的愤怒并出来作证时,他们比以前更加团结。换句话说,犯罪的刺激加快了团体内部相互作用的速度,并且促使许多单个人的个体情感融合成为一种道德常识。"因此,对埃里克森(Erikson)来讲,"犯罪通过提供一个集体情感的焦点使人们对相互之间的关系产生感觉,从而促进社会团结……偏差行为使人们对自己在团体中分享的利益以及组成社会公共道德的价值更加关注。"(1966,p. 4)"每次团体谴责偏差行为并通过正式仪式来处置违反者时,就会进一步确立行为准则的权威,重申该团体的容忍底线。"(1966,p. 13)

另外三个议题与第一个议题——犯罪的社会团结功能理论紧密相关,并且都是从中发展出来的。第二个议题是压制性司法。迪尔凯姆(Durkheim)分析了不同类型的社会如何根据其司法实践的性质来维持社会团结。他根据社会团结的基础提出了社会类型学理论。一种是机械类型,一种是有机类型。根据迪尔凯姆(Durkheim)的理论,不同社会对犯罪的反应是不同的。在机械型社会中司法往往受到限制,通过散乱的仪式性惩罚方式重申一般价值;而有机型社会往往是以恢复性司法为特征的。

关于压制性司法的历史性研究要数埃里克森(Erikson)关于发生在17世纪马萨诸塞州清教徒社区的"犯罪的三个波段"(1636年反律法主义争论,17世纪50年代后期贵格会(Quaker)迫害,1692年塞勒姆巫术恐慌)的分析。他指出,团结的瓦解,术语叫做"界限危机",会导致压制性司法剧升,造成"犯罪波段"。通过这一历史性分析,埃里克森(Erikson)证明了这些事件如何帮助定居者定义其正在形成的社会的界限。

詹姆斯·M.因韦拉里提(James M. Inverarity)(1976)用定量分析方法并建立了因果关系模型来检验巩固的南方(Solid South)民粹主义者的分裂与私刑之间的关系。因韦拉里提(Inverarity)分析了民粹主义者叛乱期间路易斯安那州的私刑状况,私刑是对所谓罪犯的仪式性的惩罚,较为典型的是,社区的大部分人都会参与对罪犯所进行的公开的私刑。因韦拉里提(Inverarity)以民粹主义者叛乱期间运用的私刑这种整个社会都参与了的惩罚仪式作为迪尔凯姆(Durkheim)压制性司法的解释。他指出,巩固的南方(Solid South)是南部白人"机械型团结"(mechanical)的一个实例。他将机械型团结描述为黑人所占比例、城市化程度和宗教的同质性这三个变量所引起的不可测因素。其分析结果支持埃里克森(Erikson)的"界限危机"导致压制性司法一说。

因韦拉里提(Inverarity)的著作一直以来遭到了广泛的批判(蒲伯(Pope)和拉金(Ragin),1977;威瑟曼(Wasserman),1977;伯恩斯提特(Bohrnstedt),1977;巴格兹(Bagozzi),1977;伯克(Berk),1977)。批评者们质疑其检验的严谨性,南北战争时期路易斯安那州的民粹主义运动是否真的形成界限危机,上述因素是否可以用来测量机械型团结。

第三个密切相关的议题是界限运动论。为了解释犯罪功能为何并且其如何促进社会团结、维持社会体系,埃里克森(Erikson)在详细阐述迪尔凯姆(Durkheim)观点的基础上提出了"界限维持论"。埃里克森(Erikson)说道:"社区就是对界限的维持:每个社会不仅在地理范畴内,而且在文化范畴内,都有其特定的范围,并在特定范围内形成该社会自己的'精神特质'或'方式'(1966,p.9)。""那么人类社会集团的成员总是将他们自己限制在特定的行为规范内,认为特定规范外的行为是不当的或者是不道德的。从这个意义上来讲,人类社会可以说是维持着它的界限。这样群体才得以保持其文化的完整性,并自发性地约束扩张,除此之外,要求严格地遵循与周围环境的相融性。"

紧张理论(Strain Theory)(莫顿(Merton),1938)、差别接触理论(Differential Association Theory)(萨瑟兰(Sutherland),1939,1947)等将犯罪当作非正常行为越过特定社会体系的道德边界的产物。与这些理论不同,埃里克森(Erikson)指出:"界限不是社会集团的不动产。当群体中的人们找到新的方法来定义其领域的外部界限,找到新的方法来扩张他们的文化,界限就改变了。"(1966,p.12)"……只有经过处于群体边缘的人的不断冲击和代表群体内部道德观的人的不断捍卫,边界才有意义。因此,每当社会集团要谴责偏差行为并举行正式仪式来处置违反者时,就会进一步确立遭受侵犯的行为准则的权威,重申该团体的容忍界限。"(1966,p.13)于是埃里克森(Erikson)认为,通过标明群体生活的外部界限,偏差行为赋予其内部结构独有特征并支撑其框架,在该框架中人们对自己的文化特性形成有序观念(orderly sense)。"(1966,p.13)

帕特·劳德代尔堡(Pat Lauderdale)(1976)详细论述了道德的边界问题。他就此问题进行了实证研究。帕特·劳德代尔堡(Pat Lauderdale)将讨论限制在"共同的"社会体系中——成员可以共同行动,人们彼此独立并负有责任。他试图解释偏差行为概念和数量如何在独立于行为人之外的特殊社会体系中改变。帕特·劳德代尔堡(Pat Lauderdale)提出了一系列假说并检测了其关于偏差行为人越过特定社会体系道德界限的产物。

他安排社会工作小组的成员讨论一个少年偏差个案。在了解了案件背景后,每个成员需要表明其喜恶程度,从十分喜爱到处以极刑。一个同伙,也是一个偏差少年,选择了一个极端立场并坚持该立场。30分钟过后参与者被告知存在有外在威胁。一个代表刑事司法权威但并未参与小组活动的观察者告诉小组的领导者(也是实验者)"这个小组或许不应当再继续下去了"。对有外在威胁和没有外在威胁这两种环境之间的变化进行评价与讨论的结果表明,当社会体系受到外部威胁时,不论其行为如何,偏差行为人会遭到更强烈的抵制或诬蔑;外在威胁是内部威胁——偏差行为者的放大器。外在威胁指向先前并不明显的内部偏差行为者的潜在危险。这种抵制或诬蔑与社会团结的流失与重建以及与道德边界的压缩有关。

第四个密切相关的理论是惩罚的稳定性假说。在谈论犯罪的正常性时,迪尔凯姆(Durkheim)提出了惩罚的稳定性假说:"如果当社会从低级形态进化到高级形态时,犯罪率(表明年度犯罪数与人口数之间关系)呈下降趋势,我们就可以认为,尽管仍然维持着表面正常,犯罪仍在丧失其正常性。然而,这一假说缺乏立论基础。许多事实表明事情在向相反方向发展。"(1982,p. 98)"如果每个社会类型没有达到或超出可能和先前准则所设立的标准,且并非不可能修复的,犯罪的存在就是正常的。"(1982,p. 98)"当侵害行为频繁发生时,人们就会去容忍这些行为。因此,行为的犯罪性与其发生频率成反比。对处于社会下层的人来讲,针对他们的犯罪要比文明社会中更为常见。"(1984,p. 98)既然假定犯罪是有功能的,犯罪也就是稳定的。

埃里克森(Erikson)(1966,p. 25)明确指出:"一个社会所遭受的偏差行为的数量总是随着时间的流逝而保持不变。"他进一步解释道,"这是一个简单的逻辑事实,社会所注意到的偏差行为的数量受到该社会所采用的监控、控制手段的局限;在此范围内,该社会的偏差率至少部分体现了社会控制手段的尺度和复杂性。"(1966,p. 24)"……社会提出其偏差行为的定义,它包含的行为范围大致相当于控制手段的可用范围——帕金森律的反用(Inverted of Parkinson's law)。"(1966,p. 25)

埃里克森(Erikson)(1966,p. 25)考察了关于一个社会的出轨行为随着时间过去而大致保持不变的假说。艾塞克斯郡(Essex County)地方法院卷宗档案被埃里克森(Erikson)誉为"全面覆盖了所有偏差行为"(1966,p. 165),以该档案为基础,他计算了1651年至1681年间每五年的犯罪率。他得出结论:在美国某地区的某个历史时期,犯罪率相当稳定(1966,p. 181)。

布鲁姆斯坦(Blumstein)和同事(布鲁姆斯坦(Blumstein)和科恩(Cohen),1973;布鲁姆斯坦(Blumstein)等,1976;布鲁姆斯坦(Blumstein)和莫特拉(Moitra),1979)致力于研究这个课题。在他们的带动下,出现了大量理论测试性研究。由于大部分建构在迪尔凯姆(Durkheim)的观点之上,这些研究旨在表明刑罚率在多个西方国家（包括美国）一定时间内都保持得相当稳定。他们试图证明刑罚的稳定性并确定其中的因果关系过程。他们用时间序列技术来检验美国 1926—1974 年间、加拿大 1880—1959 年间、挪威 1880—1964 年间监禁率的稳定性。他们将监禁率随时间而发生的变化解释为随机误差（random error）。他们认为，这些国家的监禁率是由稳定过程产生的。劳马（Rauma）（1981a）再次分析了这些数据。他认为无法清楚地说明是否由稳定过程或不稳定过程得出这些观察数据。他（1981b）进一步提出单一的时间序列分析不能揭示隐含的因果关系过程。布鲁姆斯坦（Blumstein）和陈（Chen）（1973）考察了美国重罪和轻罪的犯罪率和逮捕率之间的关系。他们的研究表明，逮捕率总体上是保持不变的。因为当总体犯罪率上升时，轻罪的逮捕率下降；当犯罪率下降时，轻罪的逮捕率又会上升。布鲁姆斯坦（Blumstein）等人（1976）也分析了加拿大的守法公民、罪犯和囚犯之间的波动与转换率。他们推论，这些组群之间的波动与其观察的结果大致相当。

批评者认为布鲁姆斯坦（Blumstein）和同事选择特定历史时期进行分析（例如：卡哈兰（Cahalan），1979）、所使用的刑罚率的概念（例如：沃勒（Waller）和陈（Chan），1974）以及运用的统计方法（劳马（Rauma），1981a，1981b）都有问题。然而，尽管他们的研究确实存在问题，比如对模型研究不足，布鲁姆斯坦（Blumstein）和其同事在模拟社会进程和检验假说稳定性方面的尝试还是在很大程度地刺激并促进了对稳定性假说这一议题的研究。

在认真考察了稳定性假说和布鲁姆斯坦（Blumstein）的著作后，伯克（Berk）等人（1981）建立了一个动态刑罚模型，该模型将布鲁姆斯坦（Blumstein）的模型作为一个特例包含在内。他们用平衡方程组来导出一套复项函数模型来表示他们的平衡趋向的假设理论。平衡方程式能够精确地模拟一个平衡系统，该系统围绕被称为系统目标的特定常数保持平衡。在这个方程式中，如果出于某种原因系统值增加并超出目标值，系统值就会开始减少；如果系统值低于目标值，它们就会开始增加。在他们的模型中，伯克（Berk）等人假定刑罚率在特定范围内的波动对维持既定社会的系统目标是有一定作用的。他们对加利福尼亚州监狱系统从 1851 年至 1970 年 120 年间的监禁率进行分析，其结果并不支持刑法稳定性的假说。

综上所述,迪尔凯姆(Durkheim)最早提出关于犯罪功能的思想。他认为犯罪是正常、规律且有其功用的。他指出,犯罪可以促进社会团结。以往有关犯罪功能的研究多是源自并围绕迪尔凯姆(Durkheim)的这一理论而进行的。这些研究主要探讨了四个问题:社会团结、压制性司法、界限维持和刑罚的稳定性。此外,研究结论多是通过观察得来的,是历史性的,但也有一些实验性的定量分析。尽管这些研究存在诸多缺陷,其结果普遍支持迪尔凯姆(Durkheim)关于犯罪促进社会团结的假说。

对迪尔凯姆(Durkheim)犯罪功能理论的研究主要集中在犯罪促进社会团结的研究上。由于研究范围狭窄,导致此方面的研究未能发展成为具有吸引力的重要领域。长久以来,对犯罪功能的研究都孤立于主流犯罪学以外的各种方面。尚未曾有人研究这些方面之间的联系。这种情况限制了对犯罪功能的研究。而事实上,犯罪学研究应关注犯罪、社会团结、犯罪后果等变量。

笔者认为,至少有两种变量在影响犯罪功能或后果方面起了重要作用。一是对犯罪的恐惧感,一是社会团结。为了在新框架中考察犯罪的功能,回答上一章的研究计划中所列出的问题,我们必须对有关恐惧感和社会团结的研究作一个回顾。

犯罪恐惧感是犯罪在现代社会中所造成的最重要的后果。学界已经广泛研究了这一现象。少数研究考察了对犯罪的反应,包括其他负面功能或社会后果。研究犯罪恐惧感的同时研究犯罪功能将会极大拓宽犯罪功能的研究视野,促使新论题的提出,并促进研究的发展。

社会团结是影响社会许多方面的一个重要变量,它是迪尔凯姆(Durkheim)理论的核心概念,认为社会团结会影响犯罪后果的想法是合情合理的。许多其他的犯罪学理论研究也涉及社会团结。比如说,社会解体理论就考察了社会一体化的重要性;社会控制理论在个体水平上考察社会联系和社会团结的功能;网络方法从新的视角研究社会团结。这些研究领域有助于我们理解社会团结的本质和效应,进一步了解犯罪的功能。在本章接下来的部分,笔者将对恐惧感研究和社会团结研究一一回顾。

## 二、恐惧感研究

自 20 世纪 60 年代中期以来,对犯罪恐惧感的研究作为一个重要研究论题出现并发展成为跨学科研究领域。恐惧感作为犯罪的显著后果受到公众和理论界的关注。诸如哈里斯、盖洛普、全国舆论研究中心(NORC)、全国犯罪调查(NCS)之类的重要调查都指出,自 20 世纪 60 年代中期以来民众对犯罪的恐惧感显著上升。有证据表明,对犯罪的恐惧感在 1965 年到 20 世纪 70 年代之间显著上升,自那以后又一直保持稳定(哈特纳格尔(Hartnagel),1979;博伊默(Baumer),1985;斯科甘(Skogan)和马克斯菲尔德(Maxfield),1981;米特(Miether)和李(Lee),1984;沃尔(Warr)和斯坦福(Starfford),1982;殷(Yin),1985)。这一时期积累了大量此领域的研究文献,基于减少恐惧感的公共项目也得到了发展(例如,施瓦茨(Schwartz)和科莱恩(Clarren),1977;罗斯(Rouse)和鲁宾斯坦(Rubenstein),1978;警察基金会(Policy Fundation),1981;福勒(Fowler)和曼吉欧尼(Mangione),1982)。大部分犯罪恐惧感研究集中于研究恐惧感产生的原因并将重点放在恐惧感跟个体人格、人口学特性之间的因果关系上。

既往研究已经建立了对犯罪的恐惧感的认知模型(吉劳法罗(Garofalo),1979;殷(Yin),1980;斯科甘(Skogan)和马克斯菲尔德(Maxfield),1981;博伊默(Baumer),1985)。犯罪恐惧感本质上被看做是对感知到的犯罪威胁的合理反应。已知的会产生恐惧感的因素基本上可以被分为三组:(1)犯罪的严重性;(2)个人的脆弱;(3)环境/社区因素。总的来说,使用多元统计方法进行的研究表明,在所有人群中,孤独的人、不满的人、被隔离的人、焦虑的人、女性、老人、有色人种和穷人的恐惧感度最高(殷(Yin),1985;肯尼迪(Kennedy)和希尔弗曼(Silverman),1985;米特(Miether)和李(Lee),1984;博伊默(Baumer),1985 等)。总之,恐惧感是作为因变量而进行研究的。

尽管很少有研究直接涉及犯罪的社会后果问题,仍有一些研究涉及个人对被害恐惧感的反应。其中,研究的最彻底的议题是通过行为改变来对付人身威胁(比德曼(Biderman)等人,1967)。康克林(Conklin)(1975)指出,人们对恐惧感的反应主要是减少同其他人尤其是陌生人的联系。戈登（Gordon）等人（1980）在妇女中作了抽样调查，了解她们处于12种正常状况下的次数（比如，"天黑后独自待在家中"）和她们在该种状况下的焦虑程度。结果显示两组反应之间有很强的负向关系。瑞法（Rifai）（1976）和劳顿（Lawton）等人（1976）指出，65岁以上的老人有69%到89%说他们晚上从不出门。另一方面，辛德朗（Hindelang）等人（1978）认为，大部分人并不会彻底改变他们的行为以应对犯罪；相反，他们更愿意微妙地改变自己做事情的方式，改变在公共场合的行为方式，以及出门时间，以此来减少他们暴露在察觉到的犯罪威胁的频率。只有少数研究将恐惧感作为在宏单元（例如，社区（泰勒（Taylor）、戈特弗雷德森（Gottfredson）和布劳尔（Brower），1984；斯科甘（Skogan）和马克斯菲尔德（Maxfield），1981；霍夫（Hough）和梅耶（Mayhew），1985）和城市（吉劳法罗（Garofalo），1979；斯科甘（Skogan）和马克斯菲尔德（Maxfield），1981；利斯卡（Liska）、劳伦斯（lawrence）和辛捷列高（Sanchirico），1982））中变化的社会后果来考察。仍然没有一种观点将研究重点放在社会对犯罪恐惧感的反应上。

总体而言，恐惧感是现代社会犯罪的主要后果。学术界广泛研究了形成恐惧感的因素。这些大多研究犯罪恐惧感；还有些研究探讨对犯罪恐惧感的个体反应，重点仍放在个体反应而不是社会反应上。在个体水平上恐惧感研究与犯罪的功能是独立的课题。但是在社会水平上这两种研究的联系就显而易见了：它们都跟社会的反应和犯罪后果相关。有关犯罪功能的研究可以显著扩展和发展。

但是仍然没有一种视角集中在社会对犯罪恐惧感的反应上。近年来，恐惧感研究集中在社区环境与恐惧感之间的联系上。研究者探询恐惧感与社区凝聚力之间的因果关系。一些研究认为恐惧感会削弱社区凝聚力；而另一些研究则认为缺乏社区凝聚力是引起恐惧感的一个原因。答案仍然待定。

# 三、社会团结研究

恐惧感研究跟犯罪的功能有关。如果我们站在社会层面将恐惧感作为一个引起社会后果的变量考察,而不是站在个体层面将恐惧感作为一个应变量来考察(大部分恐惧感研究都属于后者),我们的研究就会重点考虑犯罪恐惧感怎样影响社会。

另一个影响社会和犯罪对社会造成的后果的重要变量是社会团结。团结概念来源于许多其他表面上看起来不相干的理论和研究,是这些理论研究中的一个重要概念。许多研究领域都探讨了社会团结,并因此与犯罪功能的研究产生了一定的联系。这种联系之所以不明确,是因为对犯罪功能的研究孤立于其他研究领域。很少有研究直接针对社会团结对犯罪后果产生的效应。这方面的研究主要包括迪尔凯姆(Durkheim)关于社会团结的研究、社会解体论、社会控制论和网络途径。接下来,笔者将对它们作一一回顾。

## 1. 迪尔凯姆(Durkheim)的社会理论

社会团结是迪尔凯姆(Durkheim)社会理论的核心概念。迪尔凯姆(Durkheim)在其率先研究犯罪功能问题的著作中广泛探讨了社会团结概念,告诉我们社会团结影响社会生活。迪尔凯姆(Durkheim)的著作还指出这个抽象理论概念的概念性和可实施性。

迪尔凯姆(Durkheim)的第一部重要著作——他的博士论文《社会劳动分工》(1893),确定了他最初的理论关注点,即弄清维持和改变社会组织模式的变量。而其中的主要变量就是社会团结。这个关注点对迪尔凯姆(Durkheim)后来的著作起到了提纲挈领的作用。对迪尔凯姆(Durkheim)而言,他对社会团结的研究代表了社会组织的一般理论。

迪尔凯姆(Durkheim)认为,功能性分析给犯罪学家们提供了隔离"社会病态"的方法,使得他们能够推荐"治疗方法"。迪尔凯姆(Durkheim)倾向于将一体化和团结视同正常,而社会病态现象通常包括社会迷乱、利己主义、劳动的强行分工和功能的协调不良。对迪尔凯姆(Durkheim)而言,一个社会理论的中心议题便是确保社会团结得以实施的各种条件。离开这些条件,社会将不复存在。他之所以研究劳动分配是因为他认为劳动分配便是这样的条件之一。

犯罪的功能问题源自迪尔凯姆(Durkheim)对犯罪和社会团结之间关系

的探讨。在分析社会团结时,迪尔凯姆(Durkheim)提出了犯罪的功能论。"……犯罪伤害了在任何类型社会都认为健康的意识。"(1984,p.34)"……每个人都有自己的意识,无论它的起源和目的是什么,伤害它就是犯罪"(1984,p.40)。"……犯罪实质上存在于反公共意识的行为中"(1984,p.60)。因此,笔者认为,迪尔凯姆(Durkheim)的著作揭示了社会团结概念在发展犯罪和偏差行为功能理论中的极端重要性。迪尔凯姆(Durkheim)指出我们必须小心谨慎地检验社会团结这一概念。

尽管没有明确定义社会团结,迪尔凯姆(Durkheim)的著作仍然提及社会团结的概念化和团结的根源。因此,我们需要通过分析迪尔凯姆(Durkheim)的论述得出社会团结的定义以及如何实施这一定义。迪尔凯姆(Durkheim)说道:"因为同一社会的全体成员共同拥有的意识,社会团结才得以存在。压制性法律本质上或者至少在其最基本的要素中体现了这种团结。它在社会统一体中所占分量取决于包含在公共意识中并受公共意识调整的社会生活范围(无论大小)。行为与公共意识之间的关系变化越大,就越会使个体更紧密地联结在组群中;从而产生更大的社会凝聚力。"(1984,p.64)"因为道德存在于组群团结中并随之改变,人则因为他生活在社会中而仅仅是道德生物。"(1984,p.331)"我们可以说任何可以促进社会团结、促使人们对他人负责并超越自我制约自己行为的事情都是道德的,这些事情越多越强,道德感就越稳固。"(1984,p.331)"……意识是生活的来源。"(1984,p.53)

尽管迪尔凯姆(Durkheim)没有明确定义社会团结,其对社会团结的描述表明,社会团结就是公共意识。其关于犯罪促进团结的论述便是对这一概念的进一步深化。迪尔凯姆(Durkheim)论述道:"我们只需看一看丑闻发生后(特别是在小镇上),随之而来的事情就可以明白这一点了,人们在街上议论这一件事,他们相互拜访并尝试聚在一起谈论此事,从而使共愤得以发泄扩大。"

然而,迪尔凯姆(Durkheim)在他的著作中同样指出,社会团结不仅仅是公共意识。这一点从他研究社会团结的原因便可以看出。迪尔凯姆(Durkheim)关注将单个的人绑在一起维持社会存在的社会力量究竟是什么。在他的《劳动分工》一书中,他将团结分成两种类型:机械性团结和有机性团结。机械性团结建立在共性的基础之上,而有机性团结则建立在使人们相互依赖的个体差异上。现代社会个人利益相互依赖,从而使得组群或社会的利益成为共有利益。这种共有利益是现代社会团结的重要组成部分。尽管迪尔凯姆(Durkheim)更强调社会团结的意识成分,共有的利益成分仍是十分重要的,它可能也是意识成分形成的基础之一。

基于迪尔凯姆(Durkheim)关于集体意识和劳动分工的讨论,笔者认为团结既有文化成分,也有结构成分。例如,当个人长期生活于某个社会时,他们不光形成了共有文化、集体意识,也形成了共有利益,因为他们用自己的资源对社会进行了投资。社会团结是这两种只能在理论分析时区分的成分的结合物。在特定社会,无论哪一种成分占主导地位,团结都表现了社会成员对社会的义务和责任感。

迪尔凯姆(Durkheim)认识到团结这个概念的抽象性和其度量的困难。他指出:"社会团结完全是一种精神现象,无法精确观测,更无法对比。"(1984,p.24)就社会团结的度量,他谈道:"要想进行分类和比较,我们必须用象征性的外在数据来替代这种得不到的内在数据,通过前者来研究后者。""法律就是看得见的象征。事实上,社会团结尽管有其非物质性,其存在并非通过一种纯粹的潜在性状态而体现,而是通过可察觉的效应表明它的存在。当团结强时,它使人们互相吸引,确保人们之间的密切联系,增加人们彼此走近的机会……"(1984,p.24)"……法律(或者规则、准则)和道德代表了限制我们彼此之间以及与社会之间关系的总契约,而社会将数目众多的个体塑造成为有凝聚力的集体。"(1984,p.331)

总而言之,迪尔凯姆(Durkheim)的论述没有给团结概念下一个清楚的定义。笔者认为,团结由两种成分构成——文化性成分和结构性成分。迪尔凯姆(Durkheim)强调文化的集体意识成分,但他也谈到现代社会团结的结构性要素。笔者认为共有利益同样重要。

## 2. 社会解体理论

在犯罪学领域里,理论研究都关注同一个变量,即迪尔凯姆(Durkheim)理论所强调的"团结"。这些理论包括社会解体理论、社会控制理论和网络途径。

　　笔者认为,社会组织概念和社会团结概念在很大程度上重叠。尽管社会解体理论和迪尔凯姆(Durkheim)的传统功能理论各自独立发展,我们可以看到它们之间有许多重要的共同点。二者都强调社会的一种特殊共性,即社会统一体。社会统一体概念在二者的理论重要性中都占据中心位置。然而,由于该概念的抽象,社会解体理论和迪尔凯姆(Durkheim)的传统功能理论都被批评为概念模糊。

　　社会解体理论用社会特征——解体来解释犯罪。本质上,解体的中心含义是社会的一种状态,在这种状态中人们彼此分离,缺乏公共意识,缺乏对社会的公共义务,缺乏共有价值、行为准则,缺乏责任感。社会解体与社会团结之间的重叠是公认的。解体是对社会团结的破坏。

　　同迪尔凯姆(Durkheim)关于社会团结的概念一样,解体理论也被批评为含义不明(例如,科恩(Cohen)、何塞(Hauser),1978),并且在概念的操作性上存在问题。比如说,有人批评该理论采用解体的后果来实施解体这个概念(马茨阿(Matza),1969)。正因为概念的模糊性,其操作上的困难是不可避免的。

　　解体与犯罪的许多后果密切相关。率先提出这一理论的肖(Shaw)和麦克凯伊(Mckay),同芝加哥学派的许多社会学家一样关注大城市里滋生的社会问题。解体被认为是产生这些后果的原因。这表明社会团结是影响社会后果的一个重要变量。

## 3. 社会控制理论

　　社会控制理论考察社会键,它在个体水平上考察社会团结。在吸取迪尔凯姆(Durkheim)的社会一体化理论的基础上,赫胥(Hirschi)(1969)提出了他的社会控制理论。他认为社会键将个人束缚在传统制度上,控制人们不去做依其本性会做的事情即偏差行为。赫胥(Hirschi)(1969)明确将他的社会契约概念同迪尔凯姆(Durkheim)的社会团结概念联系在一起。赫胥(Hirschi)认为,那些跟民众和组织联系在一起的、接受传统社会目标和信仰的个人会遵从传统准则。我们能够在迪尔凯姆(Durkheim)关于社会团结的论述中找到社会契约的要素,即人们所作的承诺以及他们在社会中的共有信仰。对赫胥(Hirschi)而言,社会团结将人们联结在一起,并束缚他们的偏差行为。这表明社会团结影响社会行为和社会生活。

### 4. 社会网络途径

网络分析是研究社会的普遍方法,是社会学的一个重要领域。"个人行为的社会制约"作为其中一个概念,跟社会团结概念有关。网络分析已经被用于分析社会结构和社会进程。

社会网络是"由一系列社会关系相联系的一组节点"(劳曼(Laumann)等,1987)。个人网络以个人为中心,表现个人跟其他人的联系……(科劳恩(Krohn),1986)。网络途径中"链接"概念跟社会的相互影响概念有关。诸如"网络的多元性"、"网络密度"、"离差"、"范围"、"可到达性"等社会网络的结构性特征描述了人们之间相互关系的性质。其中"多元性"指的是任意两个人彼此之间的不同角色关系的数量,或者是某个关联中内容或焦点(例如活动、变化)的数量(费舍尔(Fischer)等,1977)。"网络密度"指的是一个社会网络中行为者的直接相连的程度(博特(Bott),1957;科瑞文(Cravan)和威尔曼(Wellman),1973)。

人们之间的相互关系是社交的结果。更为重要的是,它们是进一步社交的基础。网络特性折射出人们之间关系的不同方面,人们结合在一起的思想跟社会团结概念有关。事实上,网络研究表明在诸如社区、社会、工作组等(伯尔曼(Boorman)和怀特(White),1976;劳曼(Laumann),1973;怀特(White)等人,1976)的特定社会单元中社会网络多元性的平均水平可以决定社会团结水平。科劳恩(Krohn)在其偏差行为理论中运用社会网络方法提出,网络越是多元化,密度越大,就越能将个人行为束缚在社会网络的范围内,偏差行为就会越少。他指出,高密度网络对社区居民行为的限制是一种机械性团结。网络方法以不同形式表现社会团结,说明社会团结能够影响人们行为和社会生活。

## 四、本章小结

　　总而言之,迪尔凯姆(Durkheim)开创了对犯罪功能的研究。对他而言,犯罪是正常的,是有其功用的。他认为犯罪的主要功能是促进社会团结。围绕这一论点,以往研究将重心放在四个密切相关的问题上:社会团结、压制性司法、边界的维持和刑罚稳定性。这些研究大多是观察性的和历史性的;也有一些是实证和定量的研究。这些研究尽管存在一些问题,但普遍支持迪尔凯姆(Durkheim)关于犯罪能促进社会团结的假说。然而这种有局限的、被狭窄定义的研究没有引起多大关注。它在传统上是孤立于犯罪学研究主流而发展的;犯罪功能研究与其他犯罪学研究领域之间的关系还未曾有人涉及。这种状况同样限制了对犯罪功能的研究。事实上,在犯罪学领域里,理论研究同样关注诸如犯罪、团结、犯罪后果这些迪尔凯姆(Durkheim)论文中所涉及的变量。笔者认为,至少有两种变量在影响犯罪功能或后果方面起了重要作用,一是犯罪恐惧感,一是社会团结。

　　犯罪恐惧感对现代社会有其重要影响。学术界广泛研究了形成恐惧感的因素。少数研究探讨了个体对犯罪的反应。然而在恐惧感研究中,恐惧感仍然被当作一个个体水平上而不是社会水平上的自变量来考察;仅有少部分研究是站在宏观角度上的。我们应该将焦点移至整体层面,研究社会对犯罪威胁的反应而不是仅仅研究个人对犯罪的反应,将恐惧感当作一个带来许多社会反应的居间变量,考察恐惧感带来的社会后果。那么我们将会发现,恐惧感研究和犯罪功能或功能研究之间的联系十分明显。犯罪功能研究将会显著扩张和发展。近年来的恐惧感研究考察了社区环境和恐惧感之间的关系,以及恐惧感和社区凝聚力之间的因果关系。这些研究发现,抑或恐惧感导致社区凝聚力的降低,抑或社区凝聚力的缺乏是产生恐惧感的原因;二者间的因果关系仍不明确。

　　社会团结是影响社会许多方面的重要变量。社会团结影响犯罪后果的假定是合理的。团结观念根植于许多表面上没有联系的理论和研究。我们回顾了许多研究领域的社会团结概念,包括迪尔凯姆(Durkheim)关于团结的讨论、社会解体理论、社会控制理论和网络途径理论。社会解体理论强调社会整体的重要性。社会解体反映出社会团结遭到破坏。社会控制理论考察社会键；它在个体层面考察社会团结。网络途径从新的角度考察社会团结。这些研究帮助我们理解社会团结的本质和效应，并阐述犯罪功能研究的发展。

# 第三章　犯罪功能的理论模型

## 一、一般理论模型

我们已经将对犯罪功能的研究从迪尔凯姆（Durkheim）提出的基本问题扩展成为一个研究计划，该计划提出了三个问题。前两个具有理论重要性：第一个问题问的是犯罪的功能或后果是什么。它要求我们系统考察犯罪的功能或后果。也就是说，我们要考察犯罪引起、改变或是影响了什么样的社会过程。

第二个问题问的是犯罪在影响其后果和其他变量中如何发挥作用。它要求我们研究其他变量和社会过程，回答有关这些变量之间因果关系的问题，即犯罪和其他变量怎样影响后果、这些变量之间怎样互相影响。

在本章中，笔者提出了考察四种后果的一般理论模型。包括：某区域内的生活质量、社会经济资源、对政府的态度和社会衰退。这一理论模型认为有两个变量在解释犯罪后果方面十分重要：恐惧感和社会团结。该模型提出了犯罪、恐惧感、社会团结和后果之间的因果关系结构，解释了三个重要理论性问题。（一）模型解释了该领域的中心问题：犯罪、恐惧感和社会团结怎样影响后果。（二）模型研究了支持迪尔凯姆（Durkheim）理论的犯罪功能学说和考察犯罪如何影响社会团结的恐惧感学说之间的争论。（三）模型研究了有关恐惧感和团结的因果关系的争论，表明了恐惧感和社会团结之间的相互作用关系(图 3.1)。

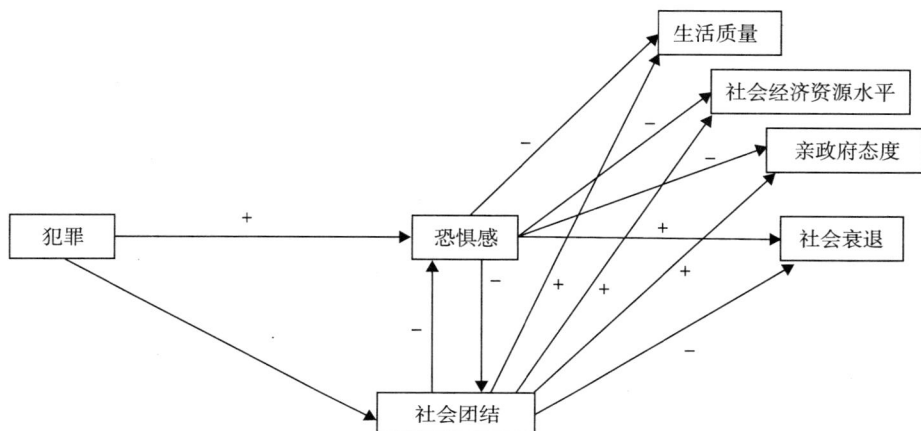

**图 3.1 一般理论模型**

接下来,笔者将一一探讨用一般理论模型解释这三个理论问题,并将明确提出涉及的理论假设,并讨论这些理论假设。本章的第二部分考察犯罪、恐惧感和社会团结如何影响犯罪后果。它包括四小部分,每小部分讨论一个犯罪后果,并提出假设。本章的第三部分考察迪尔凯姆(Durkheim)关于犯罪促进社会团结的论题。第四部分考察恐惧感和社会团结之间的因果关系。

## 二、犯罪、恐惧感和团结影响犯罪后果

首要任务是系统考察犯罪的功能或后果。犯罪能对社会产生许多重要社会后果。恐惧感学说已经广泛论证了犯罪会引起恐惧感。恐惧感反过来会影响社会的许多方面。恐惧感对人们的生活质量、社会结构、文化、人们对政府的态度以及社会衰退方面都会产生系统影响。在本书中,笔者将考察恐惧感对社会四个方面所产生的后果。在即将提到的一般理论模型中,笔者提出四个后果:生活质量、社会经济资源、对政府的态度和社会衰退。

本研究中的一般理论模型(图 3.1)表明有两个变量对解释犯罪的后果十分重要,即恐惧感和社会团结。这一理论模型指出恐惧感和社会团结直接影

响犯罪的社会后果;犯罪直接影响恐惧感和社会团结,但并不直接影响社会后果。恐惧感和团结是犯罪作用于社会团结的媒介。在下文中,笔者将逐一考察这些社会后果。假设犯罪、恐惧感和团结对不同社会后果的影响是相同的,但不同社会后果的社会进程是不同的。犯罪、恐惧感和团结以与影响社会经济资源水平不同的方式影响满意度。

有关恐惧感的著作大多将犯罪产生的恐惧感作为一个自变量来考察,并且一直在论证恐惧感是对犯罪的主要反应。针对包括在这一理论模型中的每个社会后果,笔者将阐述恐惧感和社会团结为什么以及如何影响这些后果。

## 1. 生活质量

生活质量包括许多方面。这里主要考虑受犯罪影响的社会方面和心理方面及其受影响的方式。本书的一般理论模型(图3.1)涉及五个有关生活质量的假说。

　　I.1　犯罪降低人们的生活质量。

　　I.2　犯罪不直接降低生活质量。

　　I.3　恐惧感直接降低生活质量。

　　I.4　恐惧感是犯罪作用于生活质量的媒介。

　　I.5　社会团结提高生活质量。

尽管生活质量恶化经常跟犯罪联系在一起,这些假设仍然强调恐惧感才是犯罪效应的媒介。在媒介起作用的同时,犯罪也会对生活质量产生直接影响,但模型假定犯罪对生活质量不产生直接影响。恐惧感和社会团结直接影响生活质量,它们对生活质量的作用截然相反。恐惧感降低生活质量,而社会团结则提高生活质量。

恐惧感通过许多途径降低生活质量。首先,犯罪带来的恐惧感使人们感到害怕,而危险的感觉显然会影响人们对某一区域内生活和工作的满意度;其次,犯罪的恐惧感加大了人们的心理压力,造成在某一区域生活和工作的持续负担;人们不光担心自己的安全,也担心家庭成员和朋友的安全。再次,被害经历会造成紧张,且研究表明犯罪现象会引起人们对犯罪的焦虑感。焦虑感的构成之一就是关注犯罪(富汝斯登堡(Furstenberg),1971;洛兹(Lotz),罗伊·E.（Roy E），1979）。紧张和焦虑会产生心理乃至身体上的问题。人们在面对犯罪时感到无力、软弱并易受攻击，从而导致他们消极面对周围事物（斯科甘（Skogan），1986），生活质量降低。对犯罪被害人而言，恐惧感对生活质量的降低作用更甚。学者们也推测，其他人也可能会避免与被害人接触，因为他们会感觉到被害人破损的人权，从而希望自己远离痛苦。心理学家们揭示了一种相关现象，称之为"责难被害人"现象。

有的研究着眼于研究恐惧感对人们行为的限制作用。恐惧感研究表明对暴力犯罪的一个主要反应便是限制日常行为（比德曼（Biderman）等，1967）。凯尔（Kail）和克莱曼（Kleiman）的研究表明，恐惧感、犯罪和自我行为约束会降低都市生活质量（凯尔（Kail），克莱曼（Kleiman），1985）。人们避免去自我感觉危险的地方并将行为调整到他们觉得安全的时间和地点。在高犯罪率社区生活的人们常常感到是自己家中的囚徒（鲍尔金（Balkin），1979；斯科甘（Skogan）和马克斯菲尔德（Maxfield），1981；吉劳法罗（Garofalo），1979；克拉克（Clarke）和路易丝（Lewis），1982；殷（Yin），1985；利斯卡（Liska）、辛捷列高（Sanchirico）和里德（Reed），1988）。瑞法（Rifai）（1976）和劳顿（Lawton）等人（1976）报告说65岁以上的老人有69%到89%晚上不敢出门。恐惧感限制了人们的行为，降低了人们之间的社会化程度；人们不能自由地拜访朋友，晚上不能出去娱乐。像公园这样的公共设施本来是为提高人们生活质量而修建的，夜晚却经常成为危险场所。

恐惧感还通过减少人们的相互信任使生活质量降低。人们之间，特别是邻里之间一定程度的相互信任对维持生活质量是十分重要的。相互信任使人们能够互相帮助。相互信任也有利于在人们之间建立轻松的相互关系，避免社会生活中额外的负担。缺乏相互信任则会对社会关系产生额外负担。研究表明，被害人由于自身经历而倾向于退出公共生活，对他人变得怀疑和不信任（勒琼（LeJeune）和亚力克斯（Alex），1973）。高犯罪地区的人们则倾向于心理上退出公共生活，自我孤立（基德（Kidd）和夏耶（Chayet），1984）。恐惧感作为一个隔离力量阻碍人们彼此联系，并因此减少相互理解和信任。

如前文所述，笔者假设社会团结会提高生活质量。然而，很少有研究着眼于这个假设。笔者认为社会团结提高生活质量是因为它促进了人们之间的相互作用,这种相互作用又跟社会化有关。在高度团结的社会,人们经常拜访邻居和朋友,他们晚上出门,享受社会生活。同理,社会团结促进相互理解和相互信任,因为它促进社会相互作用。通过相互作用,人们更好地相互理解,更愿意互相帮助,从而提高生活质量。此外,社会团结也有助于减少心理紧张。对社会的公共义务和共有文化为社会成员提供了社会支持。面对危机时,人们知道,对社会负有责任感的邻居和朋友会提供帮助和道义支持,这将减轻困难和心理紧张。

## 2. 社会经济资源水平

犯罪能够引起社会结构的改变。社会经济资源水平是社会结构的一个重要方面。以本书提出的一般理论模型为基础(图3.1),笔者提出五个关于社会经济资源水平的假说。

II.1　犯罪减少社会经济资源水平。

II.2　犯罪不直接减少某一区域的社会经济资源水平。

II.3　恐惧感直接减少某一区域的社会经济资源水平。

II.4　恐惧感是犯罪作用于社会经济资源水平的媒介。

II.5　社会团结增加社会经济资源水平。

这些假说强调恐惧感在犯罪效应上的媒介作用。犯罪不直接影响社会经济资源水平。恐惧感和社会团结直接影响社会经济资源水平,它们对社会经济资源水平的作用截然相反。恐惧感减少社会经济资源水平,而社会团结则增加社会经济资源水平。

恐惧感通过许多途径减少社会经济资源水平。首先,恐惧感推动人们携带资源搬离特定区域。这造成该区域商业往来减少、工作机会减少、地方政府的税收减少。其次,对暴力犯罪的恐惧感也会吓跑潜在的外来投资者和消费者。只有那些拥有较低社会经济资源的人会留下,因为他们缺乏资源搬走,这导致贫穷和社会问题集中在邻近社区。

有证据表明犯罪具有使人们搬离某个地方的作用(史密斯(Smith),1988;卡斯尔(Kasl)和 哈尔堡(Harburg),1972;左伊特布姆(Droettboom)等,1971)。桑普森(Sampson)和伍德里奇(Wooldredge)(1986)对高犯罪率促使人们从中心城市搬走的假说进行了测试。他们考察了美国 55 个大城市在 1970—1980 年间的人口变化和 1975—1980 年间的净移民值。结果表明,犯罪率对中心城市的人口衰退(对黑、白人种南北分布不均进行统计控制后)、税率、种族和年龄构成、职业、制造业基地和人口密度均起了相当作用。大多数研究者发现,高风险城市社区的现有居民更容易流露出迁移到其他地方的愿望。左伊特布姆(Droettboom)等人(1971)在一项全国性调查中发现,认为犯罪和暴力是其所在社会的严重问题的被调查者对其社区更为不满,更想搬走。卡斯尔(Kasl)和哈尔堡(Harburg)(1972)分别对底特律黑人和白人居住的高档和低档社区进行了调查。他们发现,高犯罪率地区居民生活充斥着犯罪,认为自己遭抢劫的机会很高,渴望搬走。研究还表明中产阶级家庭和其成员最渴望搬走,而暂住者往往会搬进来(斯塔克(Stark),1987;弗瑞(Frey),1980;邓肯(Duncan)和纽曼(Newman),1976)。弗瑞(Frey)(1979)和马歇尔(Marshall)(1979)在对 1965—1970 年间大城市及其郊区人口变动分析中发现,犯罪对家庭迁往郊区确实存在影响。而普莱斯(Price)和克雷(Clay)(1980)的研究表明城市人口的快速涌入会造成农村社会结构性混乱。

也有研究表明人们迁往郊区并非仅仅是因为对中心城市犯罪的恐惧感。法律实施援助管理局的城市被害调查就家庭成员过去五年内的上述迁移作了调查,问他们为什么离开原来的社区。在 1973 年进行的八城市调查中,只有 3% 的家庭将犯罪看做迁移的一个重要原因。因此,犯罪压力作为迁移证据是存在矛盾的。

然而,我们可以合理假设,拥有资源的人并不愿意迁往重罪经常发生的社区。有关这方面的调查甚少。当人们选择地方生活和开拓事业时他们会考虑犯罪这个因素。人们不愿意迁往某个地方,是因为犯罪的恐惧感影响社会经济资源的形成和改变。所以我们仍然可以证明犯罪的恐惧感导致贫穷的集中这一假设的正当性。一句话,恐惧感影响社会的经济资源水平。

尽管缺乏相关研究,笔者认为社会团结改善社会经济资源这一假设看上去是合理的。在一个高度团结的社会,人们把社会当作自己的家而不仅仅是生活的地方。社会是与他们的生活以及经济发展密切相关的地方。带着对社会的义务和责任感,人们在社会中投资、发展事业和积聚财富,商业和经济因此而稳定发展。所以说社会团结可以提高和巩固社会经济资源。

### 3. 人们的亲政府态度

笔者认为,犯罪影响人们在政治上的亲政府态度。在一般理论模型(图3.1)基础上,笔者提出五个有关政治上的亲政府态度的假说。

III. 1　犯罪降低人们的亲政府态度。

III. 2　犯罪不直接降低人们的亲政府态度。

III. 3　恐惧感直接降低人们的亲政府态度。

III. 4　恐惧感是犯罪作用于人们亲政府态度的媒介。

III. 5　社会团结提升人们的亲政府态度。

这些假说强调恐惧感是犯罪起作用的媒介。犯罪不直接影响亲政府态度。恐惧感和社会团结直接影响亲政府态度,它们对亲政府态度的作用截然相反。恐惧感降低亲政府态度,而社会团结提升亲政府态度。

对犯罪的恐惧感导致对政府的消极态度是因为犯罪被假定为是由政府来控制的。诉诸警察是市民对犯罪的正常反应。而这被认为是得到保护、减少恐惧感和提升安全感的主要途径。对犯罪的恐惧感使人们认为警察不能对付犯罪,这导致市民错过了这一减少恐惧感的基本方法。我们经常注意到,被害人不光痛恨施害者,也怨恨警察和政府。当人们和他们的朋友成为犯罪的牺牲品时,人们对警察和政府感到失望。社会的高恐惧感水平不仅引起对警察和政府的失望,也引起对警察和政府保护普通群众意愿的怀疑。这些很容易延伸到对政府其他问题的批评,比如腐败、歧视、整体的无能。这又会导致普遍的消极甚至敌视的政治态度。

然而很少有人研究这个假说。斯汀康比(Stinchcombe)等人(1978)认为对付犯罪时的无力感是犯罪的特性之一。无力感常常伴随着警察不能提供帮助而产生,对警察和政府的消极态度也随之产生。研究表明,社会经济地位较低的人被害的几率较高,他们会觉得政府对富人保护得更好。研究证明较低阶层的人和少数族裔群体对警察和政府存有敌意(比如,索伯恩里(Thornberry),1979;丹纳弗(Dannefer)和舒特(Schutt),1987)。恐惧感通过这些联系影响政治态度。

而社会团结可以改善对政府的态度和对警察的态度。社会团结提升对犯罪的公愤，促进警察和政府的协作。政府和警察的这种交互作用促进民众与政府、警察的互相理解。研究表明，高度团结的社会有更多的反犯罪合作计划，这些计划能更好地发挥作用（斯科甘（Skogan），1990）。科恩（Cohen）等人发现从事有关犯罪工作组织的成员更加相信警察能够减少犯罪。通过同政府和警察合作，人们更能理解警察和政府面临的困难和问题，他们能更好地将个别人的腐败从政府整体腐败中区分开来，这将减少对政府的消极态度。相反，社会团结度越低、社会和政府间的相互理解越少，对政府的敌意就越强。

## 4. 社会衰退

笔者所研究的社会衰退涉及一个社会的社会经济条件的综合变化趋势。社会朝哪个方向发展反映出社会的未来。这些变化存在于社会的许多方面：社会方面、经济方面、居住方面、人口统计学方面、表象和声誉。

尽管变化总会发生，大多数社会仍然相当稳定。公司和居民虽然搬进搬出，但一个稳定的社会能够自我繁衍。衰退的社会是丧失自我繁殖能力的社会。在衰退的社会里，社会经济条件恶化。居民居住条件恶化尤为明显，房价下降，房东和屋主不愿意修缮和重建房屋，房贷机构不愿意提供贷款。从经济上来讲，公司失去了顾客和利润。社会的经济条件恶化是社会衰退的一个重要方面，但不是唯一方面。衰退的社会通常显示出越来越多的逐渐恶化的表象，名声越来越差。普遍的"野蛮"或"失序"（霍普（Hope）和霍夫（Hough），1988；斯科甘（Skogan），1990）意味着社会的衰退。社会疾病包括空地上随处可见的垃圾和废物、破烂的房屋、废弃的建筑、故意破坏公共和个人财产、涂鸦、成群的少年聚集在街头角落、妓女出没等等。以一般理论模型（图3.1）为基础，笔者提出五个有关社会衰退的假说。

IV.1　犯罪加快社会衰退。

IV.2　犯罪不直接加快社会衰退。

IV.3　恐惧感直接加快社会衰退。

IV.4　恐惧感是犯罪作用于社会衰退的媒介。

IV.5　社会团结减少社会衰退。

尽管社会衰退往往跟犯罪联系在一起,这些假设强调的还是恐惧感对犯罪效应的媒介作用。犯罪不直接影响社会衰退。恐惧感和社会团结直接影响社会衰退,它们对社会衰退起相反作用。恐惧感加快社会衰退,而社会团结减少社会衰退。

恐惧感影响社会衰退。对犯罪的恐惧感使人们不愿意在这个社会生活和经商,这就会影响土地和房屋的价格。恐惧感也会将消费者和潜在消费者赶出这个地区,商业无利可图。恐惧感挫伤反犯罪的信心和行动。由于具有适合犯罪生存的土壤,外面的好生事端者被吸引进来,亲犯罪元素因而聚集在一起。一些研究表明,恐惧感和犯罪是一种分裂力量,破坏社会聚集力量对付几乎所有局部问题的能力(路易丝(Lewis),1979;康克林(Conklin),1975),混乱蔓延,社会衰退。

笔者认为,社会团结减少社会衰退。然而学界对这方面研究甚少。对社会负有责任感的人努力防止社会衰退,社会团结使人们结合在一起防止社会发生有害变化。对社会负有责任感的人愿意互相帮助,保护家庭和公司。社会团结发挥维持社会秩序的作用。在高度团结的社会,人们对社会有强烈的责任感,他们自我组织来监控有害元素,挫败有害元素,控制发生在社会中的事物,防止社会经济条件衰退。

## 5. 小结

笔者提出一般理论模型来研究计划里的基本问题。模型提出犯罪的四个后果(在许多可能性中)。犯罪影响生活质量、社会经济资源、亲政府态度和社会衰退。这一理论模型认为在解释犯罪后果上有两个重要变量:恐惧感和社会团结。模型提出犯罪、恐惧感、社会团结和犯罪后果之间的因果关系结构。

模型解释了这一领域的中心问题:犯罪、恐惧感和社会团结怎样影响这些后果。模型认为,恐惧感和社会团结直接影响社会后果;犯罪直接影响恐惧感和社会团结;犯罪不直接影响社会后果;恐惧感和团结是犯罪作用于社会后果的媒介。以这个理论模型为基础,笔者对每种后果明确提出了五个假设。这些假设致力于过去研究很少甚至没有考察的理论问题。有关恐惧感的著作大多将恐惧感看做是一个自变量,坚持恐惧感是对犯罪的主要反应。所以,针对理论模型中包括的每种社会后果,笔者主要运用现有的著作来解释恐惧感和社会团结怎样和为什么影响这些后果。

在接下来的部分,笔者将讨论有关犯罪功能的著作间的争论。争论一方支持迪尔凯姆(Durkheim)关于犯罪促进社会团结的论题;另一方,有关恐惧感的著作,则认为恐惧感削弱社会团结。

## 三、犯罪和社会团结

迪尔凯姆(Durkheim)认为,犯罪在促进社会团结上起积极功能。他解释说,犯罪聚集正义感;这种强化的社交促进社会团结。埃里克森(Erikson)认为,换句话说,犯罪产生的刺激加快组群间相互作用的节奏。总的来说,功能论者认为,犯罪产生的义愤使人们聚集在一起,促进社交,提醒人们什么是他们所共有的,从而促进社会团结。在这个理论传统里,绝大多数研究支持迪尔凯姆(Durkheim)关于犯罪促进社会团结的论断。但是当要求提供说明这个过程的历史实例时,很少有人能提供关于这个假说的测试。这个假说需要更严格的测试来证明。

与之相反的是,有关对犯罪恐惧感的著作普遍认为犯罪产生的恐惧感不是将人们聚集在一起,而是限制人们的日常行为,使人们变得疏远,减少社交,从而降低社会团结(哈特纳格尔(Hartnagel),1979;古斯汀(Gookstein)和肖特兰(Shotland),1980;康克林(Conklin),1975)。有关犯罪恐惧感的研究证据表明,由于对犯罪的恐惧感,人们将行为限制在安全的时间和安全的地点内,生活在不安全社区的人不可避免成为自己家中的囚徒(斯科甘(Skogan)和马克斯菲尔德(Maxfield),1981;吉劳法罗(Garofalo),1979;克拉克(Clarke)和路易丝(Lewis),1982;殷(Yin),1985;利斯卡(Liska)、辛捷列高(Sanchirico)和里德(Reed),1988)。尽管大多数既往研究是站在个人水平而不是社会水平上,其成果显然都跟此项研究有关。在社会水平上,利斯卡(Liska)和沃纳(Warner)(1991)的文章证明像抢劫这样带来恐惧感的犯罪抑制社交、削弱社会团结。概括而言,恐惧感研究著作表明,犯罪通过恐惧感抑制社交,从而削弱社会团结。

显然,功能论者的假说和犯罪恐惧感研究就犯罪对社会团结的功能作了不同预测。迪尔凯姆(Durkheim)认为犯罪促进社会团结;相反,恐惧感研究认为犯罪引起恐惧感,使人们疏远,从而削弱社会团结。犯罪恐惧感研究取得了持续成果,而功能论者的假说还没有运用定性研究进行直接测试。

然而,这个论题具有相当的理论重要性,因而需要进一步思考和更严格的测试。主要问题是:犯罪真的能促进社会团结么? 事实上,在现实生活中确实存在犯罪促进社会团结的情形。例如,胡里汉(Hourihan)(1987)的一项研究表明犯罪的功能是复杂的。严重罪行阻止邻里监督组织涉入,而被一些侵害行为伤害会导致更强烈的加入邻里监督组织的愿望。犯罪由于侵犯集体意识使人们聚集在一起从而促进社会团结,胡里汉(Hourihan)对这个过程的近距离观察研究表明,传统功能论者关于这个过程的论述并不完全相同。这表明人们应当对迪尔凯姆(Durkheim)最初的假说加以详述使之能够适用于现代社会,并能用现代数据加以检验。

笔者认为,在现代社会中,社会团结如迪尔凯姆(Durkheim)所说的那样是有机的,理性选择因素发挥了很大作用。在胡里汉(Hourihan)研究的过程里,集体意识和趋利避害的评价均能影响人们是否参加邻里监督组织的决定,这也是社会的共有利益。当犯罪的恐惧感压倒了集体意识,人们选择不参加;当觉得集体行动能更好地实现共有利益,人们就会参加。

笔者认为,团结有两种成分:一是文化成分,也就是集体意识;一是结构成分,包括共有利益。由于现代社会团结的有机成分,建立在现代数据基础上的测试要求详细阐述迪尔凯姆(Durkheim)的论题:社会团结包括并可能受控于共有利益这个结构成分。

在现代社会,犯罪可能促进社会团结在相当程度上是由于它提醒个人保护他们的共有利益。犯罪主要促进有机型团结。犯罪通过恐惧感使人们疏离的过程和犯罪促使人们组织起来的过程有一点是共同的,那就是都涉及个人利益考虑。当犯罪是暴力的和严重的,人们不相信集体行动有很大作用。正如有关恐惧感的著作报告的那样,他们变得疏远。当犯罪不严重时,人们不怎么害怕,他们的集体意识占主导,敢于保护自己的集体利益,所以说犯罪可以促进团结。

笔者认为,既往的研究均等对待犯罪,忽视了暴力犯罪和非暴力犯罪的重要区别。既往研究对传统的团结概念和现代社会的团结概念亦同等对待,传统的团结概念主要是机械性的,而现代的团结概念主要是有机性的,本质上是共有利益。笔者认为,在现代社会,暴力犯罪和非暴力犯罪有不同效应。暴力犯罪引起恐惧感,使人们疏离并限制人们的交互作用或行动,从而降低社会团结;非暴力犯罪促进社交,从而促进社会团结。在详细论述的基础上,通过对迪尔凯姆(Durkheim)关于非暴力犯罪理论假说的再表现,笔者对暴力犯罪和非暴力犯罪功能于社会团结的效应作了区分。笔者强调现代社会中的有机性团结,直接检验了犯罪具有促进现代社会社会团结功能的假说。笔者的解说包括以下假设:

V. 1　暴力犯罪产生恐惧感。

V. 2　非暴力犯罪不直接产生恐惧感。

V. 3　暴力犯罪降低社会团结。

V. 4　非暴力犯罪促进社会团结。

学界很少有关于这些假设的研究。斯汀康比(Stinchcombe)等人(1978)指出犯罪对引起恐惧感的特殊帮助:它使空间集中,它与危险迹象相连,我们对它没有太多办法。沃尔夫冈(Wolfgang)发现,到目前为止当人们评价犯罪的严重程度时,身体伤害和使用枪支超过了所有程度的经济损失(沃尔夫冈(Wolfgang),1978)。这些研究表明,我们有理由假设暴力犯罪在引起的恐惧感上是不同于非暴力犯罪的。

总而言之,迪尔凯姆(Durkheim)认为犯罪在促进社会团结上起积极作用。犯罪功能研究表明犯罪引起的义愤使人们聚集在一起,促进社交,提醒人们什么是他们所共有的,从而促进社会团结。与之相反,犯罪恐惧感方面的著作普遍认为,犯罪不是使人们聚集在一起,而是产生恐惧感,束缚人们的日常行为,使人们彼此疏离,减少社交,从而降低社会团结。笔者认为社会团结包括文化成分和结构成分。在现代社会,结构成分占主导,暴力犯罪和非暴力犯罪产生不同后果。暴力犯罪引起恐惧感,使人们彼此疏离,束缚人们的交互作用或行动,从而减少社会团结;而非暴力犯罪促进社交,从而提升社会团结。

## 四、恐惧感和团结之间的关系

近年来,恐惧感研究将重点放在社区条件和特征上,特别是恐惧感和社区凝聚力之间的因果关系上。一些研究指出,恐惧感减少社区凝聚力;另一些指出社区凝聚力减少恐惧感。

一方面,研究表明恐惧感减少社区凝聚力。例如,康克林(Conklin)(1975)指出,减少同其他人特别是陌生人的联系是个人对恐惧感的主要反应,这意味着社会团结的减少。一些研究认为恐惧感限制人们的行为(例如,利斯卡(Liska)和沃纳(Warner),1991),从而减少社交,降低社会团结。

另一方面,研究表明社会团结减少恐惧感。研究指出社区解体和缺乏社会凝聚力是导致高水平的犯罪恐惧感的条件(斯科甘(Skogan)和马克斯菲尔德(Maxfield),1981;亨特(Hunter)和博伊默(Baumer),1982;斯科甘(Skogan),1990)。缺乏凝聚力会增强恐惧感(福勒(Fowler)和曼吉欧尼(Mangione),1982)。人们期望社会支持能将人们从焦虑和恐惧感中释放出来。人们还期望对社区负更多责任感的个人在解释和对付相同情况时比那些较少责任感的人要更积极。

尽管双方都提到恐惧感和团结之间的消极关系,但对何者是原因存在显著分歧。一些研究认为缺乏社会凝聚力是恐惧感的后果(康克林(Conklin),1975;殷(Yin),1980)。对暴力犯罪的恐惧感限制人们的日常行为,使人们彼此疏离,减少社交(哈特纳格尔(Hartnagel),1979;古斯汀(Gookstein)和肖特兰(Shotland),1980;康克林(Conklin),1975)。一些研究提出,恐惧感是焦虑、烦恼、紧张的"都市不安"心理综合病症的一部分,跟社会解体和当代都市生活的生理上和社会上的无力有关。例如,科恩(Cohen)等人(1978)发现,参与社会组织的人感到更能控制犯罪,与没有参与社会组织的人相比较少害怕犯罪。他们还发现,接受过自卫训练的妇女感到更能控制事态并因此较少害怕犯罪。所以说,提高社会团结会减少恐惧感。

在这个思想的基础上,许多减少恐惧感的公共计划得到发展。这些计划设计方法来增加个人间交互作用和个人对社区的责任感,希望能够以此来减少犯罪和恐惧感。

笔者认为,争论说明恐惧感和团结之间存在可能的互反关系。恐惧感影响团结,团结同样也影响恐惧感。就恐惧感和团结之间的关系,笔者假设:

Ⅵ.1　恐惧感降低社会团结。

Ⅵ.2　社会团结降低恐惧感。

要解决这个争论,我们必须估计一个非递归模型,在这个模型里恐惧感影响团结,团结也影响恐惧感。

总之,既往研究检验了恐惧感对团结的功能和团结对恐惧感的作用。既往大多数研究认为恐惧感和社会团结之间是消极的单向联系,而对何者是原因存在分歧。笔者提出在恐惧感和团结之间存在一种互反关系。

## 五、本章小结

在本章中,笔者提出一个一般理论模型来回答研究计划中的基本问题。模型提出了在许多可能性之中的四种犯罪后果。犯罪影响生活质量、社会经济资源水平、民众亲政府态度和导致社会衰退。理论模型认为在解释犯罪后果时恐惧感和社会团结这两个变量十分重要。这一模型设计了犯罪、恐惧感、社会团结和犯罪后果之间的因果关系结构。该模型解释了三个重要理论问题。(1)犯罪、恐惧感和社会团结怎样影响犯罪后果。这是这一研究领域的中心问题。(2)通过阐述迪尔凯姆(Durkheim)的理论与社会团结的概念解决了一个富有争议的议题:即支持迪尔凯姆(Durkheim)的犯罪功能论与致力于解释犯罪的恐惧感影响社会团结议题的争议。(3)模型致力于解决恐惧感和社会团结之间的因果关系。模型表明了恐惧感和社会团结之间的互反关系(图3.1)。

在解释第一个问题,犯罪恐惧感和社会团结怎样影响社会后果时,笔者提出的一般理论模型认为有两个变量在解释犯罪后果上十分重要,即恐惧感和社会团结。笔者的一般理论模型认为,恐惧感和社会团结直接影响社会后果;犯罪直接影响恐惧感和社会团结;犯罪并不直接影响社会后果。恐惧感和团结是犯罪作用于社会后果的中介变量。

　　既往恐惧感相关研究著作大多视犯罪恐惧感为因变量,并一致认为恐惧感是对犯罪的主要反应。针对理论模型中包括的每种社会后果,笔者解释了恐惧感和社会团结怎样和为什么影响这些后果。

　　第二个问题是支持迪尔凯姆(Durkheim)理论的犯罪功能研究和恐惧感研究之间的争论。迪尔凯姆(Durkheim)认为犯罪在促进社会团结方面起积极功能。有关犯罪功能的研究表明犯罪产生的义愤使人们聚集在一起,促进社交,提醒人们他们的共性,从而促进社会团结。与之相反,犯罪恐惧感既往研究普遍认为犯罪并不能使人们聚集在一起,恰恰相反,犯罪引起恐惧感而限制了人们的日常行为,使人们疏离,减少社交,导致社会团结度降低。笔者认为,社会团结有文化的和结构的成分。在现代社会,暴力犯罪和非暴力犯罪有不同效果。暴力犯罪引起恐惧感,使人们疏离,限制人们的相互作用或行动,从而降低社会团结。非暴力犯罪促进社交,从而提升社会团结。

　　第三,一般理论模型致力于解决恐惧感和社会团结之间因果关系的争论。既往研究阐明并测试了恐惧感减少社会团结或社会团结降低恐惧感的作用。绝大多数研究认为恐惧感和社会团结之间是消极的单向关系,但对何者是原因存在分歧。笔者提出恐惧感和团结之间存在互反关系。恐惧感影响社会团结,社会团结也影响恐惧感。

　　接下来的章节讨论并报告对一般理论模型所采取的测试。笔者将讨论研究方法论问题,进行单变量和双变量分析,并建立和测试度量模型。笔者将测试有关犯罪、恐惧感和社会团结怎样影响社会后果的假说,以及迪尔凯姆(Durkheim)关于犯罪促进社会团结论题和认为犯罪减少社会团结的恐惧感研究之间的争论。笔者测试了一个非递归模型来解决关于恐惧感和团结之间因果关系的争论。本书最后一章将概括模型测试的结论,并讨论这些结论以及相关问题。

# 第四章　研究方法

## 一、数据

本研究所采用的数据来自马里斯·麦弗森（Marlys McPherson）、格伦·索罗威（Glenn Silloway）和戴维·弗瑞（David Frey）于1983年7月在明尼阿波利斯市（Minneapolis）和圣保罗市（St. Paul）进行的名为"社区商业中心的犯罪、恐惧感和控制"（ICPSR（大学间政治与社会研究数据库联盟）8167）的项目。这一项目的数据分两个阶段收集。第一阶段调查了明尼阿波利斯市（Minneapolis）和圣保罗市（St. Paul）的93个商业中心。每个中心依区域大小平均包括20个商店，并被距离大约3英里的居民区所包围。具体数据来自从明尼阿波利斯市（Minneapolis）和圣保罗市（St. Paul）警察局、明尼阿波利斯市（Minneapolis）和圣保罗市（St. Paul）审计局、R. L. Polk &Co.（著名市场调查公司）和美国人口普查报告得来的人口数据。研究的第二个阶段从原来的样本中挑选了24个商业中心，对这24个被选区域的每一个商业中心都选取了870位居民进行电话调查并对213名商人进行了面对面调查。

当前研究的数据出自两个文件：居民调查和商业调查，其中24个社区（商业中心）的数据来对社区内个人反应的汇总。也就是说，就居民和商业调查中的每个问题，计算出同一社区内所有参与者答案的平均值，把得出的平均值当作这个区域对该问题的答案来使用。在分析时将这两个汇总文件集合成一个文件。这样当前研究的试样量就是 24 个案例。尽管这些数据不是基于当前研究目的所收集,我们仍然可以从中获取当前研究所需要的绝大部分信息。

# 二、分析

理论问题的特殊性和研究课题的困难性决定了对分析方法和分析过程的选择。本书的研究中有两个问题尤为重要。一是理论概念的度量,一是小样本问题。在尝试建立并测试一个理论模型时,当前研究面临着度量主要理论概念(比如团结和恐惧感)的困难。团结一直都被看做是一个模糊概念,被批评为难以度量,迪尔凯姆(Durkheim)自己也认识到这一点。这样一来可靠性和有效性就成了问题。恐惧感作为一个情感状态显然面临着同样的度量问题。从数学上很容易证明,在递归分析里当一个自变量测量出现误差,系数估计值会得出偏倚的不一致的估计结果(韩舍克(Hanushek)和杰克逊(Jackson),1977)。传统方法在解决这些问题上难以让人满意。

结构方程式模型方法就可以解决这些问题,这些方法可以被用来解决难以完成的重要概念不能被准确测量的问题,因此它们是当前研究使用的首要方法。结构方程式模型方法使用潜变量来表示理论概念,并使用多项指标来度量抽象的理论概念。这种度量方法允许我们模拟结构性关系而不用假设对概念的度量完美无缺,因为对概念的所谓完美度量通常是不存在的。

典型的结构方程式模型包括两个部分:度量模型和结构模型。度量模型包括理论概念及其指标。每个理论概念由许多指标来度量。每个指标的度量误差都被包括在统计模型中。误差分布并不一定是随机的。我们从这些分析中得到的结果,也就是所谓的因子载荷,反映了由每个指标度量所度量的理论概念的净量部分。所建立的因子或潜变量被用来估计理论概念之间的结构关系。这个过程明确模拟了度量误差,从而可以确定结构参数没有被度量误差歪曲。

结构方程式模型中最常使用的估计技术是最大似然值(ML)估计(保伦

（Bollen），1989），它是两个最流行的结构方程式模型计算机程序 EQS 和 LISREL 中的缺省估计技术。该方法的实质是选择一潜在参数使产生其分布时所观察样本的可能性最大化。在一般情况下，最大似然值（ML）方法得出的估计是一致的、渐进无偏的和渐进有效的（班特勒（Bentler），1989；保伦（Bollen），1989）。在样本较小时，我们可以接受由于小样本而造成偏差的估计，也不会去使用一个不一致的估计（也就是即使当样本数目任意大时也不会收敛于总体参数的估计）（保伦（Bollen），1989）。经验研究也表明，最大似然值（ML）估计是稳健的，也就是说，它们在模型和数据偏离潜在假设时倾向于保持得较好（保伦（Bollen），1989）。在以下的分析中，笔者将用最大似然值（ML）估计来估计结构参数。

最大似然值（ML）估计的渐近性特点要求样本大小跟待估自由参数数量密切相关。至于何谓大样本，班特勒（Bentler）提出一个方针：样本大小与被待估自由参数数量的比例最低为 5∶1（班特勒（Bentler），1989）。对小一些的样本，最大似然值（ML）估计的特点还不明晰。也就是说，尽管最大似然值（ML）估计渐近无偏差，其对小样本估计的特点还不甚明了。所以当使用小样本时，我们对估计后果不太看好。

为解决小样本问题，本书分析过程被分成两个阶段以减少待估模型大小。笔者首先估计度量模型，接着再估计结构模型。第一步，笔者为每一个理论概念都建立度量模型，从所有变量中选出潜在的相应度量，通过所有可能的已确定因子分析来定位理论上有意义、实践上合适的度量模型。然后笔者用这个度量系数来建构每个理论概念的复合指标。复合指标是通过综合所有度量，使用因子载荷作为每个度量的权值而计算得来。即概念的复合指标 = b1X1 + b2X2 + b3X3…，其中 b 为因子载荷。

第二步，结构模型测试，将研究假说和对它们的测试分成三组。每组对应前一章讨论的三个理论问题中的一个。这三个理论问题是：犯罪、恐惧感和团结影响社会后果；犯罪影响团结；以及恐惧感和团结之间的关系。笔者首先测试了一个递归模型（图 4.1），这个模型主要是关于第一个问题的，即犯罪、恐惧感和团结影响社会后果。接着，笔者测试了一个非递归模型，主要解决恐惧感和团结间的因果关系问题，确认犯罪、恐惧感和团结影响后果这一假说的结果。

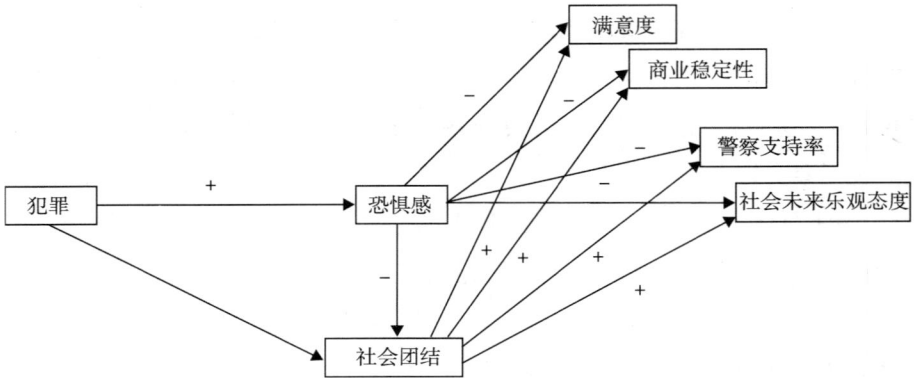

**图 4.1　一般递归模型**

在递归模型测试中,笔者将总模型分成四个子模型,每个子模型只产生一个结果(见图 4.1.1,图 4.1.2,图 4.1.3 和图 4.1.4)。一共有四个结构模型,每个模型对应犯罪的一个社会后果。笔者每次测试一个子模型来估计小部分参数,使估计的参数数量保持最小。笔者还用不同的犯罪和社会团结量度重新检测了这些模型,以确认模型的稳定性,尽管这看起来像是在作重复研究。

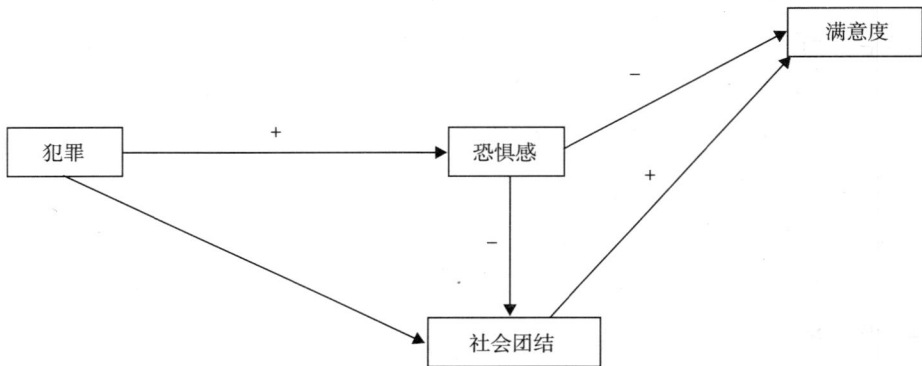

**图 4.1.1　满意度模型**

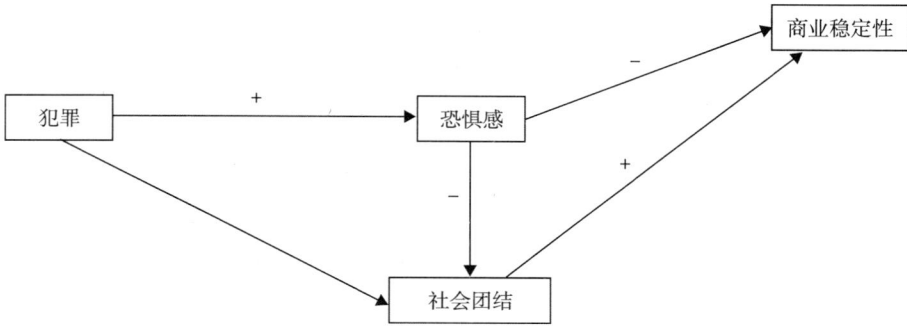

图 4.1.2 商业稳定性模型

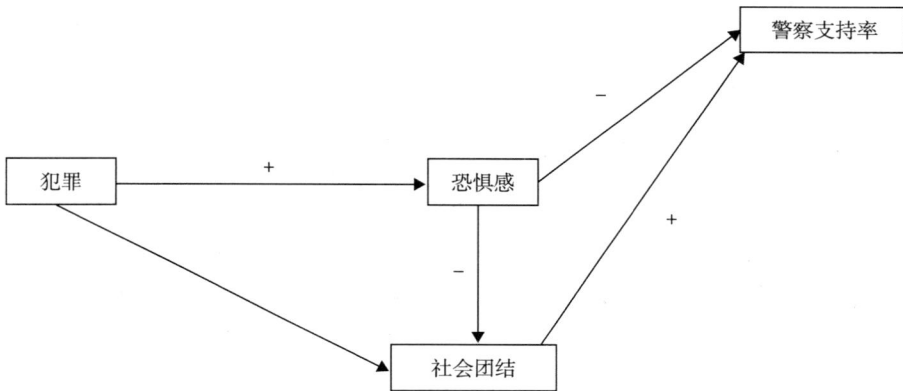

图 4.1.3 警察支持率模型

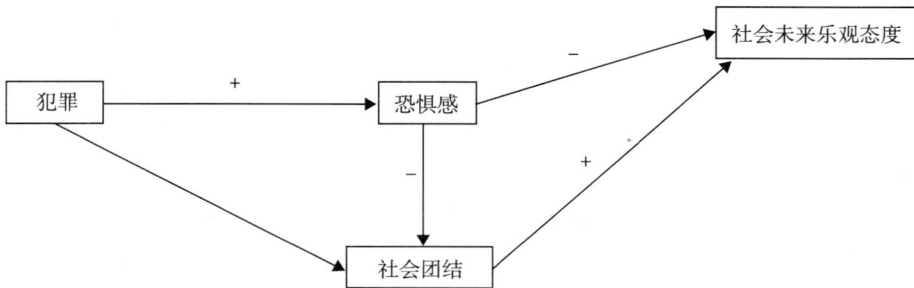

图 4.1.4 社会未来乐观态度模型

# 三、操作和假说

当前理论模型包含的理论概念有：生活质量、社会经济资源水平、亲政府态度、社会衰退、恐惧感、社会团结、暴力犯罪以及非暴力犯罪。本书第六章度量模型中将论述以多项复合量度来测量理论概念的过程以及组成理论概念的项目细节。

**生活质量**　以在地区生活和经商的满意度这个复合度量加以测量，包括三个项目。

**社会经济资源水平**　以在地区生活和经商的商业稳定性这个复合度量加以测量，也包括三个项目。

**亲政府和警察态度**　以对警察的支持率这个复合度量加以测量，它包括四个项目。

**社会衰退**　以对社会未来的乐观态度这个复合度量加以测量，它包括三个项目。复合度量使用的项目要求人们评价他们社会的社会与经济条件是在进步还是在衰退。需要注意的是，所构建的量度的值越低，表明社会衰退越厉害。

**犯罪恐惧感**　以恐惧感这个复合量度方式加以测量，包括五个项目。

**社会团结**　以对社会团结的三个不同方面以三个复合量度方式得以操作。如前所述，团结包括文化成分和结构成分，也就是说团结包括集体意识和共有利益。第一个复合度量反映了"居民对社区的义务感"（SOL1），包括三个项目。第二个复合度量反映"居民对社区的责任感"（SOL2），包括六个项目。第三个度量反映商人对商业区的责任感（SOL3），更确切地说，是他们共有利益，包括三个项目。

**自然人暴力犯罪**　通过向社区居民提问来度量：你所在社区的人们每隔多久遭到恐吓、殴打或遭遇其他类似情况？你会选择：从来没有…0；偶尔…1；经常…2；随时…3。

**非暴力犯罪**　通过对入店偷窃的提问来度量。问题向商人提出：自1981年8月以来，有人到你的商店盗窃么？有…1；没有…0。跟社区水平结合在一起后,这个度量就变成一个持续变量。

　　一般模型的操作显示在图 4.2 中,包括一系列假设。为解决犯罪、恐惧感和社会团结怎样影响社会后果问题,该模型考察了犯罪的四个社会后果:在某一区域内生活和经商的满意度、商业稳定性、对警察的支持率以及社会未来乐观态度(见图 4.2)。

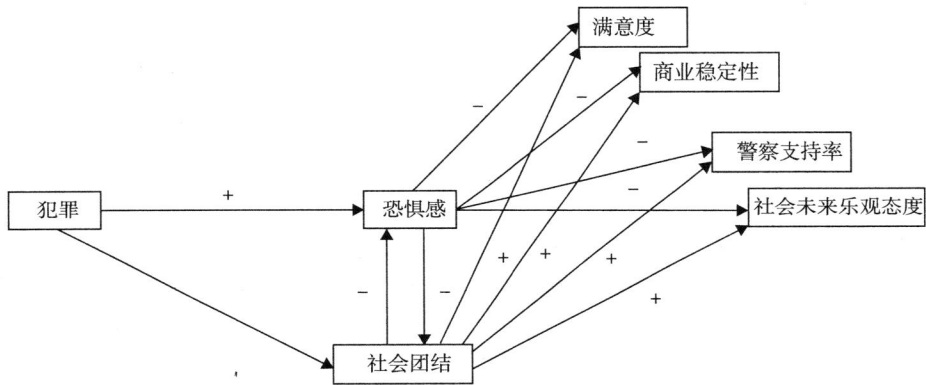

**图 4.2　理论模型的操作化**

相关假设围绕不同后果分组。对满意度的假设有:

I.1. 犯罪降低人们在区域内生活和经商的满意度。

I.2. 犯罪不直接降低满意度。

I.3. 恐惧感直接降低满意度。

I.4. 恐惧感是犯罪作用于满意度的媒介。

I.5. 社会团结提高人们在区域内生活和经商的满意度。

对商业稳定性的假设有:

II.1. 犯罪降低区域内的商业稳定性。

II.2. 犯罪不降低区域内的商业稳定性。

II.3. 恐惧感直接降低区域内的商业稳定性。

II.4. 恐惧感是犯罪作用于商业稳定性的媒介。

II.5. 社会团结提高商业稳定性。

有关人们对警察支持率的假设有:

III. 1. 犯罪降低人们对警察的支持率。

III. 2. 犯罪不直接降低人们对警察的支持率。

III. 3. 恐惧感直接降低人们对警察的支持率。

III. 4. 恐惧感是犯罪作用于对警察支持率的媒介。

III. 5. 社会团结提高人们对警察的支持率。

有关人们对社会未来乐观态度的假设有：

IV. 1. 犯罪降低人们对社会未来的乐观态度。

IV. 2. 犯罪不直接降低人们对社会未来的乐观态度。

IV. 3. 恐惧感直接降低人们对社会未来的乐观态度。

IV. 4. 恐惧感是犯罪作用于对社会未来乐观态度的媒介。

IV. 5. 社会团结提高对社会未来的乐观态度。

为解决犯罪怎样影响社会团结问题，笔者详细论述了该模型的相关部分，考察了不同犯罪的直接效应。笔者认为：

V. 1. 暴力犯罪产生恐惧感。

V. 2. 非暴力犯罪不直接影响恐惧感。

V. 3. 暴力犯罪降低社会团结。

V. 4. 非暴力犯罪促进社会团结。

针对恐惧感和团结之间的因果关系问题提出的假设有：

VI. 1. 恐惧感降低社会团结。

VI. 2. 社会团结降低恐惧感。

# 第五章　单变量和二变量分析

本书的数据分析分三步进行。第一步是单变量和二变量分析;第二步是为建立度量模型而进行的确定因素分析;第三步估计一般模型的结构参数并测试理论假设。

尽管从理论上来说,最大似然值(ML)估计要求变量是多维正态分布,但当变量是偏态分布时,其估计值通常也是稳健的。检查变量的多维正态分布是一项复杂的工作,迄今未得到很好的解决。但检查变量的单变量分布有助于发现对多维正态分布假定的违背。这是单变量分析的主要目的之一。

笔者列出了 24 个调查区域的所有变量值,检查了所有变量的频率。变量BEATIC(被殴打)是调查数据中发现的唯一过分偏斜的变量(偏斜系数 = 2.1)。BEATIC 的原始问题是:请回顾去年,从 1981 年 8 月到现在你是否在街上被人拦住,遭到恐吓、殴打或遭遇过其他类似情形(是 = 1;不是 = 0)? 量度单位是随意的,因此笔者用这个变量的平方根来转换它。新的变量SBEATIC 等于 BEATIC 的平方根,斜度仅为 0.2。

单变量分析的另一任务是识别异常值。综合从所有变量值、频率值、茎叶图、盒形图中得到的信息,笔者辨别出一个调查区域(830 号)的值异常。该区域存在许多极端变量值。笔者浏览了居民调查和个人层面的商业调查的原始文件,列表检查了所有有关犯罪、恐惧感、社会团结的案例以及一些结果变量,没有发现错误。总的来说,这个区域的所有犯罪变量都为最高值,恐惧感度量值也最高,大部分社会团结变量值为最低值,这种格局是有道理的。在因子分析中,笔者进行了包含这个区域的分析和不包含这个区域的分析。总的来说系数值没有太大改变,但是把 830 号区域剔除后,模型对数据的合适度大为改观。

在双变量分析中笔者主要检查两件事情。其一,笔者将主要变量之间的相互关系同过去的研究作比较;其二,笔者就每个理论潜变量在假设的度量模型中的合理性进行了检查。

像文献回顾中所讨论的那样,很少有定量分析来考察当前理论模型中涉及的主要理论概念的相互关系。利斯卡(Liska)和沃纳(Warner)(1991)的犯罪功能研究是这方面的重要著作。这部著作涉及犯罪、恐惧感和受限制的社交之间的关系,笔者的论著也谈到了这些。他们的样本包括全国司法研究所和审计署主持的全国犯罪调查(NCS)所调查的 26 个城市。NCS 在 1973 到 1974 年从每个城市抽取 10,000 个家庭和 20,000 个 12 岁以上被调查者。这项研究表明抢劫(自然人暴力犯罪)和恐惧感指数之间的相关度为 .60;笔者的数据表明,自然人暴力犯罪度量和恐惧感度量的相关度在 .418 到 .847 之间作用方向相同,大小相当。利斯卡(Liska)和沃纳(Warner)(1991)的研究也表明,白天的恐惧感和夜晚的恐惧感这两个潜变量跟由自评量表所测量的夜晚的社交和因犯罪而改变或受限制的社交相关度为 .88。在笔者的数据里没有关于社交或受限制的社交的度量,但有能够用来度量社会团结的项目。由五个项目组成的恐惧感指标与三项社会团结指标的相关度分别为 −.384, −.456, −.206。因为使用受限制的社交来度量社会团结,恐惧感和团结之间的关系与利斯卡(Liska)和沃纳(Warner)研究中报告的一样,负向相关。相关性大小的差异取决于度量内容的差异。

接下来,笔者检查了相同理论概念指数之间的相关性能否合理地当作相同潜变量的度量。彼此间只有微弱联系的指数不能作为相同潜变量的指标。

这样,双变量分析有助于对变量进行分类和分组,有助于为因子选择变量,有助于识别可能的理论因子。为不同理论变量而组成复合度量的度量将最终从度量模型的分析中挑选出来,度量模型将在下一章阐述。结果证明相同理论概念度量之间的相关度为中强或者较强。例如,恐惧感度量之间的相关度在 .419 到 .847 之间。

# 第六章　度量模型

当前分析的目的是建立理论上有意义、实践上合适的度量模型,所以这些分析通过全面使用数据中得到的所有信息来度量理论概念。为每一个理论概念建立良好的度量模型是有效检验结构模型的关键步骤。评估明确模拟度量误差的度量模型,注意结构系数检验的度量误差的效应,这样结构系数会更好地反映真实的母本参数。

首先,笔者运用理论和经验标准来选择所有能被潜在用于理论概念度量的所有变量并对它们进行分类。理论上的标准是备选变量理论概念的测量必须是有效的。经验标准是相同理论概念的备选量度至少达到中度相关。总计有87个变量作为潜在待选项从综合数据文件中被挑选出用来为每个理论概念建立量度模型。表6.1报道了选出变量的分布情况。

表 6.1　变量频率分布

|  | 平均数 | 标准差 | 峰度 | 偏度 | 最大值 | 最小值 |
|---|---|---|---|---|---|---|
| PEOPBEAT | .455 | .219 | .668 | .826 | 1.000 | .118 |
| CRIMEAMT | 1.036 | .417 | .246 | 1.008 | 1.917 | .500 |
| SHOPLIFT | .318 | .221 | .171 | .444 | .857 | .000 |
| ARBSBROK | .886 | .341 | .388 | −.527 | 1.556 | .125 |
| BUSBROK | 1.160 | .416 | 3.622 | 1.602 | 2.500 | .625 |
| YOURBSBU | .245 | .141 | −.296 | .578 | .556 | .000 |

| | 平均数 | 标准差 | 峰度 | 偏度 | 最大值 | 最小值 |
|---|---|---|---|---|---|---|
| FEAR31 | 1.660 | .327 | .192 | .275 | 2.432 | 1.057 |
| FEAR32 | 1.173 | .352 | .813 | 1.317 | 2.053 | .800 |
| POSSBEAT | 1.196 | .158 | 2.060 | 1.344 | 1.605 | .970 |
| SPOSBEAT | .977 | .156 | .335 | .830 | 1.342 | .706 |
| FEAR4 | 1.402 | .650 | .881 | .835 | 3.143 | .429 |
| RESYEAR | 13.420 | 3.575 | 1.928 | −1.163 | 18.588 | 3.471 |
| OPINEIBO | 1.777 | .103 | .015 | −.746 | 1.914 | 1.541 |
| COMNEIBO | 2.467 | .166 | .302 | .304 | 2.853 | 2.153 |
| LOTTOSAY | 3.277 | .305 | 5.527 | −1.966 | 3.686 | 2.216 |
| FEELRESP | 3.272 | .321 | 3.568 | −1.570 | 3.714 | 2.270 |
| TELLSTRG | 3.581 | .219 | −.091 | −.923 | 3.829 | 3.054 |
| BLOTOSAY | 2.085 | .195 | 1.878 | −1.238 | 2.412 | 1.528 |
| BFELRESP | 2.237 | .223 | .845 | −1.005 | 2.600 | 1.649 |
| BTELSTRG | 2.932 | .314 | −.198 | −.726 | 3.314 | 2.194 |
| BLOTOSA2 | 2.774 | .363 | −1.080 | .213 | 3.375 | 2.250 |
| BFELRES2 | 2.795 | .383 | .165 | −.353 | 3.667 | 2.000 |
| BTELSTR2 | 3.211 | .383 | .474 | −.353 | 4.000 | 2.333 |
| RATELIVE | 3.264 | .327 | 1.370 | −1.276 | 3.800 | 2.432 |
| AREARATE | 2.715 | .447 | −.314 | .009 | 3.714 | 2.000 |
| INVEHOME | .831 | .186 | 1.318 | −1.309 | 1.000 | .333 |
| ECOSTABL | 3.336 | .475 | −.561 | −.613 | 4.000 | 2.286 |
| OUTPLAN | .094 | .132 | .954 | 1.295 | .444 | .000 |
| LIKEMOVE2 | .699 | 2.540 | −.376 | −.662 | 3.000 | 2.125 |
| POLIWALK | .311 | .357 | 2.423 | 1.690 | 1.286 | .000 |
| POLICHAT | .350 | .377 | 1.866 | 1.526 | 1.400 | .000 |
| RATEPOLI | 2.623 | .433 | .608 | .774 | 3.714 | 1.889 |
| POLITRET | 2.457 | .433 | .608 | .774 | 3.714 | 1.889 |
| ECOTREND | 2.058 | .212 | 1.979 | 1.439 | 2.618 | 1.793 |
| ECOFUTUR | 2.204 | .415 | .680 | −.489 | 2.889 | 1.143 |
| ECOTRED2 | 2.093 | .360 | −.788 | −.068 | 2.667 | 1.429 |

　　对这些选出的变量,笔者为每个概念作了一系列验证性因子分析。笔者选择使用验证性因子分析而不使用探索性因子分析出于两个原因。其一,探索性因子分析在适应我们的理论性和实体性知识方面存在局限性,它使结论

纯粹建立在任意的统计标准上。其二,探索性因子分析不允许校正度量误差。它假定误差是纯随机的,这在我们的案例中其实是一个待检验的假设而不是一个定论。验证性因子分析克服了这些缺点。它使我们能够详细说明建立在实体性知识基础上的模型,它对度量误差不作不切实际的假定。

为了发挥这些数据的最大效用,笔者用尽了这87个度量的所有可能的交替组合来定位既有理论意义又有统计匹配性的最佳因子模型。在因子分析中,同其他项目相比较具有较低度量系数的项目不属于相同的潜变量。它们被剔除,模型被重新估计。

度量模型的分析也检验了关于度量误差是纯随机的假设。检验分两步进行。首先,笔者估计了限制所有指标的量度误差相互无关联的模型。然后,笔者估计了允许一些量度误差相互关联来提高模型对数据的适应度的模型。通过比较这两种估计值并考察模型对数据适应度的提高,笔者才可能接受或拒绝这一假设。在允许一些度量误差相互关联显著提高估计值和模型适应度的情况下,关于量度误差是纯随机的假设并不被接受。

笔者为每一个理论概念估计了一个单因子模型。对因子载荷的估计(标准最大似然值(ML)估计)见表6.2。在表6.2中,每一竖列报道一个理论概念的因子载荷。商业盗窃表示为COM,团结表示为SOL,等等(见表底部注释)。X1到X6表示每个因子的不同指标、不同因子指标变化的规格。例如,恐惧感有六个指标、商业盗窃(COM)有三个指标等等。结果表明一些度量模型低载荷,度量模型因而不理想。例如,“居民对社区的责任感”(SOL2)模型,所有载荷都在.2左右。这表明使用的度量仅反映了理论概念“居民对社区的责任感”(SOL2)的一小部分变化。然而,度量模型使我们能够用这一小部分变化来反映理论概念,克服不使用度量模型就会产生的结构系数偏差。

**表6.2　度量模型**

(标准最大似然值(ML)估计)

|  | FEAR | COM | SOL1 | SOL2 | SOL3 | SAT | BST | POL | OPT |
|---|---|---|---|---|---|---|---|---|---|
| X1 | .856 | .689 | .680 | .293 | .734 | .812 | .582 | .516 | .825 |
| X2 | .859 | .747 | .768 | .302 | .866 | .658 | -.588 | .649 | .861 |
| X3 | .946 | .645 | .668 | .182 | .654 | .739 | .848 | .714 | .931 |

续表

| | FEAR | COM | SOL1 | SOL2 | SOL3 | SAT | BST | POL | OPT |
|---|---|---|---|---|---|---|---|---|---|
| X4 | .902 | | | .152 | | | | .810 | |
| X5 | .677 | | | .178 | | | | | |
| X6 | | | | .226 | | | | | |
| Chi-Squ | 4.378 | 0 | 0 | 6.419 | 0 | 0 | 0 | .188 | 0 |
| df | 5 | 1 | 1 | 7 | 1 | 1 | 1 | 1 | 1 |
| p | .49 | .99 | .98 | .49 | .99 | .99 | .99 | .66 | .99 |
| BBNFI | .95 | 1.00 | 1.00 | .95 | 1.00 | 1.00 | 1.00 | .99 | 1.00 |
| BBNNFI | 1.01 | 1.28 | 1.13 | 1.01 | 1.61 | 1.13 | 1.28 | 1.19 | 1.28 |
| CFI | 1.00 | 1.00 | 1.00 | 1.00 | 1.00 | 1.00 | 1.00 | 1.00 | 1.00 |

注释:行标题表示不同指数。X1,X2,…X6 表示每个指数的不同指标。例如,恐惧感(FEAR)有 5 个指标(X1,…X5),不同于商业盗窃(COM)的 3 个指标(X1,…X3)。

COM = 商业盗窃
SOL1 = 居民对社区的义务感
SOL2 = 居民对社区的责任感
SOL3 = 商人对商业区的责任感
SAT = 在地区生活和经商的满意度
BST = 商业稳定性
POL = 警察支持率
OPT = 社会未来乐观态度
df = 自由度
BBNFI = Bentler-Bonett 基准契合度指标
BBNNFI = Bentler-Bonett 非基准契合度指标
CFI = 比较拟合指标

# 一、区域满意度度量模型

表 6.2 表明区域满意度(SAT)度量模型有三个指标。第一个指标的因子载荷(见标题为 SAT 的列)是 .812;第二个的因子载荷是 .658;第三个是 .739。单因子模型因而准确建立,且卡方值等于 0。为了能够评价模型跟数据的适应度,笔者修订了前文所述模型中的一个因子载荷,这样模型就过度识别了且自由度 df 等于 1。笔者重新估计了这一模型,模型跟数据适应得很好;p<.99;Bentler-Bonett 基准契合度指标 = 1.00;Bentler-Bonett 非基准契合度指标 = 1.138;比较拟合指标 = 1.000。

第一个度量问居民：综合所有因素，你认为社区作为一个生活的地方属于下面哪个等级？很好…4；好…3；一般…2；差…1。第二个度量问商人：总的来说，你认为这个商业区作为经商的地方属于下面哪个等级？很好…4；好…3；一般…2；差…1。第三个度量问商人：如果有人想在这个社区买房子安家，你会认为这是个好的投资么，或者他们在其他社区投资更好？好的投资…2；在其他社区投资更好…1。总体而言，因子反映了人们对在区域内生活和经商的满意度。

## 二、商业稳定性度量模型

表6.2表明商业稳定性度量模型有三个度量。模型识别准确，卡方值为0。为了能够评价模型跟数据的适应度，笔者修订了模型中的一个因子载荷，这样模型就过度识别了，df＝1。笔者重新估计了模型，模型跟数据适应得很好；p<.99；Bentler-Bonett 基准契合度指标＝1.00；Bentler-Bonett 非基准契合度指标＝1.289；比较拟合指标＝1.000。

第一个度量是：就商业营业额而言，这个商业区的稳定性如何？非常稳定…4；有些稳定…3；有些不稳定…2；非常不稳定…1。第二个度量是：你计划在另外一个区域重新开公司么？是…1；不是…0。第三个度量是：你在多大程度上想将公司搬到其他地方？根本不想…3；有些想…2；非常想…1。

这一因子反映商人将公司搬到其他地方的可能性。这个模型构建的复合指标反映了商业的稳定性，分值高表明商业会留在这个区域，分值低表明商业会转移到其他地方。

## 三、警察支持率度量模型

表6.2表明警察支持率度量模型有四个度量。模型识别准确，卡方值 $\chi^2$＝.118，df＝1；p<.66；Bentler-Bonett 基准契合度指标＝.994；Bentler-Bonett 非基准契合度指标＝1.191；比较拟合指标＝1.000。

四个度量分别是：据你所知，警察多久经过这个中心？很少或从来没有…0；每月一两次…1；每周一两次…2；几乎每天…3。在你工作时警察每隔多久会走访你同你聊天或者只是看看你在干什么？很少或从来没有…0；每月一两次…1；每周一两次…2；几乎每天…3。总体而言，你怎样看待警察在为这个商业区提供安保方面所做的工作？你会说：很好…4；好…3；一般…2；差…1。警察对待社区里人们的态度怎样？警察对待他们：很好…4；好…3；不太好…2；根本不好…1。这一因子反映人们对警察的评价和态度。

## 四、对社会未来乐观态度的度量模型

表6.2表明对社会未来乐观态度的度量模型有三个量度。模型识别准确，卡方值为0。为了能够评价模型跟数据的适应度，笔者修订了模型中的一个因子载荷，这样模型就过度识别了，df＝1。笔者重新估计了模型，模型跟数据适应得很好；p<.99；Bentler-Bonett 基准契合度指标＝1.00；Bentler-Bonett 非基准契合度指标＝1.289；比较拟合指标＝1.000。参数改变非常轻微。

第一个度量问居民：就你所见，你认为在未来几年里这个商业区会变得更好、保持不变还是会在经济上衰退？变得更好…3；保持不变…2；衰退…1。另外两个度量问商人：据你所见，你认为未来几年里这个商业区会在经济上变得更好、保持不变还是会在经济上衰退？变得更好…3；保持不变…2；衰退…1。过去几年你公司所在的社区的总的经济与社会条件是提高、保持不变还是衰退？提高…3；保持不变…2；衰退…1。这一因子反映出人们对所在区域总的经济和社会条件的感受。

## 五、犯罪的恐惧感度量模型

表6.2表明恐惧感的结果度量模型有五个度量。项目名称分别为FEAR31、FEAR32、POSSBEAT、SPOSSBEAT 和 FEAR4，在表6.2 中分别以 X1、X2、X3、X4 和 X5 来表示。模型跟数据适应得很好，卡方值 $\chi^2 = 4.378$；df＝5；p<.49；Bentler-Bonett 基准契合度指标＝.955；Bentler-Bonett 非基准契合度指标＝1.014；比较拟合指标＝1.000。

度量 FEAR31 是五个问题的综合：1.我经常有些担心自己会成为社区犯

罪的受害者。2. 如果在社区里晚上陌生人拦住我问路我不会感到担心。3. 当跟我关系密切的人在社区里时,我担心他们的安全。4. 当我要离开家一段时间,我担心有人试图闯入。5. 当我在社区里晚上听见身后有脚步声,我会感到不安。答案是"大部分对"和"大部分不对"。就个人回答者而言,其综合指标范围从 5 到 0,其中 5 代表最高水平的恐惧感,0 代表最低水平的恐惧感。FEAR32、FEAR4 使用同一系列问题。FEAR32 问居民关于附近商业区的问题;FEAR4 问商人关于附近商业区的问题。FEAR32 和 FEAR4 的值以跟FEAR31 相同的方法计算。

量度 POSSBEAT 的问题是:在社区里你被拦在街上、恐吓、殴打或诸如此类事情的可能性是:根本不可能…0;很少可能性…1;相当可能…2;可能性非常大…3。对 SPOSSBEAT 的问题跟对 POSSBEAT 的问题相同,问的是社区里的商业区发生类似事情的可能性。

# 六、社会团结度量模型

统计分析的结果产生了三个关于社会团结的量度模型(见表6.2)。第一个团结因子有三个度量。模型识别准确,卡方值0。为了能够评价模型跟数据的适应度,笔者修订了模型中的一个因子载荷,这样模型就过度识别了,df=1。笔者重新估计了模型,模型跟数据适应得很好;p<.98;Bentler-Bonett基准契合度指标=1.00;Bentler-Bonett 非基准契合度指标=1.133;比较拟合指标=1.000。

第一个度量是:你在现住址生活了多久了(以年数记)?第二个量度是:有人认为社区是真正的家,他们的根在这里。还有人认为社区只是他们碰巧住的地方。哪一种更接近你的想法?真正的家…2;只是住的地方…1。第三个量度是:有人对社区怀有强烈责任感,有人则没有。考虑一下你对社区的责任感,是强烈、未定还是没有?强烈责任感…3;未定…2;没有责任感…1。这些指数量度的团结因子反映了社会团结的一个方面,即"居民对社区的义务感(SOL1)"。

第二个团结模型有六个度量。模型跟数据适应得很好。卡方值 $\chi^2 =$ 6.419;p<.49;Bentler-Bonett 基准契合度指标=.958;Bentler-Bonett 非基准契

合度指标=1.009;比较拟合指标=1.000。但是,尽管仔细挑选了指数,载荷仍然很低。这也说明构建度量模型来应对度量误差而不是简单假定度量跟递归分析里的一样好是必要的。

前三个度量是对一个问题的三个陈述,要求居民从非常同意(编码4)到非常不同意(编码1)这四个选项中作出选择。问题是:首先,考虑一下正好在你家周围的地方,比如你家的前门口或后门口,如果你住的公寓还包括走廊,或者挨着你的房子还有人行道或小道。想象一下这些地方,告诉我你同意还是不同意下列说法:a. 我对发生的事情非常了解。b. 我觉得对发生的事情应负责任。c. 我能从外人中认出谁属于这里。

后三个度量是对一个问题的三个陈述,使用相同的格式和选项。问题是:考虑一下你所住街区的其他地方,告诉我你是否同意我的每个说法。a. 我对发生的事情非常了解。b. 我觉得对发生的事情应负责任。c. 我能从外人中认出谁属于这里。这个因子反映社会团结的另外一个方面,即“居民对社区的责任感(SOL2)”。

团结的第三个因子有三个度量。模型识别准确,卡方值为0。为了能够评价模型跟数据的适应度,笔者修订了模型中的一个因子载荷,这样模型就过度识别了,df = 1。笔者重新估计了模型,模型跟数据适应得很好;p<.99;Bentler-Bonett 基准契合度指标 = 1.00;Bentler-Bonett 非基准契合度指标 = 1.61;比较拟合度指标=1.000。

这三个度量是对一个问题的三个陈述,要求商人从非常同意(编码4)到非常不同意(编码1)这四个选项中作出选择。问题是:考虑一下你公司门前的人行道或旁边的停车场,告诉我当运用于这些地方时你是否同意我读的每个说法。a. 我对发生的事情非常了解。b. 我觉得对发生的事情应负责任。c. 我能从外人中认出谁属于这里。这个团结因子反映商人对社区商业区的责任感。

# 七、犯罪度量模型

笔者在一般理论模型中考察了犯罪的四种类型:自然人暴力犯罪、非暴力财产犯罪、总体犯罪水平和严重财产犯罪。因为数据里没有太多量度,或者说就自然人暴力犯罪、总体犯罪水平和非暴力犯罪不能很好地定位拟合因子模型,这四种类型更多地使用个别量度而不是总体复合量度。

自然人暴力犯罪通过向居民提问来度量:你所在社区的人们遭恐吓、殴打或其他此种情形的频率?几乎没有…0;偶尔…1;经常…2;常常…3。

非暴力犯罪通过一个关于入店偷窃的问题来度量。问题向商人提出:从1981 年8 月以来,你的公司是否遭到入店偷窃?是…1;不是…0。综合到社区水平后,度量就成为一个连续变量。

总体犯罪水平通过问商人有关社区犯罪问题来度量:针对社区总的犯罪,你会说有很多犯罪、相当多犯罪、有一些犯罪还是几乎没有犯罪?很多犯罪…3;相当多犯罪…2;有一些犯罪…1;几乎没有犯罪…0。

为严重财产犯罪建立了一个因子模型,包括商业盗窃的三个度量。模型识别准确,卡方值为0。为了能够评价模型跟数据的适应度,笔者修订了模型中的一个因子载荷,模型过度识别,df=1。笔者重新估计了模型,模型跟数据适应得很好;p =.99;Bentler-Bonett 基准契合度指标=1.00;Bentler-Bonett 非基准契合度指标=1.289;比较拟合指标=1.000。有关因子模型的问题是:这个商业区公司被打劫或破门而入的频率?几乎没有…0;偶尔…1;经常…2;常常…3。另一个问题是:你认为明年公司被盗窃或破门而入的可能性是:根本不可能…0;可能性微乎其微…1;相当可能性…2;可能性极大…3。第三个问题是:从1981 年8 月以来,你的公司遭到盗窃或破门而入过么?是…1;不是…0。因子反映了商业盗窃犯罪的程度。

概括而言,度量模型分析为犯罪恐惧感、社会团结、在一定区域内生活和经商的满意度、商业稳定性、对警察的支持率和对社会未来的乐观建立了因子。这些度量模型跟数据适应得很好。对变量"居民对社区的责任感(SOL2)"、FEAR 和POL 而言,允许量度误差相关并没有显著提高模型适合度。度量误差纯随机的假设得到确认。对其他变量,允许校正误差会导致模型识别不足。

笔者运用度量模型的因子载荷为每个理论概念建立了复合指数,复合指数被用在以下章节的结构模型分析中。在接下来的三章,笔者将阐述基于这三个问题所作出的假设的测试结果。

# 第七章　递归模型结果

## 一、递归模型测试中的问题

本书中的递归模型测试(见图4.1)主要针对犯罪后果、恐惧感和社会团结问题。笔者围绕不同后果对相关假设进行分组。

对满意度的假设有：

I.1　犯罪降低人们在区域内生活和经商的满意度。

I.2　犯罪不直接降低满意度。

I.3　恐惧感直接降低满意度。

I.4　恐惧感是犯罪作用于满意度的媒介。

I.5　社会团结提高人们在区域内生活和经商的满意度。

对商业稳定性的假设有：

II.1　犯罪降低区域内的商业稳定性。

II.2　犯罪不降低区域内的商业稳定性。

II.3　恐惧感直接降低区域内的商业稳定性。

II.4　恐惧感是犯罪作用于商业稳定性的媒介。

II.5　社会团结提高商业稳定性。

有关人们对警察支持率的假设有：

III.1　犯罪降低人们对警察的支持率。

III.2　犯罪不直接降低人们对警察的支持率。

III.3　恐惧感直接降低人们对警察的支持率。

III.4　恐惧感是犯罪作用于对警察支持率的媒介。

III.5　社会团结提高人们对警察的支持率。

有关人们对社会未来乐观态度的假设有：

IV.1　犯罪降低人们对社会未来的乐观程度。

IV.2　犯罪不直接降低人们对社会未来的乐观程度。

IV.3　恐惧感直接降低人们对社会未来的乐观程度。

IV.4　恐惧感是犯罪作用于对社会未来乐观程度的媒介。

IV.5　社会团结提高对社会未来的乐观程度。

有三个相关问题需要阐明，即测试的过程、共线性和效应分解。最大似然值（ML）估计方法要求合适的测试过程来解决小样本问题。笔者的研究设计将待估参数数量最小化以同时满足 Bentler 所提出的指标，即参数最多为5。设计方案对相同模型采用重复测试来估计系数的稳定性并测试多重共线性的影响。

首先，笔者测试了一个递归模型，在这个模型中恐惧感影响社会团结，社会团结不影响恐惧感（图4.1）。这个一般递归模型被分成四个独立模型；每个只有一个社会后果（见图4.1.1，图4.1.2，图4.1.3，图4.1.4）。笔者每次只检测具有一个社会后果的数据模型并以此估算待估参数最多为5的基本模型，由此避免了一次性测量太多参数的问题。这四个模型可以称作满意度模型、商业稳定性模型、警察支持率模型和社会未来乐观态度模型。

其次，前一章阐述的量度模型因子分析产生了一个恐惧感的复合指标、四个社会后果的复合指标以及三个社会团结的复合指标。在检测这四个结构模型时，不是将理论概念的不同量度与指标在一起检测，笔者为不同量度建立了独立结构模型。一次只放入每个理论模型的一个度量或复合指数，以使自由参数数量保持在最低。也就是说笔者使用不同度量来重复测试相同模型，所以每个后果的相同测试重复了12次。针对四个后果和四个相应子模型，笔者进行了48个重复测试。这个方案使笔者可以通过比较采用不同度量的所有测试和复制采用不同度量的研究来检查和确认所有情况下估计值的稳定性。

这48个重复测试针对不同的犯罪类型、社会团结以及社会后果,笔者估计一个规格改变了的模型,使犯罪直接影响社会后果。这一改变使我们可以对"犯罪不直接影响后果、恐惧感是犯罪发挥作用的媒介"这两个假设进行评价。同时它也表明结构系数的稳定性,从而提供共线性影响估计。后面笔者会对此作简短讨论。这样,笔者就检测了总数达96的模型。

第三,在对犯罪和团结的不同量度模型所有重复测试结果的基础上,笔者选择了在测试结果具有显著效应的犯罪和团结的量度,用所有同时影响后果的自变量来测试每个后果的模型,以估计每个犯罪和团结度量效应的相对重要性。

共线性影响也是一个应当在线性模型测试中考虑和检查的问题。共线性是有关一个样本里相关的自变量的的问题。当自变量之间的相关系数增加时,递归系数估计的标准误差也会增加。系数估计出现大量标准误差是共线性的一个主要后果。当方程式里的自变量高度相关时,不可能析出任何精度自变量的效应;系数之间高度相关;系数变得不稳定,不可信。当高度共线性时,转换样本、改变模型中变量的量度指数、给方程式减少或增加一个变量或者轻微改变模型规格都会导致系数估计戏剧性的变化。因为在一个样本里自变量通常彼此相关,不能说共线性存在或不存在,只能说它不同程度地存在。当共线性程度小时可以不考虑它的影响,但是当共线性程度增加时就会造成有害后果。

尽管简单的双变量相关性不足以诊断共线性问题,监测相关矩阵是对共线性最常用的测试。一般而言,如果自变量之间的相关系数不超过.80,共线性就不是问题(伯瑞(Berry)和费尔德曼(Feldman),1985)。在极端案例里,当一个自变量跟同一方程式里的其他一个或多个自变量线性完全相关,则共线性完全存在。所以对共线性最合理的测试是以方程式里的每一个自变量对所有其他自变量作递归测试,考察这些递归测试的R方值。如果R方值接近1.00,则共线性程度较高(伯瑞(Berry)和费尔德曼(Feldman),1985)。估计共线性影响的基本方法是用稍有不同的量度或规范重复模型校检和评估系数的改变。

对相关矩阵(表7.1)的考察表明,模型中的犯罪、恐惧感、团结等自变量的相关性高于.5。为了确认犯罪、恐惧感和团结影响社会后果的方程式中不存在共线性问题,笔者将其中之一对其他自变量进行回归测试。表7.2报道了 R 方值。没有 R 方值超过传统标准.75(费舍(Fisher)和曼松(Mason),1981),这表明除了在将"居民对社区的义务感(SOL1)"和恐惧感递归到暴力犯罪(表7.2,模型 I.1)这个案例中 R 方值为.742 外,共线性不是普遍问题。这意味着一个潜在的共线性问题。然而更进一步来看,用不同指数对相同模型重复测试的系数十分稳定。这就确定不存在共线性问题了。

表7.1　变量间的双变量相关分析

| | VIOLENT | CRIMEAMT | COM | SHOPLIFT | FEAR | SOL1 |
|---|---|---|---|---|---|---|
| VIOLENT | 1.0000 | .6635** | .1982 | .2798 | .7114** | -.7220** |
| CRIMEAMT | .6635** | 1.0000 | .6313** | .2740 | .8016** | -.5178** |
| COM | .1982 | .6313** | 1.0000 | .3914 | .4469* | -.3177 |
| SHOPLIFT | .2798 | .2740 | .3914 | 1.0000 | .3486 | -.0928 |
| FEAR | .7114** | .8016** | .4469* | .3486 | 1.0000 | -.3845 |
| SOL1 | -.7220** | -.5178** | -.3177 | -.0928 | -.3845 | 1.0000 |
| SOL2 | -.7106** | -.5338** | -.2640 | -.4174* | -.4564* | .6455** |
| SOL3 | -.2178 | -.1591 | -.0067 | .3222 | -.2069 | .2257 |
| SAT | -.6617** | -.6869** | -.2630 | -.1837 | -.7120** | .4050* |
| STA | -.5073* | -.4904* | -.0065 | .1104 | -.5615** | .2923 |
| POL | -.2214 | -.4473* | -.1755 | .1930 | -.3887 | .4104* |
| OPT | .3465 | .1500 | .0901 | .1972 | .0729 | -.5135* |

注释:VIOLENT = 自然人暴力犯罪

　　　CRIMEAMT = 总体犯罪水平

　　　COM = 商业盗窃

　　　SOL1 = 居民对社区的义务感

　　　SOL2 = 居民对社区的责任感

　　　SOL3 = 商人对社区商业中心的责任感

　　　SAT = 在地区生活和经商的满意度

　　　STA = 商业稳定性

　　　POL = 警察支持率

　　　OPT = 社会未来乐观

　　　* p<.05,双尾测试。

　　　** p<.01,双尾测试。

（续表）

| | SOL2 | SOL3 | SAT | STA | POL | OPT |
|---|---|---|---|---|---|---|
| VIOLENT | −.7106** | −.2178 | −.6617** | −.5073* | −.2214 | .3465 |
| CRIMEAMT | −.5338** | −.1591 | −.6869** | −.4904* | −.4473* | .1500 |
| COM | −.2640 | −.0067 | −.2630 | −.0065 | −.1755 | .0901 |
| SHOPLIFT | −.4174* | .3222 | −.1837 | .1104 | .1930 | .1972 |
| FEAR | −.4564* | −.2069 | −.7120** | −.5615** | −.3887 | .0729 |
| SOL1 | .6455** | .2257 | .4050* | .2923 | .4104* | −.5135* |
| SOL2 | 1.0000 | .2296 | .4802* | .2386 | −.0099 | −.3898 |
| SOL3 | .2296 | 1.0000 | .2322 | .3679 | .2440 | −.1656 |
| SAT | .4802* | .2322 | 1.0000 | .6913** | .5573** | −.0136 |
| STA | .2386 | .3679 | .6913** | 1.0000 | .4336* | .1579 |
| POL | −.0099 | .2440 | .5573** | .4336* | 1.0000 | −.1249 |
| OPT | −.3898 | −.1656 | −.0136 | .1579 | −.1249 | 1.0000 |

注释：VIOLENT＝自然人暴力犯罪

CRIMEAMT＝总体犯罪水平

COM＝商业盗窃

SOL1＝居民对社区的义务感

SOL2＝居民对社区的责任感

SOL3＝商人对社区商业中心的责任感

SAT＝在地区生活和经商的满意度

STA＝商业稳定性

POL＝警察支持率

OPT＝社会未来乐观

* $p < .05$，双尾测试。

** $p < .01$，双尾测试。

### 表7.2　共线性检查

递归自变量至自变量影响结果的 R 方

| | | 模型 1.1 | | |
|---|---|---|---|---|
| | | SOL1 | 恐惧感 | 暴力犯罪 |
| 恐惧感 | 暴力犯罪 | .555 | | |
| SOL1 | 暴力犯罪 | | .540 | |
| SOL1 | 恐惧感 | | | .742 |

60

| | | 模型 2.1 | | |
| --- | --- | --- | --- | --- |
| | | SOL2 | 恐惧感 | 暴力犯罪 |
| 恐惧感 | 暴力犯罪 | .509 | | |
| SOL2 | 暴力犯罪 | | .511 | |
| SOL2 | 恐惧感 | | | .694 |
| | | 模型 3.1 | | |
| | | SOL3 | 恐惧感 | 暴力犯罪 |
| 恐惧感 | 暴力犯罪 | .052 | | |
| SOL3 | 暴力犯罪 | | .508 | |
| SOL3 | 恐惧感 | | | .511 |
| | | 模型 1.2 | | |
| | | SOL1 | 恐惧感 | 总体犯罪 |
| 恐惧感 | 总体犯罪 | .271 | | |
| SOL1 | 总体犯罪 | | .643 | |
| SOL1 | 恐惧感 | | | .694 |
| | | 模型 2.2 | | |
| | | SOL2 | 恐惧感 | 总体犯罪 |
| 恐惧感 | 总体犯罪 | .287 | | |
| SOL2 | 总体犯罪 | | .643 | |
| SOL2 | 恐惧感 | | | .678 |
| | | 模型 3.2 | | |
| | | SOL3 | 恐惧感 | 总体犯罪 |
| 恐惧感 | 总体犯罪 | .042 | | |
| SOL3 | 总体犯罪 | | .649 | |
| SOL3 | 恐惧感 | | | .642 |
| | | 模型 1.3 | | |
| | | SOL1 | 恐惧感 | 商业盗窃 |
| 恐惧感 | 商业犯罪 | .174 | | |
| SOL1 | 商业犯罪 | | .265 | |
| SOL1 | 恐惧感 | | | .224 |
| | | 模型 2.3 | | |
| | | SOL2 | 恐惧感 | 商业盗窃 |
| 恐惧感 | 商业盗窃 | .212 | | |

| | | SOL2 | 恐惧感 | 商业盗窃 |
|---|---|---|---|---|
| SOL2 | 商业盗窃 | . 322 | | |
| SOL2 | 恐惧感 | | | . 204 |
| | | 模型 3. 3 | | |
| | | SOL3 | 恐惧感 | 商业盗窃 |
| 恐惧感 | 商业盗窃 | . 051 | | |
| SOL3 | 商业盗窃 | | . 241 | |
| SOL3 | 恐惧感 | | | . 207 |
| | | 模型 1. 4 | | |
| | | SOL1 | 恐惧感 | 入店偷窃 |
| 恐惧感 | 入店偷窃 | . 149 | | |
| SOL1 | 入店偷窃 | | . 246 | |
| SOL1 | 恐惧感 | | | . 124 |
| | | 模型 2. 4 | | |
| | | SOL2 | 恐惧感 | 入店偷窃 |
| 恐惧感 | 入店偷窃 | . 284 | | |
| SOL2 | 入店偷窃 | | . 238 | |
| SOL2 | 恐惧感 | | | . 205 |
| | | 模型 3. 4 | | |
| | | SOL3 | 恐惧感 | 入店偷窃 |
| 恐惧感 | 入店偷窃 | . 219 | | |
| SOL3 | 入店偷窃 | | . 235 | |
| SOL3 | 恐惧感 | | | . 283 |

注释:暴力犯罪 = 自然人暴力犯罪

总体犯罪 = 总体犯罪水平

商业盗窃 = 商业盗窃

SOL1 = 居民对社区的义务感

SOL2 = 居民对社区的责任感

SOL3 = 商人对社区商业中心的责任感

模型 1、2、3 代表使用"居民对社区的义务感"(SOL1),"居民对社区的责任感"(SOL2),"商人对商业区的责任感"(SOL3)的模型;1,2,3,4 代表使用暴力犯罪、总体犯罪水平、商业盗窃、入店偷窃的模型。

　　当运用从结构方程式系统中得到的估计值来测试假设时,总效益、直接效应、间接效应以及总效益分解的计算也是应当讨论的问题。要考察犯罪对社会后果的效应,就应当考察犯罪对社会后果的直接效应、间接效应和总体效应。例如,本书中的一般模型显示,犯罪的改变引起恐惧感和团结程度的改变,恐惧感和团结程度的改变又引起社会后果的改变。对社会后果的总的预期改变包括犯罪带来的恐惧感和团结引起的所有改变。犯罪对社会后果的总体效应可以分为犯罪对社会后果的直接效应和犯罪对社会后果的间接效应。如果有直接效应的话,则间接效应既可以加强也可以削弱犯罪的直接效应。总的间接效应又可以分成三个间接效应:(1)以恐惧感为媒介的犯罪对后果的间接效应;(2)以社会团结为媒介的犯罪对后果的间接效应;(3)犯罪作用于恐惧感从而影响团结,以此为媒介的犯罪对后果的间接效应(犯罪→恐惧感→团结→社会后果)。评估"恐惧感是犯罪作用于社会后果的媒介"这个中心假设的最重要的元素是以恐惧感为媒介的犯罪对后果的间接效应。因此笔者报道了犯罪对社会后果的总体效应、总的间接效应(即总体效应减去犯罪对社会后果的直接效应)和以恐惧感为媒介的犯罪对后果的间接效应(由犯罪对恐惧感的直接效应和恐惧感对社会后果的直接效应乘积计算而得)。

在总体效应分解中,我们必须记住母本数据分解和样本数据分解的重要差别。单个效应相对于从样本数据估计的总体效应的相对值的解释可能会误导我们。

在母本数据中显著性测验不是问题,所有系数反映效应的真实大小。总体效应分解成直接效应和间接效应允许我们计算具体间接效应对总体效应的比例。我们可以通过具体路径计算间接效应对总体效应的百分比,这个百分比告诉我们总体效应在多大程度上由这个路径起媒介作用(阿尔文(Alwin)和何塞(Hauser),1981)。但是对于样本数据而言,其系数是对总体系数的估计。我们的焦点首当其冲放在显著性测验上。如果一个间接效应不明显,也就意味着这个效应在总体中为零,计算这个效应在总体效应中的百分比毫无意义,因为从统计学角度讲它在母体中的效应可能为零。解释这个间接效应在总体效应中所占比例就具有误导性。这里首当其冲的是,中介变量居间作用的间接效应是否显著。只有针对统计上显著的直接和间接效应,我们才能比较效应的相对重要性。

## 二、关于犯罪、恐惧感和团结影响满意度的假设

图4.1.1是考察作为社会后果的在区域内生活和经商的满意度的递归模型。为了集中研究关于犯罪、恐惧感和社会团结怎样影响满意度的假设，笔者将只报道犯罪、恐惧感和社会团结影响满意度的结构方程式的结果。表7.3报道了通过最大似然值(ML)方法估计的结构系数。

**表7.3　犯罪、恐惧感和团结对满意度的效应**
**（标准最大似然值(ML)估计）**

| 自变量 | 满意度模型 | | | | | | | | | |
|---|---|---|---|---|---|---|---|---|---|---|
| | 1 | | | 2 | | | 3 | | | |
| | （a） | （b） | （c） | （a） | （b） | （c） | （a） | （b） | （c） | （d） |
| 恐惧感 | -.653** | -.483** | -.343** | -.623** | -.495** | -.352** | -.694** | -.482** | -.342** | |
| 自然人暴力犯罪 | | -.334 | -.328* | | -.260 | -.402** | | -.305 | -.357** | -.662 |
| SOL1 | .154 | -.022 | | | | | | | | |
| SOL 2 | | | | .196 | .069 | | | | | |
| SOL 3 | | | | | | | .089 | .066 | | |
| 卡方 | 1.442 | | | 1.051 | | | 1.331 | | | |
| 恐惧感 | -.653** | -.459** | -.360** | -.623** | -.440** | -.353** | -.694** | -.431** | -.345** | |
| 总体犯罪水平 | | -.274 | -.413** | | -.259 | -.428** | | -.327 | -.360** | -.687 |
| SOL1 | .154 | .087 | | | | | | | | |
| SOL2 | | | | .196 | .141 | | | | | |
| SOL3 | | | | | | | .089 | .090 | | |
| 卡方 | 1.148 | | | 1.097 | | | 1.883 | | | |
| 恐惧感 | -.653** | -.691** | -.309** | -.623** | -.657** | -.294** | -.694** | -.772** | -.345** | |
| 商业盗窃 | | .100 | -.363** | | .084 | -.347** | | .060 | -.323** | -.263 |
| SOL1 | .154 | .171 | | | | | | | | |
| SOL2 | | | | .196 | .202 | | | | | |
| SOL3 | | | | | | | .089 | .083 | | |
| 卡方 | .381 | | | .282 | | | .716 | | | |

续表

| 自变量 | 满意度模型 | | | | | | | | | |
| | 1 | | | 2 | | | 3 | | | |
| | （a） | （b） | （c） | （a） | （b） | （c） | （a） | （b） | （c） | （d） |
| 恐惧感 | −.653** | −.677** | −.236** | −.623** | −.651** | −.227** | −.694** | −.712** | −.248** | |
| 入店偷窃 | | .066 | −.250* | | .145 | −.329** | | .041 | −.225* | −.184 |
| SOL1 | .154 | .151 | | | | | | | | |
| SOL2 | | | | .196 | .243 | | | | | |
| SOL3 | | | | | | | .089 | .072 | | |
| 卡方 | .189 | | | | .864 | | | .056 | | |

注释:SOL1 = 居民对社区的义务感
　　　SOL2 = 居民对社区的责任感
　　　SOL3 = 商人对社区商业中心的责任感
　　　模型1、2、3 使用不同类型的团结。
　　　c 列是模型 b 的间接效应。c 列的第一个数字是犯罪通过恐惧感对满意度的间接效应;第二个数字是间接效应总和;包括犯罪通过恐惧感、团结以及既通过恐惧感又通过团结对满意度的效应。（见图5）。
　　　d 列是犯罪对满意度的效应总和。
　　　* p<.10,单尾测试。
　　　** p<.05,单尾测试。

　　在表7.3 中,列标题模型1、2、3 表明用来估计的社会团结的不同类型。模型1 使用"居民对社区的义务感"（SOL1）指数来度量团结（"居民对社区的义务感"（SOL1））;模型2 使用"居民对社区的责任感"（SOL2）指数来度量团结（"居民对社区的责任感"（SOL2））;模型3 使用商人对社区商业区的责任感指数来度量团结（"商人对商业区的责任感"（SOL3））。

　　在每个模型中,a 列报道了只有恐惧感和社会团结影响满意度的模型（图4.1.1）;犯罪不直接影响满意度。b 列报道了犯罪同时直接影响满意度的模型。模型 b 与模型 a（图4.1.1 是模型 a）的唯一不同在于其在模型 a 的基础上增加了犯罪到满意度的直接路径。这样,模型1、2、3 中的每一个都包括两个模型:模型 a 和模型 b;它们表示犯罪对团结有直接效应和没有直接效应。所以我们一共有模型1a、1b、2a、2b、3a 和 3b。

　　c 列和 d 列（表的最后一列）报道了模型 bs 的总体效应和间接效应来阐述模型 b 的总体效应分解。c 列报道了模型 b 的两个间接效应。第一个数字是犯罪通过恐惧感作用于满意度的间接效应,它由犯罪作用于恐惧感的直接效应和恐惧感作用于满意度的直接效应乘积计算得来(图4.1.1增加了一个从犯罪到满意度的路径从而得到模型b)。c列的第二个数字是犯罪对满意度的总体间接效应,通过用犯罪的总体效应(由表的最后一列,d列报道)减去犯罪对满意度的直接效应得到。包括三个间接效应(图4.1.1增加了一个从犯罪到满意度的路径得到模型b):(1)犯罪通过恐惧感作用于满意度的效应,(2)犯罪通过团结作用于满意度的效应,(3)犯罪通过恐惧感和团结作用于满意度的效应。因为本书的理论兴趣在于恐惧感是否在犯罪对满意度的作用中起中介作用,所以笔者只报道了这两种间接效应。

　　表7.3中的行标题显示的是模型1a、1b、2a、2b、3a和3b中的自变量。有四个测试通过使用自然人暴力犯罪、总体犯罪水平、商业盗窃和入店偷窃这些犯罪的不同度量来实施。笔者将以表的左上端的模型1a和模型1b的结果为例对表作更深入的解释。

　　在模型1a里,"居民对社区的义务感"(SOL1)影响满意度,自然人暴力犯罪不直接影响满意度,恐惧感作用于满意度的效应是$-.653$,$t=-4.203$,统计效应显著。团结对满意度的效应是$.154$,统计效应不显著。因为结构参数的作用方向是假设的,所以使用了单尾检验来测试统计显著性。在测定表7.3中的参数显著性时,因为样本数量小,t比的关键值随自由度而调整,$df=24-k-1=24-k$,k是待估的参数的数量。在这个案例中,k等于2。测试结果表明恐惧感降低满意度。这个模型的卡方等于1.442,模型适应良好。

　　在模型1b里,恐惧感、"居民对社区的义务感"(SOL1)和自然人暴力犯罪影响满意度,恐惧感对满意度的效应是$-.483$,$t=-2.355$,统计效应显著,表明恐惧感降低满意度。自然人暴力犯罪作用于满意度的效应是$-.334$,$t=-1.220$,统计效应不显著,表明犯罪对满意度的直接效应不显著。卡方值从模型a的1.442降到模型b的0。a列和b列代表嵌套模型,卡方值的变化在0.5的水平上并不显著,这就证明了犯罪对满意度的直接效应不显著。这些结果表明犯罪不直接影响满意度的假设得到确证。"居民对社区的义务感"(SOL1)对满意度的效应是$-.022$,仍不显著,表明"居民对社区的义务感"

（SOL1）不影响满意度，这就证明社会团结提升满意度的假设不成立。

　　模型 b 涉及一个叫做自然人暴力犯罪的自变量。这使效应图变得复杂，使在报道直接效应之外，报道理论上最为重要的间接效应和总体效应成为必要。c 列报道了模型 b 的两个间接效应：第一个数字是犯罪通过恐惧感作用于满意度的间接效应，它等于$-.343$，它由犯罪对恐惧感的直接效应积和恐惧感对满意度的直接效应乘积计算得来（见图 4.1.1 增加一个从犯罪到满意度的路径得到模型 b）。因为犯罪对恐惧感的直接效应和恐惧感对满意度的直接效应以及犯罪对满意度的直接效应都很显著，它们的乘积也一定很显著，这就证明了恐惧感居间作用于犯罪对满意度的效应的假设。c 列的第二个数字是犯罪作用于满意度的总体间接效应，它等于$-.328$，$t=1.331$；单尾检验结果在 .10 水平上显著。总间接效应包括三个间接效应：（1）以恐惧感为媒介的犯罪对后果的间接效应；（2）以社会团结为媒介的犯罪对后果的间接效应；（3）犯罪作用于恐惧感从而影响团结，以此为媒介的犯罪对后果的间接效应（犯罪→恐惧感→团结→社会后果）。表的最后一列，d 列，表明犯罪对满意度的总体效应；它等于$-.662$。它是犯罪对满意度的直接效应和所有间接效应的总和。总体效应表明犯罪的效应是降低满意度，这证明了犯罪减少人们对在区域内生活和经商满意度的假说。

　　当笔者用不同类型的犯罪和不同类型的社会团结作为替代时，结果显示基本相同。对表 7.3 报道的所有 24 个重复测试表明，恐惧感仍然影响满意度，社会团结效应仍然不显著。当允许犯罪直接影响满意度时，效应不显著。

　　为了评估恐惧感、犯罪和团结的相对重要性，笔者测试了将满意度作为应变量的方程式（表 7.4）。在第一个方程式里，笔者把恐惧感放入方程式中。笔者也将"居民对社区的义务感"（SOL1）和自然人暴力犯罪、总体犯罪水平放入方程式中，因为在重复测试（表 7.3）中尽管效应不显著，它们总的来说表现出对满意度的相对较强效应。在下述的其他方程式中，笔者一次去掉一个最低显著性犯罪变量，然后去掉其他犯罪变量，最后去掉团结变量来重新检验模型。

**表 7.4　影响满意度的变量的相对重要性**
（标准最大似然值（ML）估计）

| | 满意度 | | | |
|---|---|---|---|---|
| | 1 | 2 | 3 | 4 |
| 恐惧感 | −. 262* | −. 483** | −. 653** | −. 712** |
| SOL1 | . 107 | −. 022 | . 154 | |
| 自然人暴力犯罪 | −. 314 | −. 334 | | |
| 总体犯罪水平 | −. 294 | | | |

注释：** p<. 05，单尾测试。
　　　* p<. 10，单尾测试。

表 7.4 显示的结果跟表 7.3 一致。恐惧感显著降低满意度；犯罪不直接影响满意度，其系数不显著；团结不直接影响满意度（不显著）。恐惧感是影响满意度的最重要变量。

概括起来，模型测试结果表明犯罪的总体效应在于减少在区域内生活和经商的满意度，这证实了假设 I. 1。犯罪不直接减少满意度，这证实了假设 I. 2。恐惧感直接减少满意度，这证实了假设 I. 3。恐惧感是犯罪作用于满意度的媒介，这证实了假设 I. 4。允许犯罪直接影响满意度的效应不显著，相应的卡方改变也不显著。这证实犯罪不直接减少满意度的结论。用犯罪和团结的不同量度再次进行了模型测试，其结果与前述一致，效应相当稳定。然而，团结作用了满意度的效应在最初与重复测试中均不显著，假设 I. 5 没有得到证实。

## 三、关于犯罪、恐惧感和团结影响商业稳定性的假设

在对假设 II. 1 至 II. 5，即犯罪、恐惧感和团结影响商业稳定性的假设的测试中，笔者用社会团结的不同量度和不同类型犯罪再次进行了递归模型测试（图 4. 1. 2）。表 7. 5 报道了测试结果。此表的结构跟表 7. 3 相同。模型 1、2、3 中不同的团结量度被用来区别模型类型。a 列和 b 列是犯罪直接影响商业稳定性的模型和犯罪不直接影响商业稳定性的模型。

### 表7.5 犯罪、恐惧感和团结对商业稳定性的效应
（标准最大似然值(ML)估计）

| 自变量 | 1 (a) | 1 (b) | 1 (c) | 2 (a) | 2 (b) | 2 (c) | 3 (a) | 3 (b) | 3 (c) | 3 (d) |
|---|---|---|---|---|---|---|---|---|---|---|
| 恐惧感 | -.527** | -.393* | -.279* | -.572** | -.385* | -.273* | -.507** | -.360* | -.270* | |
| 自然人暴力犯罪 | | -.263 | -.245 | | -.381 | -.126 | | -.183 | -.325* | -.507 |
| SOL1 | .090 | -.049 | | | | | | | | |
| SOL2 | | | | -.022 | -.208 | | | | | |
| SOL3 | | | | | | | .263* | .249* | | |
| 卡方 | .611 | | | 1.542 | | | .615 | | | |
| 恐惧感 | -.527** | -.477* | -.382* | -.572** | -.475* | -.381* | -.507** | -.412* | -.330* | |
| 总体犯罪水平 | | -.071 | -.420* | | -.137 | -.353* | | -.118 | -.471** | -.490 |
| SOL1 | .090 | .072 | | | | | | | | |
| SOL2 | | | | -.022 | -.051 | | | | | |
| SOL3 | | | | | | | .263* | .264* | | |
| 卡方 | .052 | | | .204 | | | .185 | | | |
| 恐惧感 | -.527** | -.645** | -.292* | -.572** | -.698** | -.312** | -.507** | -.637** | -.285** | |
| 商业盗窃 | | .332** | -.286* | | .306* | -.312* | | .208* | -.218* | -.006 |
| SOL1 | .090 | .146 | | | | | | | | |
| SOL2 | | | | -.022 | .001 | | | | | |
| SOL3 | | | | | | | .263* | .238* | | |
| 卡方 | 3.103 | | | 2.643 | | | 2.435 | | | |
| 恐惧感 | -.527** | -.654** | -.228* | -.572** | -.647** | -.226* | -.507** | -.630** | -.220* | |
| 入店偷窃 | | .345** | -.235* | | .378** | -.268* | | .283* | -.172 | .110 |
| SOL1 | 0.090 | .073 | | | | | | | | |
| SOL2 | | | | -.022 | .101 | | | | | |
| SOL3 | | | | | | | .263* | .147 | | |
| 卡方 | 3.845 | | | 4.175 | | | 2.233 | | | |

注释:SOL1＝居民对社区的义务感

SOL2＝居民对社区的责任感

SOL3＝商人对社区商业中心的责任感

模型1、2、3使用不同类型的团结。

c列是模型b的间接效应。c列的第一个数字是犯罪通过恐惧感对满意度的间接效应,第二个数字是间接效应总和。

d列是犯罪对商业稳定性的效应总和。

* p<.10,单尾测试。

** p<.05,单尾测试。

尽管各类模型测试的结果不一,仍然存在一定的模式。在犯罪不直接影响商业稳定性模型(模型 a)和犯罪直接影响商业稳定性的两个模型(模型 b)中,恐惧感对商业稳定性的效应是一致且显著的。效应范围从 $-.36$(模型 3b)到 $-.698$(模型 2b)。这些结果证实了恐惧感减少商业稳定性的假设。

当允许犯罪直接影响商业稳定性(模型 b)时,自然人暴力犯罪和总体犯罪水平作用于商业稳定性的效应与财产犯罪(商业盗窃和入店偷窃)的效应大相径庭。自然人暴力犯罪和总体犯罪的直接效应一致且不显著,这证实了犯罪不直接影响商业稳定性的假设。相反,财产犯罪的直接效应却是显著的。商业盗窃的直接效应范围从 $.208$ 到 $.332$;入店偷窃的直接效应范围从 $.283$ 到 $.378$。效应范围的正向符号令人惊讶地显示商业盗窃和入店偷窃越多,商业稳定性越强。这些结果表明,不同的犯罪的类型与特征可能会对犯罪和商业稳定性之间的因果关系起一定影响。但是概括来讲,犯罪对商业稳定性的总体效应(d 列)是负向的,表明犯罪降低商业稳定性。

社会团结作用于商业稳定性的效应取决于团结的类型。通过对模型 3 和模型 1、2 的比较,结果表明"商人对商业区的责任感(SOL3)"(只用于模型 3)在犯罪不直接影响商业稳定性的模型 a 和犯罪直接影响商业稳定性的模型 b 中都显著影响商业稳定性。相反,在模型 1 和 2 中,所有测试都表明"居民对社区的义务感(SOL1)"和"居民对社区的责任感(SOL2)"对商业稳定性的效应不显著。测试结果表明商人的社会团结的确促进商业稳定性。

为了评估恐惧感、犯罪和团结的相对重要性,笔者用商业稳定性作为应变量来检测方程式。表 7.6 报道了这一检测的结果。在第一个方程式中,笔者只放入了表 7.5 报道的在所有重复测试中对商业稳定性均有显著效应的变量。在对模型的 12 次重复测试中都没有表现出对商业稳定性的显著效应的变量没有必要放入方程式中。笔者通过这种方式将待估参数数量保持在最小。在随后的方程式中笔者试图通过依次减去最不具显著性的犯罪变量、其他犯罪变量、团结度量和重新估计模型来观察犯罪恐惧感效应的稳定性。

**表 7.6 影响商业稳定性的变量的相对重要性**

（标准最大似然值（ML）估计）

| | 商业稳定性 | | | |
|---|---|---|---|---|
| | 1 | 2 | 3 | 4 |
| 恐惧感 | −.707＊＊ | −.637＊＊ | −.507＊＊ | −.561＊＊ |
| SOL3 | .152 | .238＊ | .263＊ | |
| 商业盗窃 | .224 | .208＊ | | |
| 入店偷窃 | .220 | | | |

注释：＊＊ p<.05，单尾测试。

＊ p<.10，单尾测试。

表 7.6 表明恐惧感显著降低商业稳定性。商业盗窃仿佛直接影响商业稳定性。"商人对商业区的责任感（SOL3）"，仿佛增加商业稳定性。而入店偷窃对商业稳定性的作用不显著，但是与"商人对商业区的责任感（SOL3）"和商业盗窃效应相比，其具有相当效应。总的来说，结果跟表 7.5 报道的重复测试一致。

概括而言，测试结果表明犯罪的总体效应是降低商业稳定性，这证实了假设 II. 1：自然人暴力犯罪和总体犯罪水平表现出不同于财产犯罪的对商业稳定性的效应。总的来说，自然人暴力犯罪和总体犯罪水平不直接影响商业稳定性，这跟假设 II. 2 一致。然而，商业盗窃和入店偷窃直接提高商业稳定性，这跟假设 II. 2 不一致。这些结果与笔者的假设不符。恐惧感直接降低商业稳定性，这证实了假设 II. 3。恐惧感是犯罪作用于商业稳定性的媒介，这证实了假设 II. 4。团结对商业稳定性的效应随团结类型的不同而改变。尽管社区居民的义务和责任感对商业稳定性的效应不显著，"商人对商业区的责任感（SOL3）"对商业稳定性的效应在 .10 水平上显著，这一结果部分证实了假设 II. 5。用犯罪和团结的不同度量对模型进行测试，其效应模式十分相似。

## 四、关于犯罪、恐惧感和团结影响对警察支持率的假设

本节将报道对假设 III. 1 到 III. 5，即犯罪、恐惧感和和团结影响民众对警

察支持率的假设的测试结果。这一模型(见图 4.1.3)使用社会团结的不同量度和不同犯罪类型进行了测试。

表 7.7 显示了犯罪、恐惧感和团结作用于对人们对警察支持率的效应结果。如前所述,模型 1、2、3 用模型中团结的不同类型区别模型。在模型 1、2、3 中,a 列报道了恐惧感和团结对警察支持率的效应,b 列报道了允许犯罪直接作用于警察支持率情况下模型的测试结果。

### 表 7.7　犯罪、恐惧感和团结对警察支持率的效应
（标准最大似然值(ML)估计）

| 自变量 | 警察支持率模型 | | | | | | | | | |
|---|---|---|---|---|---|---|---|---|---|---|
| | 1 | | | 2 | | | 3 | | | |
| | (a) | (b) | (c) | (a) | (b) | (c) | (a) | (b) | (c) | (d) |
| 恐惧感 | −.271* | −.651** | −.462** | −.497** | −.439* | −.312* | −.353** | −.449* | −.319* | |
| 自然人暴力犯罪 | | .746** | −.968** | | −.118 | −.103 | | −.138 | −.359* | −.221 |
| SOL1 | .306* | .699** | | | | | | | | |
| SOL2 | | | | −.237 | −.294 | | | | | |
| SOL3 | | | | | | | .171 | .181 | | |
| 卡方 | 4.754 | | | .123 | | | .200 | | | |
| 恐惧感 | −.271* | −.106 | −.085 | −.497** | −.112 | −.090 | −.353** | −.046 | .036 | |
| 总体犯罪水平 | | −.234 | −.213 | | −.545 | .098 | | −.383 | −.064 | −.447 |
| SOL1 | .306* | .249 | | | | | | | | |
| SOL2 | | | | −.237 | −.352* | | | | | |
| SOL3 | | | | | | | .171 | .174 | | |
| 卡方 | .506 | | | 2.913 | | | 1.518 | | | |
| 恐惧感 | −.271* | −.292* | −.131* | −.497** | −.488** | −.218** | −.353** | −.344* | −.154* | |
| 商业盗窃 | | .055 | −.231* | | −.020 | −.155 | | −.021 | −.155 | −.176 |
| SOL1 | .306* | .316* | | | | | | | | |
| SOL2 | | | | −.237 | −.238 | | | | | |
| SOL3 | | | | | | | .171 | .173 | | |
| 卡方 | .071 | | | .009 | | | .010 | | | |
| 恐惧感 | −.271* | −.403** | −.141* | −.497** | −.564** | −.197** | −.353** | −.512** | −.179** | |

| 自变量 | 警察支持率模型 | | | | | | | | | |
|---|---|---|---|---|---|---|---|---|---|---|
| | 1 | | | 2 | | | 3 | | | |
| | (a) | (b) | (c) | (a) | (b) | (c) | (a) | (b) | (c) | (d) |
| 入店偷窃 | | .360** | -.167 | | .337* | -.144 | | .365** | -.172 | .193 |
| SOL1 | .306* | .289* | | | | | | | | |
| SOL2 | | | | -.237 | -.127 | | | | | |
| SOL3 | | | | | | | .171 | .021 | | |
| 卡方 | 3.685 | | | 2.729 | | | 2.836 | | | |

注释:SOL1 = 居民对社区的义务感

　　　SOL2 = 居民对社区的责任感

　　　SOL3 = 商人对社区商业中心的责任感

　　　模型1、2、3 使用不同类型的团结。

　　　c 列是模型 b 的间接效应。c 列的第一个数字是犯罪通过恐惧感对警察支持率的间接效应;第二个数字是间接效应总和。

　　　d 列是犯罪对警察支持率的效应总和。

　　　* p<. 10,单尾测试。

　　　** p<. 05,单尾测试。

结果表明,除了允许总体犯罪水平直接影响人们对警察的支持率的模型,恐惧感对警察支持率的效应通常显著,其效应范围从-. 271 到-. 651。

各种犯罪类型对警察支持率的直接效应不一。只有入店偷窃的效益一致且显著。其效应范围从 . 337 到 .365,令人吃惊地表明入店偷窃直接提高对警察的支持率,这跟笔者的假设正好相反。在表7. 7 的一个案例中,自然人暴力犯罪表现出 . 746 的正效应(模型1b),这可以作为共线性的指征,因为恐惧感和自然人暴力犯罪的相关度高达 . 71。用"居民对社区的义务感"(SOL1)和恐惧感这两个变量对暴力犯罪工作递归分析,R 方值是 . 75,这表示可能存在共线性问题,需要进一步确证。另一方面,总体犯罪水平和盗窃对警察支持率的总体效应(b 列)是负向的,表示这些犯罪会降低对警察的支持率。

社会团结对警察支持率的效应随团结类型的不同而改变。"居民对社区的义务感"(SOL1)(模型 1)对警察支持率的效应通常是显著的,而"居民对社区的责任感"(SOL2)(模型 2)和"商人对商业区的责任感"(SOL 3)(模型 3)的效应通常不显著。只有用居民对社区义务感指数度量社会团结时,团结提高警察支持率的假设才成立。

表7.8评估恐惧感、犯罪和团结对警察支持率的相关重要性,同时帮助评估一些系数的稳定性。笔者把恐惧感、"居民对社区的义务感"(SOL1)、自然人暴力犯罪和入店偷窃放入一个方程式中,并通过一次去掉一个最不具显著性犯罪变量、最后去掉团结变量来估计方程式并观察效应的稳定性。

**表7.8　影响警察支持率的变量的相对重要性**

(标准最大似然值(ML)估计)

| | 警察支持率 | | | |
|---|---|---|---|---|
| | 1 | 2 | 3 | 4 |
| 恐惧感 | −.734** | −.651** | −.271* | −.388* |
| SOL1 | .649** | .699** | .306* | |
| 自然人暴力犯罪 | .680** | .746** | | |
| 入店偷窃 | .319* | | | |

注释:** p<.05,单尾测试。

　　* p<.10,单尾测试。

总的来说,表7.8的结果跟表7.7报道的重复测试结果保持一致,它表明恐惧感显著减少警察支持率。其效应范围从−.271到−.734。有趣的是,自然人暴力犯罪和入店偷窃直接提高警察支持率;这跟笔者的假设相反。跟假设一致的是,"居民对社区的义务感"(SOL1)提高对警察的支持率。恐惧感是影响警察支持率的最重要变量。

概括而言,这些结果表明犯罪的总体效应是降低对警察的支持率,这证实了笔者的假设 III.1。一般而言,总体犯罪水平和商业盗窃不直接影响对警察的支持率,这跟假设 III.2 不一致,是出乎意料的。自然人暴力犯罪和入店偷窃表现出直接影响警察支持率的一些迹象,这跟假设 III.2 不一致,且令人吃惊地表明存在与假设不同的反应。这些结果同时表明恐惧感直接降低对警察的支持率,这证实了假设 III.3。恐惧感是犯罪作用于警察支持率的媒介,这证实了假设 III.4。此外,社会团结对警察支持率的效应取决于团结类型。"居民对社区的义务感"(SOL1)会显著提升对警察的支持率,但是"居民对社区的责任感"(SOL2)和"商人对商业区的责任感"(SOL3)对警察的支持率并没有显著影响,表明团结的不同方面对警察支持率有不同效应。

# 五、关于犯罪、恐惧感和团结影响社会未来乐观态度的假设

本节报道了犯罪、恐惧感和团结影响社会未来乐观态度的假设,即假设IV.1至IV.5的测试结果。笔者通过替换社会团结和不同类型犯罪的不同度量测试了社会未来乐观态度模型(图4.1.4)。表7.9表现了24个重复测试得到的结果。标题和结构与前述一致。

表 7.9 犯罪、恐惧感和团结对社会未来乐观态度的效应
（标准最大似然值(ML)估计）

| 自变量 | 社会未来乐观态度模型 | | | | | | | | | |
|---|---|---|---|---|---|---|---|---|---|---|
| | 1 | | | 2 | | | 3 | | | |
| | (a) | (b) | (c) | (a) | (b) | (c) | (a) | (b) | (c) | (d) |
| 恐惧感 | −.146 | −.223 | −.159 | −.133 | −.326 | −.232 | .040 | −.364* | −.259 | |
| 自然人暴力犯罪 | | .152 | .195 | | .395 | −.049 | | .580** | −.234 | .347 |
| SOL1 | −.570** | −.490** | | | | | | | | |
| SOL2 | | | | −.450** | −.258 | | | | | |
| SOL3 | | | | | | | −.157 | −.114 | | |
| 卡方 | 1.91 | | | 1.356 | | | 4.27 | | | |
| 恐惧感 | −.146 | −.082 | −.022 | −.133 | −.168 | −.135 | .040 | −.168 | −.135 | |
| 总体犯罪水平 | | −.091 | .241 | | .050 | .100 | | .259 | −.109 | .150 |
| SOL1 | −.570** | −.592** | | | | | | | | |
| SOL2 | | | | −.450** | −.440** | | | | | |
| SOL3 | | | | | | | −.157 | −.159 | | |
| 卡方 | .081 | | | .022 | | | .576 | | | |
| 恐惧感 | −.146 | −.134 | −.060 | −.133 | −.148 | −.066 | .040 | −.001 | −.0005 | |
| 商业盗窃 | | −.033 | .123 | | .038 | .052 | | .090 | .001 | .090 |
| SOL1 | −.570** | −.575** | | | | | | | | |
| SOL2 | | | | −.450** | −.447** | | | | | |
| SOL3 | | | | | | | −.157 | −.165 | | |
| 卡方 | .027 | | | .032 | | | .091 | | | |

续表

| 自变量 | 社会未来乐观态度模型 | | | | | | | | | |
| | 1 | | | 2 | | | 3 | | | |
| | （a） | （b） | （c） | （a） | （b） | （c） | （a） | （b） | （c） | （d） |
| 恐惧感 | −.146 | −.228 | −.079 | −.133 | −.147 | −.051 | .040 | −.101 | −.035 | |
| 入店偷窃 | | .223 | −.026 | | .070 | .127 | | .326* | −.129 | .197 |
| SOL1 | −.570** | −.580** | | | | | | | | |
| SOL2 | | | | −.450** | −.428** | | | | | |
| SOL3 | | | | | | | −.157 | −.292 | | |
| 卡方 | 1.437 | | | .107 | | | 1.882 | | | |

注释:SOL1＝居民对社区的义务感

　　　SOL2＝居民对社区的责任感

　　　SOL3＝商人对社区商业中心的责任感

　　　模型1、2、3使用不同类型的团结。

　　　c列是模型b的间接效应。c列的第一个数字是犯罪通过恐惧感对社会未来乐观态度的间接效应;第二个数字是间接效应总和。

　　　d列是犯罪对社会未来乐观态度的效应总和。

　　　* p<.10,单尾测试。

　　　** p<.05,单尾测试。

　　　模型测试结果显示恐惧感作用于社会未来乐观态度的效应为负向,这跟恐惧感降低社会未来乐观态度的假设一致。但是,效应普遍不显著。恐惧感降低社会未来乐观的假设没有得到有力支持,表明跟假设相反,犯罪的恐惧感对人们的乐观态度直接影响不大。

　　　犯罪对社会未来乐观态度的直接效应普遍不显著。其中的一个例外是模型3b中自然人暴力犯罪这一变量,显示出.580的显著正效应。这个单一案例是异常的。总的来说,犯罪对社会未来乐观的总体效应（b列）令人吃惊地为正向,显示犯罪会提高社会未来乐观态度。

　　　跟假设不同的是,社会团结效应的改变取决于模型中的团结类型。跟假设相反,作为"居民对社区的义务感"（SOL1）度量的"居民对社区的义务感"（SOL1）和作为居民对社区责任感度量的"居民对社区的责任感"（SOL2）,普遍显示对社会未来乐观态度的负效应（模型1）;但是"商人对商业区的责任感"（SOL3）的效应都是不显著的。"居民对社区的义务感"（SOL1）和"居民对社区的责任感"（SOL2）越强,社会未来乐观程度就越低。

表 7.10 报道了恐惧感、犯罪和团结对社会未来乐观态度的相关重要性测评结果。第一个方程式包括作为自变量的恐惧感、"居民对社区的义务感"（SOL1）、"居民对社区的责任感"（SOL2）和自然人暴力犯罪，因为这些变量已经在表 7.9 报道的重复测试中表现出对社会未来乐观态度的显著效应。在接下来的方程式中，笔者将恐惧感留在方程式里，一次去掉一个最不显著变量，对模型进行了重估。

**表 7.10　影响社会未来乐观态度的变量的相对重要性**

（标准最大似然值（ML）估计）

| | 社会未来乐观态度 | | | |
|---|---|---|---|---|
| | 1 | 2 | 3 | 4 |
| 恐惧感 | -.219 | -.187 | -.133 | .073 |
| SOL1 | -.450* | -.478** | -.450** | |
| SOL2 | -.148 | -.167 | | |
| 自然人暴力犯罪 | .072 | | | |

注释：** p<.05，单尾测试。
　　　* p<.10，单尾测试。

同重复测试结果一致，表 7.10 表明恐惧感对社会未来乐观态度的效应并不显著。居民对社会的义务会提高他们对社会未来的乐观程度。而自然人暴力犯罪不直接影响居民对社会未来的乐观态度。

概括来讲，结果表明犯罪的总体效应是提高社会未来乐观态度，这证明假设 IV.1 不成立。一般而言犯罪不直接影响社会未来乐观态度，这跟假设 IV.2 一致。恐惧感并不显著减少社会未来乐观态度，假设 IV.3 没有得到确证。所以恐惧感在犯罪和社会未来乐观态度之间的媒介效应并不显著，假设 IV.4 没有得到确证。此外"居民对社区的义务感"（SOL1）和"责任感"（SOL2）会降低社会未来乐观程度，这证明假设 IV.5 不成立。

# 六、犯罪后果假设测试小结

犯罪作用于社会后果的检测结果显示：一些研究假设获得了验证，一些研究假设的检验结果并不明朗,而另一些则未能通过验证。就犯罪后果而言,一些社会后果,表现出一定的规律;而另一些,其规律不甚明了。

在所有模型测试中,满意度模型的结果最为清晰明了。总的来说,有四个假设均得到数据支持,只有一个未通过检验。检测结果表明犯罪的总体效应是降低民众在区域内生活和经商的满意度,这确证了假设 I.1;犯罪不直接降低满意度,这确证了假设 I.2;恐惧感直接降低满意度,这确证了假设 I.3;恐惧感在犯罪对满意度的效应上起居间作用,这确证了假设 I.4;允许犯罪直接影响满意度时,效应不显著,相应的卡方值改变也不显著,这确证了犯罪不直接降低满意度的结论。使用犯罪和满意度的不同度量再次进行检测,其结果与前述一致,效应相当稳定。然而反复测试的结果都证明,团结作用于满意度的效应不显著,因而假设 I.5 未能得到证实。

商业稳定性模型的形态更加复杂。结果表明犯罪的总体效应是降低商业稳定性,这确证了假设 II.1;自然人暴力犯罪和总体犯罪水平表现出不同于财产犯罪的对商业稳定性的直接效应。总的来说,自然人暴力犯罪和总体犯罪水平不直接影响商业稳定性。令人吃惊的是,商业盗窃和入店偷窃直接提高商业稳定性,这跟假设 II.2 不一致。恐惧感直接降低商业稳定性,这证实了假设 II.3。恐惧感是犯罪作用于商业稳定性的媒介,这证实了假设 II.4。团结作用于商业稳定性的效应随团结类型的不同而改变。尽管社区居民的义务和责任感作用于商业稳定性的效应不显著,"商人对商业区的责任感"(SOL3)作用于商业稳定性的效果显著($p<.10$),这跟假设 II.5 一致。

警察支持率模型的检验结果不如满意度和商业稳定性模型般清楚。其结果表明犯罪的总体效应是降低民众对警察的支持率,这证实了笔者的假设 III.1。一般而言,总体犯罪水平和商业盗窃不直接影响警察支持率,这跟假设 III.2 一致。而犯罪作用于社会后果的检验结果比较复杂:自然人暴力犯罪和入店偷窃表现出直接影响警察支持率的一些迹象,这跟假设 III.2 正相反。恐惧感直接降低警察支持率,这证实了假设 III.3。恐惧感是犯罪作用于警察支持率的媒介,这证实了假设 III.4。社会团结对警察支持率的效应取决于团结的不同类型。"居民对社区的义务感"(SOL1)显著提升时警察的支持率。"居民对社区的义务感"（SOL2）和"商人对商业区的责任感"（SOL3）并不显著影响对警察的支持率，恐惧感是影响居民对警察支持率的最重要变量。

社会未来乐观态度模型的检测结果最出人意料。大部分假设未被证实。结果表明犯罪的总体效应是提高民众对社会未来的乐观态度，这证明假设IV.1不成立。一般而言犯罪不直接影响民众对社会未来的乐观态度，这跟假设IV.2一致。恐惧感并未显著降低人们对社会未来的乐观态度，假设IV.3没有得到确证。所以恐惧感在犯罪对社会未来乐观态度的效应中所引起的媒介效应并不显著，假设IV.4没有得到确证。此外，"居民对社区的义务感"和"责任感"会降低社会未来乐观态度，这跟假设V.5相反。

对不同后果模型的结果进行比较，结果表明恐惧感和团结的效应改变，一些规律就会出现。像预期的那样，恐惧感显著降低满意度、商业稳定性和警察支持率。但是恐惧感对社会未来乐观的效应不显著，这是出乎意料的。团结对不同后果的效应是不一致的，大部分不显著，表明除了极少数情况外，大多数情况下团结不像预期的那样影响社会后果。"居民对社区的义务感"（SOL1）显著提高警察支持率；"商人对商业区的责任感"（SOL3）显著提高商业稳定性。但是，跟假设相反的是，"居民对社区的义务感"（SOL1）显著降低社会未来乐观态度；"居民对社区的责任感"（SOL2）显著降低社会未来乐观态度。

# 第八章　犯罪影响团结的结论

迪尔凯姆（Durkheim）提出犯罪促进社会团结，而恐惧感研究一直以来认为犯罪产生恐惧感从而直接或间接降低社会团结。为了解决关于犯罪促进还是降低社会团结的争论，笔者认为我们必须考虑团结和共有利益的结构成分，必须区分和测试不同类型犯罪的相关效应。暴力犯罪和非暴力犯罪的直接效应是不同的。笔者提出几个假设：

V.1. 暴力犯罪产生恐惧感。

V.2. 非暴力犯罪不直接影响恐惧感。

V.3. 暴力犯罪减少社会团结。

V.4. 非暴力犯罪促进社会团结。

笔者估计暴力犯罪和非暴力犯罪的效应，以及暴力犯罪和非暴力犯罪对三种不同类型社会团结的效应。在笔者的数据所包含的犯罪的四种度量（自然人暴力犯罪、总体犯罪水平、商业盗窃、入店偷窃）中，自然人暴力犯罪是对暴力犯罪的最合理度量，入店偷窃是对非暴力犯罪的最合理度量。所以我们考察自然人暴力犯罪和入店偷窃如何影响恐惧感和团结。

表8.1报道了自然人暴力犯罪、总体犯罪水平、商业盗窃、入店偷窃对恐惧感的效应。笔者首先使用各种类型犯罪对恐惧感进行回归分析，然后每次去掉一个效应最低的变量。结果表明自然人暴力犯罪显著影响恐惧感（.286到.330），这确证了假设 V.1。入店偷窃对恐惧感的效应不显著（.118，t =

.927），这确证了假设 V.2。结果也表明总体犯罪水平对恐惧感的显著效应（表8.1），这意味着如果不区别暴力犯罪和非暴力犯罪，如同犯罪的恐惧感文献研究中所说的那样，犯罪总体上会产生恐惧感。

表 8.1　犯罪对恐惧感的效应
（标准最大似然值（ML）估计）

| 犯罪 | 恐惧感 | | |
|---|---|---|---|
| | 1 | 2 | 3 |
| 自然人暴力犯罪 | .286 * (1.695) | .330 ** (1.998) | .321 ** (2.101) |
| 总体犯罪水平 | .603 ** (2.898) | .569 ** (2.728) | .589 ** (3.858) |
| 商业盗窃 | −.036 (−.214) | .023 (.143) | |
| 入店偷窃 | .118 (.927) | | |

注释：** p<.05，单尾测试。
　　　* p<.10，单尾测试。

为测试假设 V.3 暴力犯罪降低社会团结的假设和假设 V.4 非暴力犯罪促进社会团结的假设，笔者使用不同类型的犯罪和恐惧感量度对社会团结作回归分析。对每一类型团结，笔者首先检验恐惧感和所有犯罪对团结的效应，然后每次去掉一个最不显著或最不重要的犯罪类型，对模型进行重估。表8.2、表8.3 和表8.4 报道了分步检测结果。

表 8.2　犯罪和恐惧感对社会团结的效应
（标准最大似然值（ML）估计）

| 犯罪 | SOL1 | | |
|---|---|---|---|
| | 1 | 2 | 3 |
| 恐惧感 | .461 * | .446 ** | .466 ** |
| 自然人暴力犯罪 | −1.004 ** | −1.014 ** | −.988 ** |
| 商业盗窃 | −.374 * | −.389 ** | −.330 ** |
| 入店偷窃 | .183 | .188 | |

续表

| 犯罪 | SOL1 | | |
|---|---|---|---|
| | 1 | 2 | 3 |
| 总体犯罪水平 | − . 036 | | |

注释: * * p<. 05, 单尾测试。

　　 * p<. 10, 单尾测试。

### 表 8.3　犯罪和恐惧感对社会团结的效应
（标准最大似然值（ML）估计）

| 犯罪 | SOL2 | | |
|---|---|---|---|
| | 1 | 2 | 3 |
| 恐惧感 | . 347 | . 374 | . 180 |
| 自然人暴力犯罪 | − . 712 * * | − . 709 * * | − . 764 * * |
| 商业盗窃 | − . 269 * | − . 270 * | − . 266 * |
| 入店偷窃 | − . 284 | − . 289 | |
| 总体犯罪水平 | − . 005 | | |

注释: * * p<. 05, 单尾测试。

　　 * p<. 10, 单尾测试。

### 表 8.4　犯罪和恐惧感对社会团结的效应
（标准最大似然值（ML）估计）

| 犯罪 | SOL3 | | |
|---|---|---|---|
| | 1 | 2 | 3 |
| 恐惧感 | − . 301 | − . 293 | − . 243 |
| 自然人暴力犯罪 | − . 249 | − . 186 | − . 172 |
| 商业盗窃 | . 498 * * | . 456 * * | . 455 * * |
| 入店偷窃 | . 203 | . 074 | |
| 总体犯罪水平 | − . 146 | | |

注释: * * p<. 05, 单尾测试。

　　 * p<. 10, 单尾测试。

　　就变量"居民对社区的义务感"（SOL1）而言,结果（表 8.2）表明模型 1、

2、3 中自然人暴力犯罪对作用于居民对社会的义务系数分别是 -1、-1 和 -.98。这意味着暴力犯罪和恐惧感之间的高相关性可能引起共线性问题，这在前面已经讨论过了。但是三个方程式的系数都一致显示相同的方向和近似的大小，这反映了一定的稳定性。因此笔者很谨慎地得出初步结论，暴力犯罪会减少居民对社会的义务感，这跟假设 V.3 一致。结果表明入店偷窃不显著影响居民对社会的义务感，假设 V.4 未得到确证，理论思想未获支持。

就"居民对社区的责任感"（SOL2）而言，结果（表 8.3）表明自然人暴力犯罪显著减少"居民对社区的责任感"（SOL2），假设 V.3 得到确证。结果表明入店偷窃显著减少"居民对社区的责任感"（SOL2），假设 V.4 被剔除，表明理论思想可能不正确。

就变量"商人对商业区的责任感"（SOL3）而言，结果（表 8.4）表明自然人暴力犯罪不显著减少"商人对商业区的责任感"（SOL3），假设 V.3 未得到确证。结果表明入店偷窃显著提高"商人对商业区的责任感"（SOL3），假设 V.4 得到确证。考虑到变量"商人对商业区的责任感"（SOL3）只询问了商人有关商业区的问题，它不能代表社会范围的团结，因此结果只表明入店偷窃提醒商人他们的共有利益、激发他们对商业区的责任感。也就是说，入店偷窃主要激发团结的结构成分。

总的来说，与假设一致，自然人暴力犯罪会提高人们对犯罪的恐惧感，入店偷窃显著影响恐惧感。当我们不区分暴力犯罪和非暴力犯罪时，结果表明，如同恐惧感研究文献所说的那样，犯罪总体会提升恐惧感。恐惧感和犯罪对社会团结的效应随社会团结的不同类型而改变。总的来说，关于暴力犯罪（由居民报道的自然人暴力犯罪度量）降低社会团结的假设 V.3 得到支持，但其对商业团结的效应不显著。当使用居民团结度量时，关于非暴力犯罪（入店偷窃）促进社会团结的假设 V.4 的结论未获支持；然而，结果表明入店偷窃显著促进"商人对商业区的责任感（SOL3）"，所以假设 V.4 对商人来讲得到确证。这些结果表明，团结的度量形成测量的不同方面，它们反映出团结的不同维度，而这些维度与恐惧感和犯罪的关系各不相同。

# 第九章　非递归模型

## 一、非递归模型的理论探索

　　大部分恐惧感研究文献尽管不是结论性的，都报道了恐惧感跟社会凝聚力之间的消极联系。就像第三章所讨论的那样，在关于恐惧感和社会团结的因果关系上存在争论。一些研究表明恐惧感降低社会团结；另一些则表明社会团结降低恐惧感。尽管两种说法都表明恐惧感和社会团结之间是消极的单向联系，但在谁是因谁是果上面没有达成一致看法。

　　争论表明恐惧感和团结之间存在可能的互反关系。正如递归模型所显示的那样，恐惧感影响团结，团结也影响恐惧感。为了解决这个争论，我们应当检测一个非递归模型，在这个模型里，恐惧感对团结的效应和团结对恐惧感的效应可以被同时估测。

　　团结和犯罪的社会后果之间的互反效应的可能性也是值得探索的，可以用来观察是否存在民众满意度对社会团结的效应、商业稳定性对社会团结的效应、警察支持率对社会团结的效应以及社会未来乐观态度对社会团结的效应。

　　不幸的是，如前所述，很少有研究从集体层面解决诸如恐惧感、社会团结、在区域内生活和经商的满意度、商业稳定性、警察支持率和社会未来乐观态度这样的理论概念。没有合适的数据集可用来测试非递归模型，因为这一模型需要同时估计至少十个参数。也就是说,除了六个结构参数外,至少还需要两个工具变量(或媒介变量)来估计团结和社会后果之间的互反效应。这样就增加了四个参数(两个工具变量的直接效应和每个的方差)(见图9.1)。最大似然(ML)估计的渐进性要求样本大小同待估自由参数的数量密切相关。根据 Bentler 指标,对于最大似然估计,样本大小跟待估自由参数数量的比率可以低至5:1(班特勒(Bentler),1989)。

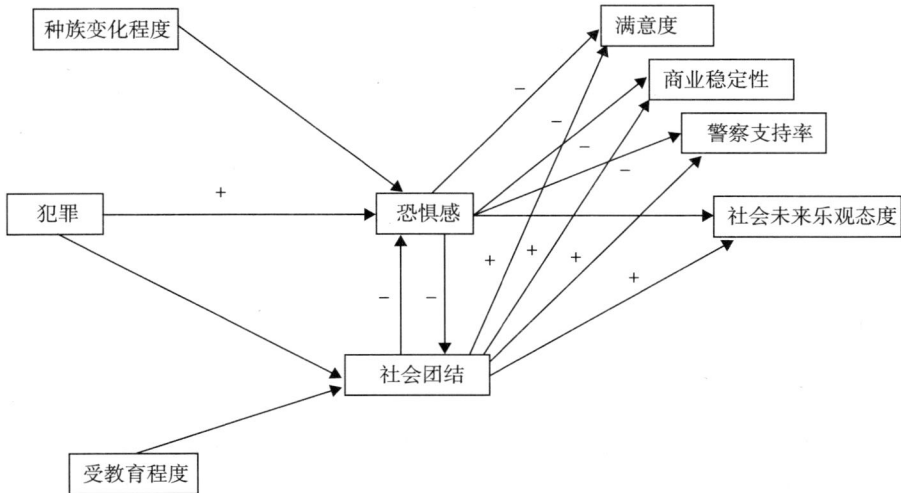

**图9.1 非递归模型估测**

因为没有足够的数据集可用于对非递归模型的可信测试,我们面对这样一种状况:我们要么谨慎探索来提高我们对因果关系的理解,要么什么也不做等着合适数据集的出现。最近几年不可能出现合适的数据集,因为在集合层面大部分数据集不可能包括像恐惧感、团结这样的变量。在个人层面从众多的地理区域或社区中收集数据成本太高。只有用在许多不同的地理集合单位比如城市、社区中收集到的数据,我们才能把个体数据汇集到集体层面来获得大量案例。无论如何,探索性工作都是有价值的,因为它为以后的研究提供思想支持。例如,对充分工具变量的理论探讨有助于为以后的调查选择工具变量。

出于这些考虑,笔者试着对数据集作了初步测试。因为样本含量很小,也就是说,必须估计的参数和样本中案例数量的比率十分低,测试的统计学力度会太低而不能体现效应的显著性。因此,相当一部分变量的效应可能是不显著的。

要估计两个变量之间的互反效应,两个互相影响的变量都需要工具变量。要估计恐惧感和团结之间的互反效应,至少需要一个对恐惧感的辅助变量、一个对社会团结的工具变量。对恐惧感的辅助变量要能导致恐惧感而不是团结的变化。同样,对社会团结的工具变量要能引起社会团结而不是恐惧感的变化。尽管从理论上来讲存在合适变量,但由于数据集的特殊性质,实践中很难找到符合这些条件的工具变量,这就使得实践中估计互反关系比较困难。所以从实践角度看,我们应该从考察相关性矩阵出发寻找可能的备选工具变量。恐惧感的备选工具变量应当跟恐惧感高度显著相关,因此这一变量也许就是恐惧感产生的一个原因。它跟团结的相关性在统计学上应当不显著,因此不是团结产生的原因。社会团结的备选工具变量应当跟社会团结高度显著相关但跟恐惧感不显著相关,所以它是团结产生的原因而不是恐惧感产生的原因。这是实践中最有可能符合工具变量定义的变量。

笔者从理论设想出发,对相关性进行了检验以寻找恐惧感的工具变量。大量的研究都集中在个人的易遭受犯罪侵害的特点上。除了少数特例外(比如,莱伯维茨(Lebowitz),1975),个人层面的研究一致发现性别和年龄跟犯罪的恐惧感密切相关(克莱门茨(Clemente)和凯曼(Keiman),1977;博伊默(Baumer),1978;斯科甘(Skogan)和马克斯菲尔德(Maxfield),1981;斯坦福(Starfford)和伽勒(Galle),1984;皖得沃夫(Van der Wurff)、艾椎(Adri)等人,1989;帕克(Parker)和瑞(Ray),1990;帕克(Parker),1988;夏普(Sharp)和多德(Dodder),1985;拉格阮志(LaGrange)和佛拉若(Ferraaro),1987;利斯卡(Liska),散彻寇(Sanchirco)和里德(Reed),1988;等等)。女人和老人更容易感到恐惧感,因为他们更容易遭到犯罪侵害。也有研究发现,社会弱势群体比如穷人和有色人种比其他人更易感到恐惧感(斯科甘(Skogan)和马克斯菲尔德(Maxfield),1981;克莱门茨(Clemente)和凯曼(Keiman),1977;殷(Yin),1985;肯尼迪(Kennedy)和希尔弗曼(Silverman),1985;米特(Miether)和李(Lee),1984;博伊默(Baumer),1985;等等)。

但是,如果从集体层面考虑而不从个人层面考虑这些结论,性别、年龄和种族跟恐惧感在当前研究中并不高度相关。性别跟恐惧感的集合度量之间的相关性为-.16,统计学上不显著。所以性别不能用作恐惧感的工具变量。在当前的数据集里,年龄和恐惧感的复合度量之间的相关性为.34,不具显著性。这表明年龄也不能作为恐惧感的工具变量。

也有研究发现社会弱势群体,比如有色人种,比其他人更易感到恐惧感。在目前的数据集里,种族和恐惧感的集合度量之间的相关性为.01,也不具显著性。这表明在这次调查中,社区的少数族裔比例在社区层面跟恐惧感没有太大相关性。种族跟社会团结的任何方面也都没有太大相关性;种族跟居民对社会的义务的相关性为.02,跟居民的责任感的相关性为.19,跟商人责任感的相关性为.14,在统计学上都不显著。因为种族跟恐惧感和团结的相关性都不显著,它也不能作为恐惧感或团结的充分工具变量。

当前研究的数据集只提供了一个可用作恐惧感工具变量的变量,即种族变化程度。发生种族变化和种族冲突的地方跟稳定地方相比具有较高水平的恐惧感。有关种族变化的调查问居民:过去两年左右时间里社区的种族构成发生了怎样变化?少数族裔大量减少…1;少量减少…2;保持不变…3;少量增加…4;大量增加…5。种族变化和恐惧感的集合指数的相关性为.44,十分显著。另一方面,种族变化跟社会团结的任何方面都没有太大相关性,跟居民对社会的义务的相关性为.09,跟居民的责任感的相关性为.01,跟商人责任感的相关性为-.14,在统计学上都不显著。

概括而言,理论设想和实际数据在恐惧感和社会团结的互反关系中为我们提供了一个恐惧感的可能工具变量,即社会的种族变化程度。

为了测试恐惧感和社会团结的互反关系,我们也需要社会团结的工具变量。如前所述,从实践上讲社会团结的工具变量应当跟社会团结显著相关但跟恐惧感不显著相关。在寻找社会团结的工具变量时可供参考的研究不多。有相当多的研究考察恐惧感和团结的因果关系,但很少有研究提出除恐惧感之外可以影响团结的变量。

除了恐惧感研究之外,社会解组理论也跟社会团结概念相关,它们之中有很多共性。二者都跟社会的特殊状态——社会一体化有关。社会解组可以被看做与对社会一体化的破坏这一概念相似的概念。但是大部分引起社会解组的变量也很有可能引起犯罪和恐惧感。这意味着以解组理论为基础寻找团结的工具变量是很难的。测试社会团结和恐惧感的互反效应的研究具有特殊的实际困难。当前数据集中有两个变量可以被用来度量贫穷,一是住房类型,一是就业与否。其中住房类型跟恐惧感和团结高度相关;就业与否跟恐惧感和团结弱相关。这使得住房类型和就业与否都不能用作工具变量。

　　然而,在现有数据集里,笔者发现了另一个变量——受教育水平,其在理论上没有,但在实际上跟这一变量有适度相关性($-.47$)。它跟恐惧感弱相关($-.15$),但相关性不显著,因此它不是导致恐惧感的原因。所以尽管理论上不是很清楚,出于探索目的笔者将它作为"居民对社区的义务"(SOL1)这一变量的工具变量,并对恐惧感和"居民对社区的义务"(SOL1)之间的相互关系作了探索性测试。

　　总的来说,恐惧感的唯一可能工具变量是种族变化程度。在寻找团结的工具变量的过程中,当前数据没有提供在理论上清晰明了的充分工具变量。但是它提供了一个在实际上可作用"居民对社区的义务"(SOL1)这一变量的工具变量,即受教育水平。在当前的探索性测试中,犯罪的量度是总体犯罪水平,因为它最能在总体上反映犯罪。笔者也用自然人暴力犯罪作为犯罪的量度对模型进行了再次测试,并检查系数的稳定性。这一非递归模型由图9.1表示。

# 二、模型识别

　　要估计结构方程式模型,首先必须进行模型识别。模型检测的过程是一个得出结构方程式模型的未知参数的解的过程。我们必须确定检测前这些结构方程式模型的未知参数是否存在唯一值。

　　模型识别通过表示未知参数是已识别参数的唯一函数而这些函数只引起唯一值来演示。如果能做到这一点,未知参数就能识别;否则,一个或更多参数不能识别。演示结构方程模型的识别就是以已知参数(例如观测变量的方差和协方差)表达未知参数唯一解,而已知参数对于观测变量而言已经获得了一致的样本估计。

识别对于样本和极少的案例来讲都不是问题。它由母本参数定义。已识别信息来源于母本协方差矩阵。参数涉及母本而不涉及样本值。无论样本多大，未识别模型不可能有未知参数的唯一值，所以识别跟样本大小无关。

模型的识别有时很容易建立，有时又很复杂。对非递归模型，阶条件和秩条件在建立模型识别上运用最广。

我们要测试的非递归模型是由三个方程式组成的复合方程式体系：

$$Y1 = 0 \quad + \quad b12Y2 + 0 \quad + \quad r11X1 + \quad r12X2 + 0 \quad + \quad D1$$
$$Y2 = b21Y1 + \quad 0 \quad + \quad 0 \quad + \quad r21X1 + \quad 0 \quad + \quad r23X3 + \quad D2$$
$$Y3 = b31Y1 + \quad b32Y2 + \quad 0 \quad + \quad 0 \quad + \quad 0 \quad + \quad 0 \quad + \quad D3$$

方程式系统用矩阵表示为：

$$\begin{bmatrix} Y1 \\ Y2 \\ Y3 \end{bmatrix} = \begin{bmatrix} 0 & b12 & 0 \\ b21 & 0 & 0 \\ b31 & b12 & 0 \end{bmatrix} \begin{bmatrix} Y1 \\ Y2 \\ Y3 \end{bmatrix} + \begin{bmatrix} r11 & r12 & 0 \\ r21 & 0 & r23 \\ 0 & 0 & 0 \end{bmatrix} \begin{bmatrix} X1 \\ X1 \\ X1 \end{bmatrix} + \begin{bmatrix} D1 \\ D1 \\ D1 \end{bmatrix}$$

$$c = \begin{bmatrix} 0 & -b12 & 0 & | & -r11 & -r12 & 0 \\ -b21 & 0 & 0 & | & -r21 & 0 & -r23 \\ -b31 & -b12 & 0 & | & 0 & 0 & 0 \end{bmatrix}$$

阶条件可以表述为：识别一个方程式的必要条件是从方程式中排除的变量数量至少为 $p-1$，$p$ 是模型中自变量 $y$ 的数量。如果模型中所有的方程式都被识别了，那么这个模型就被识别了。就当前研究的非递归模型而言，$p=3$，$p-1=2$。C 矩阵的第一行有 3 个 0，多于 2 个，符合阶条件，所以系统的第一个方程式得到识别。第二行有 3 个 0，多于 2 个，符合阶条件，所以系统的第二个方程式得到识别。第三行有 4 个 0，多于 2 个，符合阶条件，所以系统的第三个方程式也得到识别。既然所有的方程式都得到识别，模型就能得到识别。阶条件的运用使我们能够快速检查模型的识别状况，但阶条件是一个必要条件。一个模型要想得到识别，必须满足必要条件。笔者运用秩条件来进一步保证非递归模型的识别状况。

秩条件也从 $C = [(I-B) | -R]$ 开始。为了检查 ith 方程式的识别，笔者删除了所有在 C 的 ith 行中没有 0 的列，用剩下的列建了一个新矩阵，Ci。秩条

件规定识别 ith 方程式的必要且充分条件是 Ci 的阶等于（p－1）（保伦（Bollen），1989）。

为考察第一个方程式的识别,我们通过删去 C 矩阵中所有列的第一行不包括 0 的列并组成矩阵 C1。同样,我们通过删去 C 矩阵中所有列的第二行不包括 0 的列并组成矩阵 C2。我们通过删去 C 矩阵中所有列的第三行不包括 0 的列并组成矩阵 C3。C1、C2、C3 如下所示:

$$c1 = \begin{bmatrix} 0 & 0 \\ 0 & -r23 \\ 1 & 0 \end{bmatrix}$$

$$c2 = \begin{bmatrix} 0 & -r12 \\ 0 & 0 \\ 1 & 0 \end{bmatrix}$$

$$c3 = \begin{bmatrix} -r11 & -r12 & 0 \\ -r21 & 0 & -r23 \\ 0 & 0 & 0 \end{bmatrix}$$

矩阵或向量的阶指的是独立的行和列的数量。C1、C2、C3 矩阵的阶都等于 2。就当前非递归模型,p＝3,p－1＝2。ith 方程式的阶条件是 Ci 的阶等于（p－1）,每个 Ci 的阶都等于 p－1＝2。这样系统中所有方程式都得到识别。

总而言之,笔者将阶条件和秩条件运用于非递归模型中,并描述了模型的识别状态。

# 三、结果和结论

当前的非递归模型测试结果显示在图 9.1 中。这个模型包括每个后果的四个子模型:满意度、商业稳定性、警察支持率、社会未来乐观态度。表 9.1 显示了这四个模型中的分析结果。每个子模型都是同时发生的方程式系统,由三个方程式组成;恐惧感、团结和四个社会后果是其中这三个方程式各自的因变量。

**表 9.1　非递归模型**

（标准最大似然值(ML)估计）

| | | 非递归模型 | | | |
|---|---|---|---|---|---|
| | | 1 | 2 | 3 | 4 |
| FEAR | SOL1 | SAT | BST | PLO | OPT |
| 恐惧感 | | −.777 | −.653 | −.527 | −.271 | −.146 |
| | | −1.317 | −4.246 | −2.863 | −1.382 | −.772 |
| 团结 | .405 | | .154 | .090 | .306 | −.570 |
| | 1.156 | | .986 | .479 | 1.537 | −2.959 |
| 总体犯罪水平 | 1.007 | .134 | | | | |
| | 4.524 | .266 | | | | |
| 种族变化程度 | .002 | | | | | |
| | .014 | | | | | |
| 受教育程度 | | −.600 | | | | |
| | | −3.012 | | | | |
| 卡方值 | | | 12.25 | 8.795 | 7.893 | 9.239 |
| Df 自由度 | | | 6 | 6 | 6 | 6 |
| p | | | .057 | .185 | .246 | .161 |
| BBNFI | | | .840 | .865 | .871 | .856 |
| BBNNFI | | | .747 | .860 | .897 | .835 |
| CFI | | | .899 | .944 | .959 | .934 |

注释:SAT=在地区生活和经商的满意度
　　　BST=商业稳定性
　　　POL=警察支持率
　　　OPT=社会未来乐观
　　　SOL1=居民对社区的责任感
　　　df=自由度
　　　BBNFI=Bentler-Bonett 基准契合度指标
　　　BBNNFI=Bentler-Bonett 非基准契合度指标
　　　CFI=比较拟合指标

在每个包括一个社会后果作为因变量的子模型中,笔者允许恐惧感与团结互相影响,并使用种族变化作为恐惧感的工具变量,用受教育程度作为团结的工具变量(见表 9.1)。模型的剩余部分跟我们前面测试过的递归模型一样。

　　结果显示恐惧感减少团结,这跟理论假设一致。标准化系数是$-.777$;$t=-1.317$。单尾测试自由度$=n-3-1=4$,显著性测试当$p<.10$时临界$t$值为$1.325$。效应几乎是显著的。考虑到样本非常小,其大小与参数数量的比率为$2:1$,我们可以预计即使效应大到$-.777$,其统计上的显著程度可能仍然不够。

　　在递归模型里,恐惧感减少社会团结的假设是不确定的:使用"居民对社区的义务感"(SOL1)作为因变量的测试中,这一假设被驳回;恐惧感对"居民对社区的义务感"(SOL1)的效应系数为$.45$(表8.2)。对比递归模型中得到的系数$.45$和非递归模型中得到的系数$-.777$,我们可以看到效应发生了戏剧性变化。

　　结果也表明团结对恐惧感有相当大的效应,其系数是$.405$。跟笔者的假设相反,结果显示社会团结会增加恐惧感,而不是单向研究所提出的减少恐惧感。尽管效应大小适中,$t(1.156)$在统计学上仍不够显著。考虑到样本极小,这是可预期的。

　　表9.1中有两个变量值得关注。首先,总体犯罪对恐惧感的效应是$1.007$;标准化系数超过$1$通常意味着共线性问题。如果这样的话,系数将不稳定、不可信。其次,种族变化对恐惧感的效应是$.002$,不显著。种族变化是恐惧感的工具变量,预计会对恐惧感有相当大的效应。这些结果要求进一步检查结果的稳定性和稳健性。

　　总的来说模型跟数据匹配。结果跟关于恐惧感减少团结的假设一致。然而,跟过去关于恐惧感和团结的因果关系的研究不同,结果表明团结积极影响恐惧感;模型的其他结果表现出与递归模型同样的形态。犯罪产生恐惧感,恐惧感消极影响所有后果;系数保持相同,$t$值改变轻微。团结对社会后果的效应跟递归模型相同,$t$值改变轻微。但还需要进一步检查结果的稳定性以增加结果的可信度。

　　为进一步检查结果的稳定性,笔者改变了模型中的一些度量,对模型进行了再测试。数据允许的唯一可能改变是改变犯罪的度量,因为团结只有一个可用工具变量,恐惧感也只有一个可用工具变量,满意度、商业稳定性、警察支持率和社会未来乐观态度亦只有一个复合指数。

　　笔者将犯罪的度量从总体犯罪改变至自然人暴力犯罪,重复测试了同样四个非递归模型,结果见表9.2。非递归模型结果表明恐惧感降低社会团结,这跟理论假设以及表9.1中的模型和结果一致。标准化系数为$-.264$,t $=$ $-.693$,不具显著性。

**表9.2 非递归模型稳定性测试**

**(标准最大似然值(ML)估计)**

| | | 非递归模型 | | | |
|---|---|---|---|---|---|
| | | 1 | 2 | 3 | 4 |
| FEAR | SOL1 | SAT | BST | PLO | OPT |
| 恐惧感 | | $-.264$ | $-.653$ | $-.527$ | $-.271$ | $-.146$ |
| | | $-.693$ | $-4.185$ | $-2.821$ | $-1.362$ | $-.760$ |
| 团结 | .352 | | .154 | .090 | .306 | $-.570$ |
| | 1.035 | | .948 | .461 | 1.478 | $-2.847$ |
| 自然人暴力犯罪 | .919 | $-.446$ | | | | |
| | 3.652 | $-1.501$ | | | | |
| 种族变化程度 | .255 | | | | | |
| | 1.843 | | | | | |
| 受教育程度 | | $-.417$ | | | | |
| | | $-2.552$ | | | | |
| 卡方值 | | | 10.54 | 7.143 | 9.534 | 7.233 |
| Df 自由度 | | | 6 | 6 | 6 | 6 |
| p | | | .104 | .307 | .145 | .299 |
| BBNFI | | | .867 | .894 | .858 | .891 |
| BBNNFI | | | .823 | .946 | .830 | .940 |
| CFI | | | .929 | .978 | .932 | .976 |

注释:SAT=在地区生活和经商的满意度

　　　BST=商业稳定性

　　　POL=警察支持率

　　　OPT=社会未来乐观

　　　SOL1=居民对社区的责任感

　　　df=自由度

　　　BBNFI=Bentler-Bonett 基准契合度指标

　　　BBNNFI=Bentler-Bonett 非基准契合度指标

　　　CFI=比较拟合指标

结果也显示团结作用于恐惧感的相当大的效应,系数是.352,表明社会团结不是像单向研究认为的那样降低恐惧感,而是增加恐惧感。尽管效应大小适中,t(1.035)在统计学上不具显著性。考虑到样本极小,这也是可预期的。

其他系数普遍遵循与表9.1中的递归模型和原始非递归模型分析结果相同的形态。犯罪对恐惧感的效应是正向、重要且显著的。

总的来说,稳定性测试模型跟数据相匹配(表9.2)。模型测试结果显示与表9.1相同的形态。恐惧感消极影响团结;团结积极影响恐惧感;恐惧感消极影响所有后果,系数保持相同,t值改变轻微。团结对各类社会后果的效应跟前述相同,t值改变轻微;暴力犯罪产生恐惧感、降低团结度。结果相当稳定。

概括起来,笔者发现,当同时估计恐惧感对团结的因果关系和团结对恐惧感的因果关系时,结果显示出恐惧感对团结的消极效应。这跟既往的研究一致。但是,结果也显示团结对恐惧感的相当大的积极效应。改变犯罪的度量再测试模型后,结果一致。而既往的研究没有测试过互反效应。

以往的研究指出团结减少恐惧感,而缺乏凝聚力会增加恐惧感;因此,提高人们对社区的义务是减少恐惧感的重要方法。许多公共恐惧感减少计划被用来增加人们之间的相互作用,提高个人对社区的义务,目的就在于减少犯罪和恐惧感。

笔者根据非递归模型得出的结果提出相反结论:"居民对社区的义务感(SOL1)"增加他们的恐惧感。这在理论上十分有趣并具有重要的政策启示意义。

笔者推测,这可能是因为对社区负有较高义务的人对犯罪问题更敏感、反应更强烈。对社区义务越多,对社区就越关心;对犯罪问题越敏感,就会越恐惧。同样,社会团结度越高,人们之间的社交就越频繁,恐怖的犯罪故事散播得就越广越快。有研究认为新闻报道会增加人们的恐惧感(利斯卡(Liska),1990),因为新闻报道可以广泛、快速传播恐怖的犯罪故事。这跟笔者的推理是一致的。

笔者称这种效应为"敏感反应效应"。在现代美国都市社区里,团结减少犯罪,例如与社区义务相关的高度社会支持也许能减少一些恐惧感,但不能平衡"敏感反应效应"。所以当人们对社区负有更多义务时,人们不可避免地会感到更加恐惧。

但是,观察这些结果必须十分审慎,因为样本很小,工具变量也不理想。要使结果达到更高的可信度,将来的研究应当运用更大的样本并使用在理论上更合理、实践上更完美的工具变量进行更深入的研究。

# 第十章　结论和探讨

## 一、问题和方法

犯罪的功能是社会学长期存在的经典问题。迪尔凯姆(Durkheim)提出犯罪是影响社会秩序和社会组织的重要社会事实。与认为犯罪是社会的异常现象的现代犯罪学研究主流不同,迪尔凯姆(Durkheim)探讨了犯罪的正常性。迪尔凯姆(Durkheim)认为犯罪"在社会生活中扮演了正常角色"(1982,p. 102),"犯罪是必需的"(1982,p. 101)。现代犯罪学主流大都聚焦于犯罪事件和犯罪涉及的个人。与之相反,迪尔凯姆(Durkheim)考察了犯罪对社会的功能,他的研究焦点在于社会。迪尔凯姆(Durkheim)的著作认为犯罪的功能是一个理论上十分重要的论题。他的著作蕴涵着现代犯罪学的不同方向,但被现代犯罪学研究所广泛忽视。

同样,对迪尔凯姆(Durkheim)关于犯罪功能论的研究是有限的,仅涉及少数问题。由于缺乏系统性指导,对犯罪功能研究的关注显得十分松散。既往相关研究局限于迪尔凯姆(Durkheim)的功能说,孤立于犯罪学的其他研究领域。犯罪功能论大致围绕以下四个论题进行:社会团结、压制性司法、边界维持和刑罚稳定。研究绝大部分是观察得来的,是历史性的(埃里克森(Erikson),1966;斯科特(Scott),1976;康纳(Connor),1972;本耶胡达(Ben-Yehuda),1980;登特勒(Dentler)和埃里克森(Erikson),1959),但也有一些理论测试(劳德戴尔(Lauderdale),1976;劳德戴尔(Lauderdale)等,1984)。尽管存在一些批评外,这些研究普遍支持迪尔凯姆(Durkheim)关于犯罪起到促进社会团结功能的假说。

概括迪尔凯姆(Durkheim)关于犯罪功能的论断,笔者认为他提出了关于犯罪的两个问题:(1)犯罪在社会体系中起什么作用?(2)犯罪怎样发挥作用?

回答第一个问题时,迪尔凯姆(Durkheim)指出犯罪在维持社会秩序方面起了重要功能。他提出犯罪在促进社会团结上的功能。为解释犯罪怎样在促进社会团结中发挥功能,迪尔凯姆(Durkheim)说道:"犯罪汇集人们的正直良心并将它们集中起来。当出现丑行时,我们不得不注意到将会发生什么。这种情形在小镇上表现得尤为明显。人们在街道上互相拦住对方,相互拜访,一起谈论发生的丑行,以至引起的公愤越来越大。"(1933,p. 102)

考虑到除了促进团结外犯罪还有其他功能或后果,笔者认为我们应当将这两个问题扩大到两个近似问题:犯罪的作用是什么?犯罪在实现其作用或后果时怎样发挥功能?这种扩大使这个论题得到发展。第一个问题要求我们系统考察犯罪对每个社会进程和每个社会机构的功能或后果。第二个问题关注对犯罪功能或后果的解释。它要求我们首先找到犯罪发挥功能影响社会进程的重要变量;然后回答有关这些变量之间因果关系的问题,亦即提出犯罪功能理论。最后,我们还要问:理论的政策启示是什么?这些问题展示了这个领域的新的研究日程。

在本书中,笔者提出了一个一般理论模型来回答这些基本问题。模型显示了犯罪的四种后果(在众多可能后果中)。犯罪影响生活质量、社会经济资源、亲政府态度和社会衰退。这一理论模型认为有两个变量在解释犯罪后果上十分重要:恐惧感和社会团结。因此该模型提出犯罪、恐惧感、社会团结和社会后果间的因果关系结构并致力于解决三个重要理论问题。(一)该模型解释了该领域的中心问题:犯罪、恐惧感和社会团结怎样影响社会后果。(二)该模型研究了支持迪尔凯姆(Durkheim)理论的犯罪功能学说和考察犯罪如何影响社会团结的恐惧感学说之间的争论。(三)该模型研究了有关恐惧感和团结的因果关系的争论,表明了恐惧感和社会团结之间的互反关系

（图3.1，理论模型）。

在解释关于犯罪、恐惧感和社会团结怎样影响社会后果的第一个问题时，该理论模型提出，恐惧感和社会团结直接影响社会后果，犯罪直接影响恐惧感和社会团结，犯罪不直接影响社会后果。恐惧感和社会团结是犯罪功能与社会后果的媒介。

第二个问题是关于支持迪尔凯姆（Durkheim）论题的犯罪功能研究和恐惧感研究之间的争论。迪尔凯姆（Durkheim）认为犯罪在促进社会团结上起积极功能。犯罪功能研究认为犯罪引起的义愤使人们聚在一起，促进社交，提醒人们他们所共有的，从而促进社会团结。与之相反，当代关于犯罪恐惧感的文献普遍认为犯罪的结果不是使人们聚集在一起，而是产生恐惧感，束缚人们的行为，使人们彼此疏离，减少社交，从而降低社会团结。笔者认为暴力犯罪和非暴力犯罪在现代社会有不同效应。暴力犯罪引起恐惧感，使人们彼此疏离，束缚人们的交互作用/行为并降低社会团结。非暴力犯罪不引起恐惧感而是刺激社交，从而促进社会团结。

第三，该模型想解决恐惧感和团结之间因果关系的争论。一些既往研究指出，恐惧感通过使人们疏离来降低团结度。一些研究也表明缺乏凝聚力会提高恐惧感（福勒（Fowler）和曼吉欧尼（Mangione），1982）。学者们认为社区解组和缺乏社会凝聚力会导致高水平的对犯罪的恐惧感（斯科甘（Skogan）和马克斯菲尔德（Maxfield），1981；亨特（Hunter）和博伊默（Baumer），1982；斯科甘（Skogan），1990）。因此，提高"居民对社区的义务感"（SOL1）是减少恐惧感的重要途径。以这个假设为基础，许多恐惧感减少计划设法增加个人间的交互作用和"居民对社区的义务感"（SOL1），希望以此减少犯罪及其所带来的恐惧感。

既往研究测试了恐惧感减少社会团结或社会团结降低恐惧感的作用。大多数研究认为恐惧感和社会团结之间是消极的单向关系，但对谁是原因存在分歧。笔者提出恐惧感和团结之间存在互反关系。恐惧感影响团结，团结也影响恐惧感。

当前研究的数据由马里斯·麦弗森（Marlys McPherson）、格伦·索罗威（Glenn Silloway）和戴维·弗瑞（David Frey）于1983年7月在明尼阿波利斯市

（Minneapolis）和圣保罗市（St. Paul）进行的名为"社区商业中心的犯罪、恐惧感和控制"（ICPSR 8167）的项目中收集。数据分两个阶段收集。第一阶段调查了明尼阿波利斯市（Minneapolis）和圣保罗市（St. Paul）的 93 个商业中心。研究的第二个阶段从原始样本中挑选了 24 个商业中心。对其中的每一个商业中心都进行了 870 个居民电话调查并亲自会见了 213 名商人。

当前研究的量度出自两个文件：居民调查和商业调查，24 个社区（商业中心）层面的量度由个人回答汇总而得。就居民和商业调查中的每个问题，计算出同一社区所有回答者答案的平均值，把得出的平均值当作这个区域对该问题的答案来使用。在分析时这两个集合的文件就会聚成一个文件。这样，当前研究的样本大小就是 24 个案例。尽管这些数据并不是为当前研究目的所收集，本书研究所需要的绝大部分信息仍然可以从中获取。

本研究中有两个问题尤为重要。一是理论概念的量度，一是小样本问题。在尝试建立并测试一个理论模型时，当前研究面临着测量主要理论概念，比如团结和恐惧感的困难。团结一直都被看做是一个模糊概念，被批评为难以度量。迪尔凯姆（Durkheim）自己也认识到这一点。团结量度的可靠性和有效性问题在使用回归分析方法时大为突出。恐惧感作为一个情感状态显然面临同样的度量问题。而传统方法无法解决这些问题。结构方程式模型方法的优势就在于它可以解决这些问题，因此它是当前研究使用的首要方法。

第二个问题是小样本问题。结构方程式模型最常用的估算方法是最大似然估计，它对样本大小敏感。也就是说，当渐近性地无偏差时，最大似然估计对小样本估计的特性不太清楚。所以当使用小样本时，我们对估计后果不太看好。为解决小样本问题，分析过程被分成两个阶段以减少被估计模型大小。笔者首先估计量度模型，接着再评估结构模型。第一步，笔者为每一个理论概念建立合适的量度模型，从所有变量中选出潜在度量，进行所有可能的因子分析来定位理论上有意义、实践上合适的量度模型。然后笔者用这个估算结果来建构每个理论概念的复合指标。第二步，结构模型测试，笔者首先测试了一个递归模型（图 4.1），接着测试了一个非递归模型。笔者将递归模型分成四个子模型，每个子模型只产生一个后果（见图 4.1.1，图 4.1.2，图 4.1.3 和图 4.1.4）。因此，一共有四个结构模型，每个模型对应犯罪的一个社会后果。

笔者通过测试这些子模型来每次估计少数参数,避免同时估计太多参数,使估计的参数数量保持在最小。为检查确认模型的稳定性,笔者还用犯罪和社会团结的不同度量重估模型,重复进行模型测试。

笔者详细测试了下述假设。这些假设被分成六组:前四组考察犯罪、恐惧感和团结对社会后果的效应。

对满意度的假设有:

I. 1. 犯罪降低人们在区域内生活和经商的满意度。

I. 2. 犯罪不直接降低满意度。

I. 3. 恐惧感直接降低满意度。

I. 4. 恐惧感是犯罪作用于满意度的媒介。

I. 5. 社会团结提高人们在区域内生活和经商的满意度。

对商业稳定性的假设有:

II. 1. 犯罪降低区域内的商业稳定性。

II. 2. 犯罪不直接降低区域内的商业稳定性。

II. 3. 恐惧感直接降低区域内的商业稳定性。

II. 4. 恐惧感是犯罪作用于商业稳定性的媒介。

II. 5. 社会团结提高商业稳定性。

有关人们对警察支持率的假设有:

III. 1. 犯罪降低人们对警察的支持率。

III. 2. 犯罪不直接降低人们对警察的支持率。

III. 3. 恐惧感直接降低人们对警察的支持率。

III. 4. 恐惧感是犯罪作用于人们对警察支持率的媒介。

III. 5. 社会团结提高人们对警察的支持率。

有关人们对社会未来乐观态度的假设有:

IV. 1. 犯罪降低人们对社会未来的乐观态度。

IV. 2. 犯罪不直接降低人们对社会未来的乐观态度。

IV. 3. 恐惧感直接降低人们对社会未来的乐观态度。

IV. 4. 恐惧感是犯罪作用于人们对社会未来乐观态度的媒介。

IV. 5. 社会团结提高人们对社会未来的乐观态度。

为解决犯罪怎样影响恐惧感和社会团结这一问题,笔者详细考察了不同犯罪的直接效应。笔者提出:

V.1. 暴力犯罪产生恐惧感。

V.2. 非暴力犯罪不直接影响恐惧感。

V.3. 暴力犯罪减少社会团结。

V.4. 非暴力犯罪促进社会团结。

针对恐惧感和团结之间的因果关系问题提出的假设有:

VI.1. 恐惧感减少社会团结。

VI.2. 社会团结减少恐惧感。

概括而言,迪尔凯姆(Durkheim)的著作蕴涵着犯罪学的重要方向,即考察犯罪对社会的功能或后果。然而,尽管现代犯罪学理论研究从迪尔凯姆(Durkheim)处借鉴甚多,这一重要蕴涵仍被忽视了。关于犯罪功能的研究局限于少数问题,且孤立于犯罪学主流之外。笔者认为迪尔凯姆(Durkheim)已经提示了这一领域的主要问题。我们应当系统考察犯罪后果。我们要解释重要社会变量怎样影响犯罪后果以及这些变量之间的因果关系。据此,笔者提出了一个一般理论模型来解释恐惧感和社会团结怎样影响满意度、商业稳定性、亲政府态度和社会衰退。笔者致力于解决支持迪尔凯姆(Durkheim)论题的犯罪功能研究和考察犯罪怎样影响社会团结的恐惧感研究之间的争论。笔者从恐惧感和团结的因果关系入手解决这个争论,提出恐惧感和社会团结之间存在一种互反关系。

## 二、发现:思想的重塑

对这三个问题中的每一个,测试的结果都不明晰。有的假设得到证实,有的则被驳回。对于犯罪、恐惧感和团结怎样影响犯罪的社会后果这一中心问题,不同的社会后果作用不同。未料到的结果在许多方面重塑了笔者的思想。

大部分关于满意度的假设获得了数据支持。其结果表明犯罪的总体效应是减少在区域内生活和经商的满意度。犯罪直接产生恐惧感,恐惧感直接降低人们的满意度。用犯罪直接影响满意度,效应不显著。这证实了关于犯罪不直接降低人们满意度的假设。恐惧感居间功能于犯罪对满意度的效应,居间效应显著。

　　然而,不同类型团结对满意度的效应是一致的,且不显著。这更新了笔者关于团结怎样影响犯罪的社会后果的思想。笔者推测,现代美国社会是一个非常崇尚个人主义的社会,在这样一个社会里满意度绝大部分来自个人生活的成功和个人对生活的感觉。像社会团结这样的集体特征可能不会影响个人满意度。笔者预期在强调集体主义的社会中团结对满意度的作用应该具有显著效应。

　　商业稳定性模型的测试结果跟满意度模型结果一致,一些假设得到证实,另一些则出乎意料而且很有趣。结果像预期的那样表明犯罪的总体效应是减少商业稳定性。犯罪直接产生恐惧感,恐惧感又会减少商业稳定性。恐惧感居间作用于犯罪对商业稳定性,其媒介效应显著。这些发现跟假设一致。然而,当考察犯罪对商业稳定性的直接效应时,自然人暴力犯罪和总体犯罪表现出跟财产犯罪不同的形态。总的来说,自然人暴力犯罪和总体犯罪不直接影响商业稳定性,但令人吃惊的是,商业盗窃和入店偷窃直接促进商业稳定。结果表明像商业盗窃和入店偷窃这样的财产犯罪除了居间作用于恐惧感对商业稳定性的效应外,还直接影响商业稳定性。

　　这个意料之外的发现更新了笔者关于犯罪对商业稳定性效应的理解。它表明这一因果关系与犯罪的性质有关。财产犯罪大多数是为了利润。暴力犯罪和总体犯罪将商业赶出某一区域,而财产犯罪不这样。企业集中财富,这使罪犯们实现目的的机会最大化。

　　笔者推测财产犯罪和商业稳定性之间的因果关系方向与笔者以前假设的正好相反。企业的主要目的是追求利润,地区的利润越多,商业就越稳定。商业越稳定,财产犯罪就越多,因为它们为财产犯罪提供了更多的获取利益的机会。相较不稳定的商业而言,罪犯更易熟悉稳定的商业周围环境,所以商业稳定性会增加财产犯罪。机会理论(科恩(Cohen)和菲尔森(Felson),1979)认为合适的目标是犯罪机会论的三个要件之一。

　　笔者假设团结会促进商业稳定。然而结果表明团结对商业稳定的效应随团结的不同类型而改变。"居民对社区的义务感"(SOL1)和责"居民对社区的责任感"（SOL2）对商业稳定性的效应并不显著，而"商人对商业区的责任感"（SOL3）以及它们对商业稳定性的效应却是显著的。这意味着居民的团结（"居民对社区的义务感"（SOL1）和"居民对社区的责任感"（SOL2））和商人的团结（"商人对商业区的责任感"（SOL3））对商业稳定性的效应差别很大。商人的团结像理论假设的那样提高商业稳定性；笔者假定团结的绝大部分是有机的，能够反映商人的共有利益。然而居民的团结对商业稳定性的效应并不显著。这意味着居民和企业的行为分属不同领域。

对于警察支持率，结果更复杂。跟预料的一样，犯罪的总体效应是降低民众对警察的支持率。一般来讲，犯罪直接产生恐惧感，恐惧感直接减少警察支持率。恐惧感居间作用于犯罪对警察支持率的效应，居间效应在统计学上显著。

关于犯罪对警察支持率的直接效应，结果表明总体犯罪水平和商业盗窃不直接影响警察支持率，直接效应在统计学上不显著。这跟假设一致。然而，跟假设相反的是，入店偷窃仿佛会直接提高民众对警察的支持率；暴力犯罪亦然。这是没有料到的，因此，它更新了笔者对因果关系过程的理解。

可能因为警察对入店偷窃报道的反应让人们满意，警察的支持率获得提高。《统一犯罪报告》反复报道了对窃盗罪的高破获率，这也许支持了笔者的假设。例如，1991 年盗窃罪的破获率是 21%，在城市是 25%。比财产犯罪破获率 18% 要高，比夜盗罪的破获率 13% 要高出很多（FBI，1991）。相比之下，夜盗可能比入店偷窃要难对付，在动用警力上又没有那么急迫，这就是为什么商业盗窃对警察支持率没有积极的直接效应。同样，警察通常优先处理暴力犯罪。例如，1991 年谋杀罪的破获率是 67%（FBI，1991）。这也许是暴力犯罪同样可以提高警察支持率的原因。

笔者假设团结可以直接提高民众对警察的支持率。假设的结果比较复杂。社会团结对警察支持率的效应随团结类型而改变。"居民对社区的义务感"（SOL1）显著提高警察支持率。"居民对社区的责任感"（SOL2）和"商人对商业区的责任感"（SOL3）对警察支持率没有显著影响。义务和责任感在对警察支持率的效应上存在差异。居民的义务像理论上假设的那样影响对警察的支持率，因为它促进了和警察的协作、相互作用以及对警察的理解。"居民对社区的责任感"（SOL2）、"商人对商业区的责任感"（SOL3）同义务不同，它反映了人们对所在社区和区域内企业的控制感。这可能是一种独立于警察行为之外更少依赖警察行为的控制，因此它不显著影响警察支持率。

关于社会未来乐观模型，大部分假设都没有得到证实，模型规律不甚清楚。测试结果表明，尽管系数符号正确，恐惧感不显著降低社会未来乐观态度。恐惧感在犯罪对社会未来乐观的效应上的媒介作用不显著，犯罪不直接影响社会未来乐观。这可能意味着人们对社会未来的乐观态度很大程度上由模型之外的其他因子决定。例如，政府对社会的政策可以提高人们对社会未来的乐观态度。测试结果也表明"居民对社区的义务感"（SOL1）和责任感会降低社会未来乐观态度。这可能是因为义务和责任感越强，对社会的期望就越高，对社会未来的估计就越不乐观。

第二个问题是犯罪是否会促进社会团结。像预料的那样，由自然人暴力犯罪度量的暴力犯罪显著影响恐惧感；而由入店偷窃度量的非暴力犯罪对恐惧感没有显著影响。至于暴力犯罪和非暴力犯罪对团结的效应，结果是混合型的，并呈现出一些有趣形态：其效应随社会团结类型不同而改变。

由"居民对社区的义务感"度量的暴力犯罪对"居民对社区的义务感"（SOL1）的效应，以及由居民的责任感度量的暴力犯罪对"居民对社区的责任感"（SOL2）的效应，跟预料的一样是消极的、显著的；然而，由商人责任感度量的暴力犯罪对"商人对商业区的责任感"（SOL3）的效应是不显著的。这些结果表明居民和商人对暴力犯罪的反应方式不同。暴力犯罪降低居民团结，但对商人团结影响不显著。这可能是商人感到对商业区负有责任而导致的，因为无论暴力犯罪是否发生，对利润的追求要求他们具有这种责任感。

由入店偷窃度量的非暴力犯罪对团结的效应也是不一致的，随模型中使用的团结类型而改变。只有对商人的责任感这一变量，非暴力犯罪像预料的那样具有促进团结的功能。这里团结的概念主要是现代社会的有机型团结，是商人之间的共有利益，这一点应当注意。研究假设来源于迪尔凯姆（Durkheim）关于传统社会的思想。就居民团结这一变量而言，其结果也是不一致的。"居民对社区的义务感"（SOL1）这一变量的效应如预料的那样是积极的，但不显著。对"居民对社区的责任感"（SOL2）这一变量而言，其效应是消极的、显著的。为什么会出现这种情况笔者也感到难以理解。

第三个问题是论及恐惧感和团结之间的因果关系。当同时估计恐惧感对团结的因果关系和团结对恐惧感的因果关系时,结果显示恐惧感对团结具有消极效应。这和以往的研究一致。但是,结果也显示出团结对恐惧感的相当大的积极效应:"居民对社区的义务感"(SOL1)增加恐惧感。这在理论上十分有趣,并具有重要的政策启示意义。

笔者推测这可能是因为对社区有较高义务的人对犯罪更敏感、对犯罪问题的反应更强烈。对社区越负有义务,就越谨慎;对犯罪问题越敏感,就越感到恐惧感。同样,社会团结度越高,人们之间的社会交往就越频繁,恐怖的犯罪故事传播得就越广越快。研究表明新闻报道增加恐惧感(利斯卡(Liska),1990),因为新闻报道广泛而迅速地传播恐怖的犯罪故事。笔者称这种效应为"敏感反应效应"。在当今的美国城市社区,尽管团结可能起着减少恐惧感的效应,但它不能平衡"敏感反应效应",所以矛盾的是,当人们对社区负有更多义务时他们会感到更加恐惧。

## 三、政策启示

这三个问题的主要发现都有其政策启示意义。这三个问题被综合在围绕恐惧感的一般理论模型中。在考察犯罪、恐惧感和团结怎样影响社会后果时,研究结果表明恐惧感居间作用于犯罪对社会后果的效应。总的来说,结果表明恐惧感是犯罪影响社会后果过程中的关键变量。这为当前工作提供了最重要的政策启示。要控制社会后果,我们必须控制恐惧感。

在处理第二个问题——迪尔凯姆(Durkheim)关于犯罪促进团结的论题时,测试结果表明暴力犯罪会增加恐惧感。这表明暴力犯罪在引起社会后果方面更加突出。政策启示是,控制犯罪的社会后果中最为重要的是控制暴力犯罪。

第三个问题测试了恐惧感和团结之间的关系。矛盾的是,促进社会团结会增加恐惧感,因为社会交往的增加会使恐惧感的传播更加便利。这可能是因为人们之间的社交有两个相反效应:一方面它提供减少恐惧感的社会支持,另一方面它传播恐怖的故事。如果社交传播的恐惧感比提供的社会支持要多,团结就会导致恐惧感增加。从政策制定的角度出发,一个恐惧感减少计划不能仅仅依靠提高社交来实现其目的。恐惧感减少计划必须被设计成控制社交的机理从而增加社会支持、减少恐惧感传播。这很难做到,需要周密的努力和更多关于影响社会支持和恐惧感传播过程的深入知识。

　　总的来说,犯罪功能是一个重要研究领域,强调的是社会而不是犯罪事件和个人。与着眼于犯罪事件和个人的犯罪学主流不同,笔者认为聚焦于社会是犯罪学一个重要方向。笔者提出和测试了一个理论一般模型,试图回答关于犯罪的功能或后果是什么、犯罪在影响社会后果上怎样发挥作用等重要理论问题。笔者考察了理论上具有重要性的重要变量之间的因果关系,试图解决犯罪怎样影响社会团结、恐惧感和社会团结之间的因果关系等理论上的重要问题。有的发现支持假设,有的更新了笔者对因果关系的理解。发现具有重要政策启示意义。

# 四、当前研究的局限

　　当前的研究有许多局限。数据没有包括可能会同时影响社会后果和模型中自变量的变量,因而在估计模型变量对社会后果的效应时应当受控。

　　就商业稳定性模型而言,政府的绩效既影响商业稳定又影响社会团结。如果当地政府在本地发展上很有能力,商业会更稳定,人们会更有信心,对本地会有更多义务。因而,当估计团结对商业稳定的效应时,应当对政府绩效加以控制。

　　就警察支持率模型而言,警力资源影响警察绩效,从而影响警察支持率和犯罪。警察拥有更多资源,犯罪就会降低,警察就会获得更高支持率,这样的假定是合理的。当估计犯罪对警察支持率的直接效应时,应当对警力资源加以控制。

　　就社会未来乐观模型而言,政府发展计划的效果应当被关注。如果有有效的政府计划支持地区发展和扩展,人们会对社会未来持乐观态度,他们对社会会更加关心,社会也会更加团结。所以在估计团结对人们对社会未来的乐观态度的作用时应当对政府计划加以控制。

由于缺乏合适的工具变量,现有的数据还不允许我们考察社会后果与犯罪可能存在的互反关系。笔者假设社会团结提高在地区生活和经商的满意度,然而满意度促进社会团结也是可能的。满意度会加强人们对社会的义务。理论模型假设恐惧感影响警察支持率,有可能警察支持率也同样影响恐惧感。警察支持率反映出对警察抓捕和惩治罪犯能力的信心。这种信心给人们感觉事情是受控制的,从而减少恐惧感。

笔者指出,当前研究的另一个局限性是样本太小,因此,我们应该审慎对待模型测试结果。如果我们能使用更大的样本来进行重复测试,结果会更有效可信。

总之,笔者建议有些变量因为会影响模型中的其他变量与结论而应当被剔除;同时,当检测变量间潜在的相互作用时,工具变量亦不应当囊括其中。即使当数据库中存在这些变量时,小样本依然会限制理想检测的实施。因此,对当前研究的结果应当持谨慎的态度。今后的研究应当克服这些局限性。

# 五、展望未来

前一部分讨论了研究的局限,指出今后的研究要克服这些局限。至于今后的工作,首当其冲的是要采集更大样本来对理论模型进行重复测试。我们要采集关于社会的更大的样本,比如街道、社区、城市、国家。今后的研究要像本书前面部分建议的那样将数据集没有包括的变量包括进去,这跟采集更大的样本一样重要。

一个理想的纵向设计应当考虑到理论模型的进一步发展。如果可能我们应当采集足够多的时间点的数据,比如,在几年内每隔六个月采集一次数据。用这些数据,我们不仅能测试理论模型中提出的假设,也能测试关于因果关系在过程中怎样运行的新的假设。也许犯罪对不同社会后果的效应需要不同的时长来实现;也许不同犯罪需要不同时长来实现对同一后果的效应;抑或许相同犯罪对同一后果在不同时间段有不同效应。例如,暴力犯罪对商业稳定性的作用很小,除非暴力犯罪率保持持续高的水平。这些假设从理论上来讲既有趣且重要,因为它们可以提高我们对犯罪影响后果这一社会进程的理解。

然而,今后研究最重要的任务是超越前人,使关于犯罪功能的研究得到发展,开辟犯罪学发展的新方向。我们应当更深入细致地考察更广泛的犯罪后果。笔者认为迪尔凯姆(Durkheim)的著作说明社会是一个重要的逻辑出发点,应当成为犯罪学的重要焦点。但这一点被现代犯罪学研究所广泛忽视。我们应当把犯罪学的新的焦点放在以下两个方面:犯罪对社会进程和社会组织的功能或后果是什么以及犯罪怎样影响这些社会后果和社会组织。

在新的研究计划里,我们应当考察何种社会进程和社会组织受到犯罪的影响、通过何种方式受到影响。为了激发关于犯罪功能或后果的思考,笔者指出犯罪对社会更多的可能后果,并提出新的研究课题或总的研究方向。

笔者提出,犯罪至少可以通过好几种方式来影响社会经济。工业与商业机构的投资行为对社会经济有重要影响。银行和借贷公司这样的金融机构会考虑犯罪对财产价值的影响,比如房屋价值就明显受到犯罪的影响。保险公司制定政策时会考虑犯罪可能造成的生命或财产损失。

犯罪会影响人口分布。研究表明犯罪在都市郊区化中起到了一定的作用(斯科甘(Skogan)和马克斯菲尔德(Maxfield),1981)。这对许多社会进程和社会机构都有重要影响。人口分布的改变产生许多影响。它加剧城市中心的贫穷化,加剧种族居住隔离和学校隔离,因为它影响拥有不同社会资源的不同社会群体的迁移,而这样又会影响不同地方不同人口群体的分布。

犯罪也影响政府部门行为。例如,城市规划部门会考虑这样一个事实:修建公园可能会带来犯罪并造成混乱。绝大部分城市政府面临着重建衰败的城市街道的问题,因此它们不得不对犯罪有所反应。犯罪可能影响诸如警察机构在内的司法体系的组织情况,这些体系在不同时间不同地点应对犯罪时可能会改变其形式与行为。

犯罪对社会规范、消费者以及人们的生活方式都有影响。居住在犯罪高发地区的人们会更加害怕帮助陌生人,因为他们更警惕。经常听说黑帮故事的人会更难容忍像青少年酗酒和吵闹这样的行为,因为他们把这些行为看做混乱和犯罪的导火线。犯罪影响人们的休闲活动,因为公园常常被认为是危险的地方。日常行为理论认为生活方式的改变会促进犯罪率的提高,犯罪也会促进人们生活方式的改变。在犯罪高发的城市中心地带人们避免夜晚出门，而在郊区居住的人害怕晚上进城使用娱乐设施。

我们对犯罪是否真的产生这些后果知之甚少。即使犯罪真的产生这些后果，我们对这些后果怎样发生也不太了解。尽管笔者也无法提出具体的思想与答案，我们仍然可以提出更多关于犯罪功能或后果的问题来探索可能存在的研究领域。例如：犯罪对街道组织的影响。在犯罪高发区域，街道组织的主要任务是对付犯罪。犯罪对家庭产生后果，因为许多犯罪就发生在家庭中，对家庭产生影响。我们对家庭外部的犯罪和内部的犯罪怎样影响家庭知之甚少。犯罪会引起社会中家庭结构的改变。此外，我们也不太了解犯罪是否影响和怎样影响教育机构。青少年犯罪状况的改变会引起学校里的某些变化么？如果是，这些影响的启示是什么？

总之，一旦我们转向犯罪学研究的新方向，我们将会发现许多可能的犯罪功能或后果应当被考察，许多问题应当被提出并解答。对犯罪功能的研究面临着巨大挑战，前景也十分灿烂。

# Functions of Crime

# Chapter I. Introduction

The functions of crime are a long standing classic issue in sociology. The issue was originally formulated in Durkheim's profound theoretical conception of social order and social organization. Not looking at crime as an abnormality of a society as many criminologists do, Durkheim looks at crime as a social fact integrated into a social system. Different from mainstream criminology, Durkheim's argument about crime focuses on how crime affects society, rather than criminal events and individuals involved in crime. However, although modern criminological theories and research have drawn a lot from Durkheim's work, this implication of his work is largely ignored by modern criminological research.

Summarizing his arguments on functions of crime, I think that he asks two questions about crime: One, what is the role that crime plays in a social system? Two, how does crime play its role? The focus of these questions clearly is on society, rather than criminal events and individuals.

In answering the first question, Durkheim (1982) argues that crime "plays a normal role in social life" ( p. 102 ) and that "crime is necessary" ( p. 101 ). He suggests that crime has an important function for maintaining the social order. From this functional perspective, crime and deviance are viewed as regular, integrative and normal aspects of a society. Durkheim argues about the functionality of crime in

113

increasing social solidarity.

In explaining how crime plays its role for increasing social solidarity, Durkheim states: "Crime brings together upright consciences and concentrates them. We have only to notice what happens, particularly in a small town, when some scandal has just been committed. They stop each other on the street, they visit each other, they seek to come together to talk of the event and to wax indignant in common" (1933, p. 102). The functionality hypothesis is derived from Durkheim's general functional approach to social systems. It is an important and integrated part of Durkheim's general theory of social order and social organization; however, theories and research have not articulated the significance of this theme.

## A. Significance of the Subject

Although some work has been done (for example, Erikson, 1966; Inverarity, 1976; Lauderdale, 1976; Blumstein et al. 1976 etc.), the functions of crime issue has not attracted as much attention as it should have. Very few studies have been published over the years, compared with the rapid development of social science, especially criminology. Even fewer studies use rigorous quantitative methods, considering the recent dramatic development in quantitative methodology. The topic has been basically a "cool" subject in the studies of crime. The lack of development of the topic is because the issue does not apparently show a strong theoretical and practical significance. The research on Durkheim's thesis has been limited to a few issues; it has been isolated from other theories and research of crime; the research is not well developed and integrated into the broad criminological theory and research enterprise; and the theoretical importance of the subject is not revealed on a broad theoretical and research background and connected to other research fields in the studies of crime. There have been no systematic efforts to develop a theory of the functions of crime, nor do we have a systematic research agenda. Clearly, the significance of the subject has to be discussed before any further pursuit of the issue.

First, the functions of crime issue are very important theoretically. Crime occurs in society, so studies of crime have two logical starting points: one is crime, the other is society. Most criminological theories and research focus on criminal events and individuals involved in crime, while the other starting point, ie., society, rarely becomes a focus of criminology.

I argue that Durkheim's work on crime largely represents this direction, but this is mostly ignored. Functions of crime are involved in many important social processes that are critical for understanding society and crime. Durkheim's work is a classic illustration of this point. He shows us that the understanding of the function of crime is vital in understanding social order and organization. Without a good understanding of the functions of crime, we can not say that we understand crime; and we also can not say that we understand society.

Durkheim mainly examines one function of crime: crime increases solidarity. Modern society exhibits innumerable new features. The functions of crime are changing and developing. Today, it may not be an exaggeration to say that crime alters many social processes and that crime has important functions or consequences on many aspects of society. Without understanding what is the role that crime plays and how crime plays its roles in these important social processes, we cannot have a complete understanding of these social processes. Studying the functions of crime takes criminology back to the broad understanding of general social system and social processes, and puts the studies of crime in a broad background of the studies of societies. It is important for both developing general social theory and studies of crime.

Second, crime has both causes and consequences. Most criminological theory and research studies the causes of crime. Theorists and researchers in criminology focused principally on explaining what factors cause individuals to commit crimes. Major inquiries have been on why some individuals commit crime while others do not. Numerous theories have been proposed and tested. Theories and research have identified many social, cultural, economic, psychological, and biological factors that cause crime. Theoretical work and research in this direction have been developing and our knowledge on the causes of crime has been systematically developed. In this direction of criminology, crime is the logical starting point and major focus of criminology.

However, crimes cause consequences. People are concerned about crime because of its consequences. The reason that we study the causes of crime is largely because we perceive and believe that crime has serious functions or consequences for our social life. It is primarily the consequences(mostly negative consequences) of crime that makes criminological study important. It is the consequences of crime that press people to search for the causes of it. Understanding the causes of crime is very important, but equally important is to study functions or consequences of crime. A fully developed criminology not only should study the causes of crime, but also should research the functions or consequences of crime for society. The central concern is not why people commit crime, but what functions or influences of crime have on society as a normal social process.

Third, from a practical point of view, studying the functions or consequences of crime is important to social control. Many criminological theories have suggested that the causes of crime are rooted in the social structure and the culture structure of society. Merton ( 1938 ), for example, argues that American culture places imbalanced emphases on goals and means. It emphasizes material success as goals and does not emphasize the norms that identify proper ways to achieve those goals. American social structure, characterized by an unequal distribution of opportunities economically and socially, pressures disadvantaged persons toward deviant behavior in order to adapt to the strain created by the discrepancy between the available means and the goals that are unattainable through conventional activities. Research has identified that economic inequality, poverty, and racial inequality are all correlates of crime. Practically, we admit that we can not manipulate these structural causes to control crime. However, an equally important alternative is to control the consequences of crime. Studying the functions or consequences of crime opens up an additional alternative direction for crime control, that is, to directly control the consequences of crime. I argue that the relationship between the consequences of crime and the seriousness of crime is not a simple one to one linear relationship; the same crime rate can cause different consequences in different communities. Crime rate is not necessarily proportionate to the seriousness of social consequences. Other social variables play important roles in the process.

For example, consider one social consequence of crime: fear. Research suggests that high crime rates in neighborhoods are not closely related to the fear of crime (Donnelly, 1989). Citizens "assessments of neighborhoods" specific crime problems and personal risks do not consistently correspond to official crime rates. This suggests that our knowledge of the consequences of crime can be used to control the consequences of crime and alter the social processes in which crime plays a part.

In studying the functions of crime, I suggest an analytical distinction between two consequences of crime. One is the direct consequences of crime on victims, which can be termed the individual consequences of crime. The other, which in fact is much more detrimental for society, is the social consequences. After crimes occur in a community, they affect not only the victims' life but also, more profoundly, the life of the community. Durkheim states that: "assuredly murder is always an evil, but nothing proves that it is the greatest evil. What does one human being the less matter to society? Or one cells fewer in the organism? It is said that public safety would be endangered in the future if the act remained unpunished (1984, p. 33)". So it is the social consequences of crime that are much more serious and profound and that makes the study of criminology an important academic field, and makes the study of functions of crime important. The present work studies the social consequences of crime at the level of social aggregates.

# B. A Research Agenda

A good understanding of what the central questions of the area are is a precondition for any substantial development of a research area. The literature review in next chapter will show that the concerns and foci of the research on the functions of crime have been very loosely organized without any systematic direction. Past research on this topic is limited to Durkheim's functionality thesis, and the research is isolated from other research areas in criminology. The research is mostly around a few issues to illustrate and develop Durkheim's thesis of functionality of crime in increasing social solidarity. The topic is understood and defined very narrowly. In fact, Durkheim's work on the functionality of crime is to answer two basic questions: what is the function of crime and how does crime plays its role for society? Summarizing the topic this way, we can see that the questions imply a new direction of research. Considering that crime has other functions or consequences beyond increasing solidarity, we should expand the two questions into two similar questions: what are the functions of crime? How does crime play its role in realizing its functions or consequences?

The firstquestion asks us to examine systematically the functions or consequences of crime in every social process and for different social institutions. That is, we should examine what social processes are caused, or altered, or affected by crime? More specifically, what are the consequences of crime on people's social life, on a community's socioeconomic resources, on a community's culture, on people's political attitudes, on important characteristics of social organization, and on a community's development? What are the social institutions that are affected by crime? What are the changes in these institutions affected by crime?

The second question concerns the explanation of the functions or consequences of crime for aspects of social process and social institutions. It requires us first to find important variables influencing the social processes and social institutions where crime plays its roles, and then to answer questions about the causal relationships among these variables, that is, to propose theories about the functions of crime. Many functions of crime in modern society have never been systematically examined and documented. Naturally, there is no systematic theory about how crime and other variables affect consequences and how these variables affect each other in the processes of affecting the consequences. Finally, we will also ask: what are the policy implications of the theory?

These broad questions in fact redefine the research area of the functions of crime, making it possible to organize the research and theoretical inquiry in a new systematical framework. Past research and a broad range of related studies can be organized into this broad new framework. These questions suggest a new research agenda for the field. These tasks require us to examine the topic in a broad background and examine all the relevant research areas, rather than limit the research to only the narrowly defined traditional Durhkeimian thesis.

# Chapter II. Review of Literature

## A. Durkheim's Thesis

The functions of crime research are developed separately from other research areas in criminology. Around Durkheim's thesis of the functionality of crime, research regarding the functions of crime has been very limited and has involved a few very limited issues. Most studies are historical and field observational ( Erikson, 1966; Scott, 1976; Connor, 1972; Ben-Yehuda, 1980; Dentler and Erikson, 1959). A few of them are theory testing ( Lauderdale, 1976; Lauderdale et al. , 1984). Research can be classified roughly around four closely related issues: social solidarity, repressive justice, boundary maintenance, and the stability of punishments.

First, a central issue of past research is to document the functionality of crime for strengthening social solidarity. The traditional functional perspective assumes that social structures function is to maintain society's values, goals, and needs. In his analysis of the distinction between the normal and the pathological ( 1982, pp. 85 – 107) , Durkheim suggests ( 1982, p. 98 ) that crime " ··· is a factor in public health, an integrative element in any healthy society. " He states ( 1982, p. 99 ) : " crime is normal because it is completely impossible for any society entirely free of

120

it to exist". For him, deviance and crime play a function of promoting social solidarity. It is only when rates of deviance exceed what is typical of a certain societal type that abnormality is present.

To illustrate the normality of crime, he suggests: "Imagine a community of saints in an exemplary and perfect monastery. In it crime as such will be unknown, but faults that appear venial to the ordinary person will arouse the same scandal as does normal crime in ordinary consciences. If therefore that community has the power to judge and punish, it will term such acts criminal and deal with them as such. It is for the same reason that the completely honorable man judges his slightest moral failings with a severity that the mass of people reserves for acts that are truly criminal." (1982, p. 100) Durkheim also says: "By this is explained why some acts have so frequently been held to be criminal, and punished as such, without in themselves being harmful to society." (1984, p. 61)

The studies documenting the functions of crimes are mostly historical (Erikson, 1966; Currie, 1968; Connor, 1972; Ben-Yehuda , 1980) and field observational (Dentler and Erikson 1959, Scott 1976). These studies try to illustrate how crime either functions to increase solidarity (Erikson, 1966) or fails to do so (Ben-Yehuda, 1980). For example, an influential work is Erikson's "Wayward Puritans". He suggests that deviant forms of behavior are often a valuable resource in society, providing a kind of scope and dimension which is necessary to all social life. He elaborates on how deviance and crime function to strengthen solidarity, the social process that Durkheim did not very clearly describe. Erikson states: "The deviant individual violates rules of conduct which the rest of the community holds in high respect; and when these people come together to express their outrage over the offense and to bear witness against offender, they develop a tighter bond of solidarity than existed earlier. The excitement generated by crime, in other words, quickens the tempo of interaction in the group and creates a climate in which the private sentiments of many separate persons are fused together into a common sense of morality." (1966, p. 4) So, to Erikson, crime promotes social solidarity by creating"a sense of mutuality among the people of a community by supplying a focus for group feeling···deviance makes people more alert to the interests they share in common and draws attention to those values which constitute the 'collective conscience' of the community. "( 1966, p. 4 ) " Each time the community moves to censure some act of deviation, then, and convenes a formal ceremony to deal with the responsible offender, it sharpens the authority of the violated norm and restates where the boundaries of the group are located. "(1966, p. 13 )

The other three issues are closely related and are developed from the first issues, the functionality thesis. The second issue is the repressive justice issue. Durkheim analyzes how solidarity is maintained in different types of societies in terms of the nature of their social justice practices. Durkheim develops a typology ofsociety's in terms of their basis of solidarity. One type is termed mechanical and the other organic. According to Durkheim, the reactions of society to crime are different in different societies. Mechanical society is associated with repressive justice, which reaffirms a common value through diffuse forms of ritual punishment. Organic society is associated with restitutory justice, which is characterized by restorative justice.

A good historical study on repressive justice is Erikson's( 1966 )analysis of the three"crime waves" ( Antinomian controversy of 1636, Quaker persecution of the late 1650's, and witchcraft hysteria of 1692) which took place in the seventeenth century Puritan community in Massachusetts. He argued that disruptions of solidarity, termed as"boundary crisis", produce a sudden and dramatic increase in repressive justice, "crime wave". By this historical analysis, Erikson evidenced how these episodes helped the settlers define the boundaries of their emerging society.

James M. Inverarity ( 1976 ) provides a quantitative analysis and develops a causal model to examine the relationship between the Populist disruption of the Solid South and the incidence of lynching. Inverarity analyzes lynching in Louisiana during the Populist revolt. Lynchings were ritual punishments of alleged criminals.

Typically, lynching involved large segments of the community participating in an open, public reaction against an accused criminal. Inverarity uses lynching during the Populist revolt period as the indicator of Durkheim's concept of repressive justice, which is a ritual punishment in which the whole society participates. He suggests that the Solid South is an instance of mechanical solidarity among Southern whites. He represents mechanical solidarity as an unmeasured factor caused by three variables: percent black, urbanization, and religious homogeneity. The results of the analysis support Erikson's thesis that boundary crises produces repressive justice.

Inverarity's work has been extensively criticized( Pope and Ragin, 1977; Wasserman, 1977; Bohrnstedt, 1977; Bagozzi, 1977; Berk, 1977 ). Critics have questioned the rigorousness of the test, whether the post-civil war Populist movement in Louisiana really constituted a boundary crisis, and whether the above indicators constitute a valid operationalization of mechanical solidarity.

The third closely related issue is the boundary movement argument. Elaborating on Durkheim, to explain why and how crime functions to promote social solidarity and sustain a social system, Erikson proposes a "boundary maintaining" argument. Erikson states: " communities are boundary maintaining: each has a specific territory in the world as a whole, not only in the sense that it occupies a defined region of geographical space but also in the sense that it takes over a particular niche in what might be called cultural space and develops its own "ethos" or "way" within that compass ( 1966, p. 9 ). "A human community can be said to maintain boundaries, then, in the sense that its members tend to confine themselves to a particular radius of activity and to regard any conduct which drifts outside that radius as somehow inappropriate or immoral. Thus the group retains a kind of cultural integrity, a voluntary restriction on its own potential for expansion, beyond that which is strictly required for accommodation to the environment. " ( 1966, p. 10 )

Unlike many other theories, such as strain theory ( Merton, 1938 ) and

123

differential association theory ( Sutherland, 1939, 1947 ) that approach crime as the products of the movement of the deviants across the moral boundaries of a particular social system, Erikson states: "Boundaries are never fixed property of any community. They are always shifting as the people of the group find new ways to define the outer limits of their universe, new ways to position themselves on the larger cultural map." ( 1966, p. 12 ) "…boundaries remain a meaningful point of reference only so long as they are repeatedly tested by persons on the fringes of the group and repeatedly defended by persons chosen to represent the group's inner morality. Each time the community moves to censure some act of deviation, then, and convenes a formal ceremony to deal with the responsible offender, it sharpens the authority of the violated norm and restates where the boundaries of the group are located." ( 1966, p. 13 ) Therefore, Erikson suggests "Deviant forms of behavior, by marking the outer edges of group life, give the inner structure its special character and thus supply the framework within which the people of the group develop an orderly sense of their own cultural identity." ( 1966, p. 13 )

Pat Lauderdale ( 1976 ) elaborates on the moral boundaries issue. He does an experimental study on the issue. He restricts his discussion to "corporate" social systems structures that possess an ongoing social organization through which members can act collectively and to which they feel responsible independent of their sentiments toward one another. He tries to explain how the definition and volume of deviance can change in a particular social system independent of the actions of the deviants associated with that system. He proposes and tests a set of hypothesis based on his argument that deviance can be thought of as a product of the movement of the actors across the moral boundaries of a particular social system.

He assigned subjects to social work groups to discuss a juvenile delinquent case. After reading the case history, each member announced their position on a scaled list of alternative recommendations ranging from extreme love and affection to extreme punishment. One confederate, the deviant, chose an extreme position and maintained it throughout the discussion. An outside threat condition was introduced to the group after the first 30 minutes of interaction. An observer, claiming to represent a criminal justice authority, who was not involved in the interaction of the group, made a statement to the leader of the group ( experimenter ) that " this group should probably not continue ". The assessment of the changes between two conditions, one with an outside threat and one without an outside threat, was made and discussed. The experimental results show that deviants, independent of their actions, will be more severely rejected and stigmatized following an external threat to their corporate social system; the external threat serves as a magnifier of the internal threat—the deviants. The external threat points to the potential dangers of the internal deviants that was not apparent prior to the threat. The rejection and stigmatization have been related to the loss and then reestablishment of solidarity of that system and to the constriction of the moral boundary.

The fourth closely related issue is the stability of punishment hypothesis. In arguing for the normality of crime, Durkheim suggests a stability of punishment hypothesis: " If at least, as societies pass from lower to higher types, the crime rate ( the relationship between the annual crime figures and population figures ) tended to fall, we might believe that, although still remaining a normal phenomenon, crime tended to lose that character of normality. Yet there is no single ground for believing such a regression to be real. Many facts would rather seem to point to the existence of a movement in the opposite direction. " ( 1982, p. 98 ) " What is normal is simply that criminality exists, provided that for each social type it does not reach or go beyond a certain level which it is perhaps not impossible to fix in conformity with the previous rules. " ( 1982, p. 98 ) " Where acts of violence are frequent, they are tolerated. Their criminal character is in inverse proportion to their frequency. Thus with the lower people, crimes against the person are more usual than in our civilized societies. " ( 1984, p. 98 ) Since crime is assumed to be functional, it must be also stable.

Erikson ( 1966, p. 25 ) explicitly states that " the amount of deviation a community encounters are apt to remain fairly constant over time. " He further explains that this is because " it is a simple logistic fact that the number of deviancies which come to a community's attention are limited by the kinds of equipment it uses to detect and handle them, and to that extent the rate of deviation found in a community is at least in part a function of the size and complexity of its social control apparatus. " ( 1966 , p. 24 ) " ⋯ community develops its definition of deviance so that it encompasses a range of behavior roughly equivalent to the available space in its control apparatus—a kind of inverted Parkinson's Law. " ( 1966 , p. 25 )

He examines the hypothesis that the volume of deviance found in a community is likely to remain constant over time. Based on the Essex County Court records, which is believed by Erikson to be "a complete coverage of all deviant activities" ( 1966 , p. 165 ), he computes crime rates from 1651 - 1680 per five year. He concludes that " in one region of America, during one period of its history, the offender rate seems to have remained quite stable. " ( 1966 , p. 181 )

Blumstein and associates ( Blumstein and Cohen, 1973 ; Blumstein et al. , 1976 ; Blumstein and Moitra, 1979 ) have addressed the issue and their work has stimulated considerable theory testing research. Building heavily on Durkheim's views, these studies purport to show that rates of punishment are quite stable over relatively long intervals in a variety of Western countries and throughout political jurisdictions in the United States. They have tried to document the stability of punishment( definition ) of crime and to identify the causal processes that underlie it. They use time series techniques to examine the stability of imprisonment rates in the United States from 1926 to 1974, in Canada from 1880 to 1959, and in Norway from 1880 to 1964. They interpret the variation in imprisonment rate over time as a random error. That is, they argue, the imprisonment rates in these countries are generated by a stationary process. Rauma( 1981a ) reanalyzes these data. He argues that there is no clear evidence to decide whether a stationary process or a nonstationary one generates these observations. He ( 1981b ) further argues that a univariate time series analysis can not reveal the underling causal process. Blumstein and Chen (1973) have examined the relationship between crime and arrest rates for serious and nonserious crime in the United States. Their findings suggest that a stable general arrest rate is maintained because as the general crime rate increases, the arrest rate of nonserious crimes decreases, and as crime rate decreases, the arrest rate of nonserious crimes increases. Also, Blumstein et al (1976) analyze the flow rates between conformists, criminals, and prisoners in Canada. They deduce flow rates among these groups that generally approximate the observed rates.

Blumstein and his associates have been criticized for the particular historical periods analyzed (e. g. , Cahalan, 1979), definitions of the punishment rate used (e. g. Waller and Chan, 1974), and the statistical procedures employed (Rauma, 1981a, 1981b). Although there are problems with their work, for example, their model is underidentified, Blumstein and his associates' attempts to model the social process and test the stability hypothesis have considerably stimulated the debate and advanced the development of research on the stability hypothesis issue.

Carefully examining the stability hypothesis and Blumstein's work, Berk et al. (1981) develops a dynamic model of punishment that includes Blumstein's model as a special case. They use equilibrating equations to formally derive a set of polynomial function models that specify the hypothesized equilibrating tendencies. Equilibrating equations can mathematically model a equilibrating system, a system that equilibrates around a specified constant called the system target. In this equation, if for some reason the system values increase and exceed the target value, they will start to decrease; if the system values fall below the target, they will start to increase. In their model, Berk et al assume that the punishment rate varies around a specific level that is functional for a given society, that is, the system target. Using data on imprisonment rates from California for the period from the opening of the prison system in 1851 to 1970, they find no empirical evidence for the stability of punishment hypothesis.

To summarize, the earliest thought on the functions of crime comes from Durkheim. He argues that crime is normal, regular, and functional. He suggests that crime has a function in increasing social solidarity. Past research on the functions of crime is mainly around and derived from this Durkheimian thesis. The research centers on four closely related issues: social solidarity, repressive justice, boundary maintenance, and the stability of punishment. The studies are mostly observational and historical, but there is some experimental and quantitative testing. Despite some criticism, the research generally supports Durkheim's hypothesis that crime is functional in increasing social solidarity.

The research following Durkheim's thesis treats only one function of crime, that is, crime increases social solidarity. This limits and narrowly defines the research area to only a few issues, and limits the research from developing into an attractive and important area. Traditionally, this research developed isolated from the major criminological enterprise and other areas of research on crime. The connection between them has never been made. This situation also limits the development of the study of functions of crime. In fact, in criminology, theories and research have been concerned with the same variables that the Durkheimian thesis was concerned, such as crime, solidarity, and consequences of crime.

I think that there are at least two variables that play important roles in affecting the functions or consequences of crime: one is fear of crime, and the other is social solidarity. To examine the functions of crime in a new framework, and to answer questions in the research agenda proposed in previous chapter, we should review research on fear and social solidarity.

Fear of crime is one of the most important consequences of crime in modern society. Research has extensively studied fear of crime. A few studies examine the reactions to crime, and these involve other negative functions or social consequences. Joining fear research with the function of crime tradition will greatly increase the scope of the functions of crime research, will stimulate new topics, and will promote the development of research.

Social solidarity is an important variable that affects many aspects of society. It is a central concept in Durkheim's theory. It is reasonable to think that social solidarity plays important roles in influencing the consequences of crime. Many other criminological theories and research also study social solidarity. Social disorganization theory, for example, examines the importance of social integration. Social control theory examines social bonding and social solidarity at the individual level. Network approach treats social solidarity from a new perspective. These areas of research will help us understand the nature and effects of social solidarity and therefore shed light on the development of the functions of crime research. In next few sections of this chapter, I will review fear research and social solidarity research.

# B. Fear Research

The fear of crime has emerged as an important research topic and has developed into a multidisciplinary research areasince mid-1960s. The fear of crime has become a distinct consequence of crime that has attracted both public and academic attention. Important surveys, such as Harris, Gallup, National Opinion Research Center (NORC), and National Crime Survey (NCS) all report that the fear of crime has significantly increased since the mid-1960s. Basically, evidence suggests that fear of crime rose significantly between 1965 and the mid – 1970s, and since then it has remained stationary (Hartnagel, 1979; Baumer, 1985; Skogan and Maxfield, 1981; Miethe and Lee, 1984; Warr and Stafford, 1982; Yin, 1985). A large body of literature in this area has accumulated over years and public programs related to fear reduction have also been developed (e. g. Schwartz and Clarren, 1977; Rouse and Rubenstein, 1978; Police Foundation, 1981; Fowler and Mangione, 1982). Most fear research is on sources of fear. Most studies focus their attention on the causal relationships between fear and individual personality and demographic characteristics.

The research has identified a cognitive model of fear of crime (Garofalo, 1979; Yin, 1980; Skogan and Maxfield, 1981; Baumer, 1985). Fear of crime is viewed essentially as a rational response to a perceived threat of crime (Baumer, 1985). Basically, factors found contributing to fear can be categorized into three groups: 1. seriousness of crime. 2. individual vulnerability to crime. 3. environmental / neighborhoods conditions. In general, research using multivariate statistical techniques reports that the highestlevel of fear exists among the lonely, dissatisfied, alienated, and anxious, and among females, the elderly, nonwhites, and the poor (Yin 1985; Kennedy and Silvermanr 1985; Miethe and Lee 1984; Baumer 1985 etc.). In general, fear is studied as a dependent variable in fear research.

Although little fear research has directly addressed the issue of the social consequences of crime, a few studies deal with the reactions of individuals to fear of victimization. Changing one's activities to deal with personal threats is perhaps the most thoroughly researched behavior (Biderman et al., 1967). Conklin (1975) reports that a predominate individual reaction to fear is reducing contact with other people, especially strangers. Gordon et al. (1980) asked a sample of women about how often they found themselves in 12 common situations (for example, "home alone after dark") and how worried they were in these situations. The two sets of responses were strongly negatively correlated. Rifai (1976) and Lawton et al. (1976) report that between 69 percent and 89 percent of those over 65 years of age say they never go out at night. On the other hand, Hindelang et al. (1978) conclude that most people do not alter their behavior drastically in response to crime; rather, they subtly change the way in which they do things, the manner in which they conduct themselves in public places, and the time of day when they go out, in order to reduce their frequency of exposure to what they perceive to be the threat of crime. Only a few studies examine fear as a social consequences varying across macro units, such as neighborhoods (Taylor, Gottfredson, and Brower, 1984; Skogan and Maxfield, 1981; Hough and Mayhew, 1985), and cities (Garofalo, 1979; Skogan and Maxfield, 1981; Liska, Lawrence, and Sanchirico, 1982). There is not yet a perspective focusing on reactions of society to fear of crime.

In recent years, research on sources of fear has developed a focus on conditions and characteristics of neighborhoods. These include signs of incivility, social disorder, physical disorder ( e. g. Biderman et al. , 1976; Hunter, 1978; Skogan and Maxfield, 1981 ). Skogan ( 1990 ) suggests that disorder has effects on the fear of crime independent of the seriousness of crime. Also, other research suggests that neighborhood disorganization and lack of social cohesion are the conditions that lead to a high level of fear of crime ( Skogan and Maxfield, 1981; Hunter and Baumer, 1982; Skogan, 1990 ).

Among the factors contributing to fear, the effects of a neighborhood's condition, especially the neighborhood's social cohesion and the individuals ' commitment to their neighborhood, are of particular interest and of particular theoretical importance for the study of functions or consequences of crime. Research has found that public programs on crime and fear reduction are more likely to be successful in neighborhoods where individuals' commitments to their neighborhood are high ( Skogan, 1990 ). However, this research mostly focuses on the causal relationship between a neighborhood's cohesion and the fear of crime. There is a considerable disagreement about which is the cause; some argue that lack of cohesion increases fear ( Fowler and Mangione, 1982 ); some argue that it is the consequence of fear ( Conklin, 1975; Yin, 1980 ).

To summarize, fear is a major consequence of crime in modern society. Research extensively studies factors that contribute to fear. In fear research, fear is mainly considered as a dependent variable; some research studies individual reactions to fear of crime, but the focus is mostly on individual reactions, not social ones. At the individual level, the fear research and functions of crime are separate topics. However, at the society level, the link between the two researches will be easier to see; both are concerned with society's reactions to and consequences of crime. The research on the functions of crime can be significantly expanded and developed.

However, there is not yet a perspective focusing on reactions of society to fear of crime. In recent years, fear research has developed a focus on the relationship between neighborhood conditions and fear. Research studies the causal relationship between fear and neighborhood cohesion. Some research argues that fear leads to the reduction of neighborhoods cohesion; others argue that the lack of neighborhoods cohesion is a cause of fear. The answers remain inconclusive.

# C. Research on Social Solidarity

Fear research is relevant to the functions of crime. If we examine fear as a variable that causes social consequences at the societal level, rather than examine fear as a dependent variable at the individual level, which is the case in most fear research, we will develop a focus on how society is influenced by fear of crime.

Another important variable that affects society and the consequences of crime for society is social solidarity. The notion of solidarity has roots in many other seemingly unrelated theories and research, and is an important concept in those theories and research. Many fields of research have studied social solidarity and therefore have implicit links to the study of functions of crime. The connections have not been explicitly made, because functions of crime research develop isolated from these areas. Little research directly addresses the effects of social solidarity on consequences of crime. The major areas include Durkheim' study on social solidarity, social disorganization theory, social control theory, and network approach. In the following sections, I will review their research on social solidarity.

## 1. Durkheim's Social Theory

Social solidarity is the central concept of Durkheim's social theory. Durkheim's work, from which the function of crime issue originated, discusses the concept of social solidarity extensively, and informs us that social solidarity influences a community's social life. Durkheim's work also informs us about the conceptualization and operationalization of this abstract theoretical concept.

Durkheim's first important work, his doctorate dissertation, "The Division of Labor in society" ( 1893 ), establishes his primary theoretical concern, that is, understanding the variables that maintain and change patterns of social organization. The major variable is social solidarity. The concern guides almost all Durkheim's subsequent works. To Durkheim, his study of social solidarity presents a general theory of social organization.

Durkheim believes that functional analysis gives sociologists a means for isolating "social pathologies" so that they can recommend "treatments" for them. He tends to equate integration and solidarity with normality, while pathologies are those conditions that deviate from integration, such as anomie, egoism, the forced division of labor, and the poor coordination of functions. To Durkheim, the central subject of a social theory is the conditions that ensure solidarity of societies. Without these conditions, society can not exist. He studies the division of labor because he thinks that it is such a condition ( 1984, p. 22 ).

The functions of crime issues originated from Durkheim's discussion of the relationship between crime and social solidarity. It is in the analysis of social solidarity that Durkheim suggests the thesis of the functions of crime. " ··· crime disturbs those feelings that in anyone type of society are to be found in every healthy consciousness" ( 1984, p. 34 ) " ··· a sentiment, whatever may be its origin and purpose, is found in every consciousness and that disturbs it is a crime" ( 1984, p. 40 ). " ··· crime consisted essentially in an act contrary to strong, well-defined states of the common consciousness" ( 1984, p. 60 ). Therefore, I argue that Durkheim's work suggests to us the great importance of the concept social solidarity in our development of a general theory of the functions of crime and deviance. Durkheim suggests that we should carefully examine the concept of social solidarity.

While he does not clearly define social solidarity, Durkheim's work does inform us about the conceptualization of social solidarity, as well as the sources of solidarity. We need to reach a definition of social solidarity and an operationalization of it through analyzing Durkheim's statements. Durkheim states: "a social solidarity exists which arises because a certain number of states of consciousness are common to all members of the same society. It is this solidarity that repressive law materially embodies, at least in its most essential elements. The share it has in the general integration of society plainly depends upon the extent, whether great or small, of social life included in the common consciousness and regulated by it. The more varied the relationships on which that consciousness makes its action felt, the more also it creates ties that bind the individual to the group; the more, consequently, social cohesion derives entirely from this cause and bears this imprint" (1984, p. 64). "Man is only a moral being because he lives in society, since morality consists in solidarity with the group, and varies according to that solidarity." (1984, p. 331) "We may say that what is moral is everything that is a source of solidarity, everything that forces man to take account of other people, to regulate his actions by something other than the promoting of his own egoism, and the more numerous and strong these ties are, the more solid is the morality." (1984, p. 331) "…consciousness is a source of life" (1984, p. 53)

Although Durkheim does not clearly define the concept of social solidarity, his illustrations suggest that social solidarity is the collective consciousness. His hypothesis that crime increases solidarity is also a further illustration of the concept of solidarity. He states: "We have only to notice what happens, particularly in a small town, when some scandal has just been committed. They stop each other on the street, they visit each other, they seek to come together to talk of the event and to wax indignant in common" (1984, p. 58).

However, in Durkheim's work, he also suggests the social solidarity is not only collective conscience. This can be seen from why he studies social solidarity. He is concerned about what are the social forces that bind the individuals together that support the existence of society. In his "Division of Labor", he classifies solidarity as two types: mechanical solidarity and organic solidarity. Mechanical solidarity is based on shared commonness, while organic solidarity is based on the differences among individuals, which make them interdependent. In modern society, individual's interests depend on each other so some interests for a group or a society become shared interests. This shared interests is an important component of social solidarity in modern society. Although Durkheim emphasizes mostly the conscience component of social solidarity, the shared interest component is important, and it perhaps is also a basis for the formation of the conscience component.

Considering both Durkheim's discussion on the collective conscience and division of labor, I argue that solidarity has both cultural and structural components. For example, when individuals live in a community for a long period, they not only develop their shared culture, the collective conscience, but also develop shared interests, because they invest their resource in the community. Social solidarity is the combination of the two components, which can only be analytically distinguished. No matter which component is dominant in a particular community, solidarity manifests itself as the commitment of society's members to the society and a sense of responsibility for the society.

Durkheim recognizes the abstractness of the concept and the difficulty in its measurement. He stated: "Social solidarity is a wholly moral phenomenon which by itself is not amenable to exact observation and especially not to comparison." (1984, p. 24) On measuring social solidarity, he states: "To arrive at this classification, as well as this comparison, we must therefore substitute for this internal datum, which escapes us, an external one which symbolizes it, and then study the former through the latter." "That visible symbol is the law. Indeed where social community solidarity exists, in spite of its non-material nature, it does not remain in a state of pure potentiality, but shows its presence through perceptible effects. Where it is strong it attracts men strongly to one another, ensures frequent contacts between them, and multiplies the opportunities available to them enter into mutual relationships". (1984, p. 24) "··· law, (also rules, norms) and morality represent the totality of bonds that bind us to one another and to society, which shape the mass of individuals into a cohesive aggregate" (1984, p. 331).

In sum, the concept solidarity is not clearly defined in Durkheim's illustration. I argue that solidarity has two components, the cultural and the structural components. Durkheim emphasizes the cultural, collective conscience component, but he also talks about the organic element of solidarity in modern society. I argue that the shared interest is also important.

## 2. Social Disorganization Theory

In criminology, theories and research have been concerned about the same variable that the Durkheimian theory emphasizes: solidarity. These include disorganization theory, social control theory, and the network approach.

I argue that to a large extent, the concept social organization and social solidarity overlap. Although the research in disorganization theory and Durkheimian functional traditions developed independently, we can recognize that among them there are some important commonalities. Both emphasize a particular state of community: social integration. For both, the notion of social integration occupies a central position of theoretical importance. Because of the abstractness of the concept, both are criticized for vagueness.

Social disorganization theory explains crime in terms of community characteristics: disorganization. In essence, the central notion of disorganization is a state of a community that is characterized by people's staying apart from each other, lack of common conscientious, lack of common commitment to the community, lack of shared values, norms, and lack of sense of responsibility. The overlap between the disorganization and social solidarity is recognizable. Disorganization is the destruction of social solidarity of a community.

Like Durkheim's concept of social solidarity, disorganization theory also has been criticized for vagueness (e. g. Kornhauser, 1978), and for problems in the operationalization of the concept. For example, it has been criticized for using the consequences of disorganization to operationalize the concept (Matza, 1969). Given the vagueness of the concept, difficulties in operationalization are inevitable.

Disorganization is closely related to many consequences of crime. Like many other sociologists from the Chicago school, Shaw and Mckay, who first proposed the theory, were concerned with growing social problems in large cities. Disorganization is thought as contributing to these consequences. This suggests that social solidarity is an important variable that affects social consequences.

## 3. Social Control Theory

Social control theory examines social bonding; it examines social solidarity at the individual level. Drawing from the Durkheimian theory of social integration, Hirschi(1969) develops his social control theory. He argues that social bonds bind individuals to the conventional institutions and control people from doing what they will otherwise naturally do: commit deviant behavior. Hirschi (1969) explicitly links his concept social bonding to Durkheim's concept of social solidarity. Hirschi argues that those individuals who are attached to people and institutions, and who accept goals and beliefs of conventional society, will conform to conventional norms. The major elements of social bonding, the commitment that people make, and the beliefs they share with their community, can be found in Durkheim's statement about social solidarity. To Hirschi, social solidarity bonds people together and constrain them from committing deviant behavior. This suggests social solidarity influences social behavior and social life.

## 4. Social Network Approach

The network analysis is a general approach in studying society and is an important area of sociology. One of its concepts, social constraints on individual's behavior, is relevant to the concept of social solidarity. Network analysis has been used to analyze community structure and social processes.

A social network is "a set of nodes linked by a set of social relationships" (Laumann et al. , 1987). A personal network is one that is centered on the individual and represents his or her links to other people ( Krohn, 1986 ). The critical concept of"link"in the network approach bears on the notion of social interaction. The structural characteristics of a social network such as"network multiplexity" , " network density " , " dispersion " , " range " , " reachability " describe properties of relationship among people. Multiplexity refers to the number of different role relations any two people have with one another, or the number of contexts or foci ( e. g. activities, exchanges ) in a relationship ( Fischer, et al. , 1977 ). Network density is the extent to which all actors in a social network are connected by direct relations( Bott,1957; Cravan and Wellman,1973 ).

Relationships among people are the results of social interaction. More importantly, they are the basis for further social interaction. Network properties reflect different aspects of relationships among people and the idea that people are combined together relates to the concept of social solidarity. In fact, network research suggests that the level of social solidarity can be determined by identifying the mean level of multiplexity in social networks within a given social unit: neighborhood, society, work group ( Boorman and White,1976; Laumann,1973; White et al. , 1976 ). In his theory of delinquent behavior, using the social network approach, Krohn( 1986 ) proposes that the greater network multiplexity and network density, the greater the constraint on individual's behavior within the purview of the social network, and therefore the less the delinquency. He suggests that high density networks constrain the behavior of community inhabitants, which is precisely a type of mechanical solidarity. The network approach expresses social solidarity in a different form and shows social solidarity can influence human behavior and social life.

# D. Summary

To summarize, Durkheim originated research on the functions of crime. To him, crime is normal, regular, and functional. He argued that the major function of crime is to increase social solidarity. Around this argument, past research centers on four closely related issues: social solidarity, repressive justice, boundary maintenance, and the stability of punishment. The studies are mostly observational and historical; and some are experimental and quantitative. The research generally supports Durkheim's hypothesis that crime is functional in increasing social solidarity despite some criticisms. This limited and narrowly defined research has not attracted much attention. It has traditionally developed isolated from mainstream criminological research; the connection between the function of crime research and other areas of criminology has never been made. This situation limits the development of the area of functions of crime. In fact, in criminology, theories and research have been concerned about the same variables that the Durkheimian thesis concerns, such as crime, solidarity, and consequences of crime. I think that at least two variables play important roles in affecting functions or consequences of crime: one is fear of crime, and the other is social solidarity.

Fear of crime has important consequences for modern society. Fear research extensively studies factors that contribute to fear. A few studies examine the individual reactions to crime. However, in fear research, fear is mainly examined as a dependent variable at the individual level, not at the society level; a few studies are at the macro level. We should move our focus to the aggregate level, to study reactions of society to fear rather than only to study individual reactions to crime, to consider fear as a mediating variable that cause many societal reactions, and to examine the social consequences caused by fear. We will then find that the link between fear research and functions or consequences of crime research is apparent. Research on functions of crime will be significantly expanded and developed. In recent year, fear research addressed the relationships between neighborhood conditions and fear. Research studies the causal relationship between fear and neighborhood cohesion. Research either argues that fear leads to the reduction of neighborhoods cohesion or argues that the lack of neighborhoods cohesion is a cause of fear; the causal direction between the two remain inconclusive.

139

Social solidarity is an important variable that affects many aspects of society. It is reasonable to assume that social solidarity influences the consequences of crime. The notion of solidarity has roots in many seemingly unrelated theories and research, and is an important concept in those theories and research. We review the concept in several areas of research, including Durkheim's discussion on solidarity, social disorganization theory, social control theory, and network approach. Social disorganization theory emphasizes the importance of social integration. Disorganization reflects the destruction of social solidarity. Social control theory examines social bonding; it examines social solidarity at the individual level. The network approach treats social solidarity from a new perspective. These areas of research help us understand the nature and effects of social solidarity and therefore shed light on the development of the functions of crime research.

# Chapter III. A Theoretical Model of Functions of Crime

## A. A General Theoretical Model

We have expanded the functions of crime from Durkheim's basic questions to a research agenda that asks three questions. The first two are theoretically important. One question asks what are the functions or consequences of crime; it requires us to examine systematically the functions or consequences of crime. That is, we should examine what social processes are caused, altered, or affected by crime.

The second question asks how crime plays its role in affecting the consequences and other variables. It requires us to study other variables and social processes and to answer questions about the causal relationships among these variables, that is, how crime and other variables affect the consequences, and how these variables affect each other.

In this chapter, I propose a general theoretical model that examines four consequences. They include the quality of life in an area, socioeconomic resources, the attitudes toward government, and community decline. The theoretical model argues that two variables are important in explaining the consequences of crime: fear and social solidarity. The model proposes a causal structure among crime, fear, social solidarity, and consequences. The model explains three theoretically important issues. One, the model explains the central question of the field: how crime, fear, and social solidarity affect consequences. Two, the model addresses a controversy between functions of crime research supporting the Durhkeimian thesis and fear research in examining how crime affects social solidarity. Three, the model addresses a controversy on the causal relationship between fear and solidarity. The model suggests a reciprocal relationship between fear and social solidarity ( Figure III. 1 ).

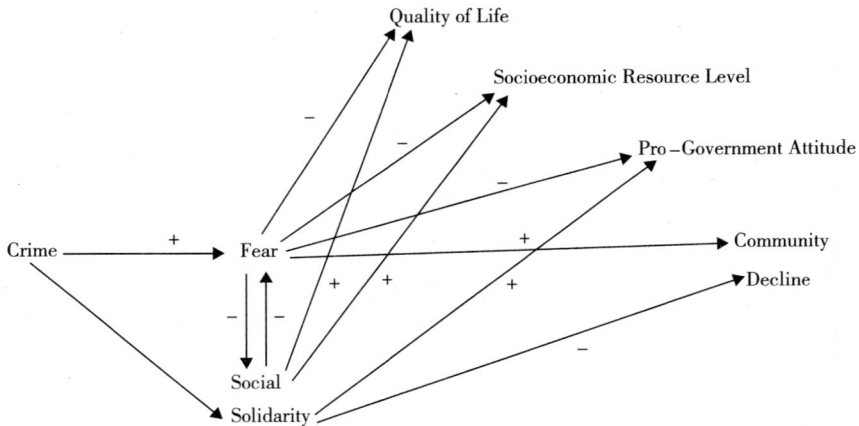

**Figure III. 1　General Theoretical Model**

In the following sections, I discuss each of the three theoretical issues explained by the general theoretical model. I explicitly state the theoretical hypotheses involved, and discuss the theoretical hypotheses. Section B addresses how crime, fear, and social solidarity influence consequences of crime. It includes four subsections; each discuss one consequence and states the hypotheses for the consequence. Section C addresses the Durkheimian thesis that crime increases social solidarity. Section D addresses the causal relationship between fear and social solidarity.

# B. Crime, Fear, and Solidarity Influencing Consequences

The first task is to systematically examinefunctions or consequences of crime. Crime can have many important social consequences for society. Fear research has extensively documented that crime cause fear. Fear can in turn influence many dimension of society. Fear has systematic consequences for people's quality of life, for social structure, for culture, for people's attitudes toward government, and for community decline. In this work, I examine the consequences for four dimensions of society. In the theoretical model, I suggest four consequences: the quality of life, social economic resources, attitudes toward government, and community decline.

The theoretical model( Figure III. 1 ) argues that two variables are important in explaining the consequences of crime: fear and social solidarity. The theoretical model suggests that fear and social solidarity directly affect social consequences; crime directly affects fear and social solidarity; and crime does not directly affect social consequences. Fear and solidarity mediate the effects of crime on social consequences. In the following sections, I examine each of these consequences. The hypothesized relationships of how crime, fear, and solidarity affect different consequences are the same, but the social process is not the same for different consequences. Crime, fear, and solidarity affect satisfaction in a different way than they affect socioeconomic resource level.

The fear literature mostly treats fear of crime as a dependent variable, and has consistently demonstrated that fear is the major reaction to crime. For each of the social consequences included in the theoretical model, I explain how and why fear and social solidarity affect these consequences.

## 1. The quality of Life

The quality of life consists of many aspects. The concern here is mainly on social and psychological aspects that are affected by crime and the way they are affected. Based on the general theoretical model ( Figure III. 1 ) , five hypotheses involve the quality of life are derived:

I. 1.  Crime reduces people's the quality of life.

I. 2.  Crime does not directly reduce the quality of life.

I. 3.  Fear directly reduces the quality of life.

I. 4.  Fear mediates the effect of crime on the quality of life.

I. 5.  Social solidarity increases the quality of life.

Although deterioration of the quality of life is often associated with crime, the hypotheses emphasize that fear mediates the effect of crime. Also, when the mediating effect presents, crime could meantime has direct effect on the quality of life, but the model hypothesizes that crime does not directly affect the quality of life. Fear and social solidarity directly affect the quality of life, and they have opposite effects on the quality of life. Fear reduces the quality of life, while social solidarity improves the quality of life.

Fear reduces the quality of life through several processes. Fear of crime threatens people. A feeling of danger considerably affects people's satisfaction with living and doing business in an area. Fear of crime adds psychological pressures on people; it can be a constant burden on living and working in the area. People not only worry about the safety of themselves, they also worry about the safety of their family members and friends. The victimization experience induces strain. Research suggests that crime causes anxiety about crime. One of the components of anxiety is concern of crime( Furstenberg, 1971; Lotz, Roy E. , 1979). Strain and anxiety can induce psychological problems and even physical problems. People feel powerless, impotent, and vulnerable in the face of crime. They are passive in response to events around them ( Skogan, 1986) and reduce the quality of life. For victims of crime, fear reduces the quality of life even worse. Researchers also speculate that other people may shun victims, sensing their " spoiled" identities and wishing to dis-associate themselves from suffering. Psychologists have uncovered a related phenomenon that they call " blaming the victim".

Fear constrains people's activity. Some research bears on this point. Fear research shows that a major reaction to violent crime is constrained daily activities ( Biderman et al. , 1967 ). Research by Kail and Kleinman suggests that fear, crime, and self-imposed restrictions on activities lower the quality of urban life ( Kail, Kleinman, 1985 ). People avoid going to perceived dangerous places and adjust activities to times and places perceived safe. People live in high crime rate neighborhoods frequently become prisoners in their own homes ( Balkin, 1979; Skogan and Maxfield, 1981; Garofalo, 1979; Clarke and Lewis, 1982; Yin, 1985; Liska, Sanchirico, and Reed, 1988 ). Rifai ( 1976 ) and Lawton et al. ( 1976 ) report that between 69% and 89% of those over 65 years of age say they never go out at night. Fear constrains people's activity, and reduces people's socializing with others. People can not freely go to friends' houses and go out for entertainment at night. Public facilities, such as parks, built for enhancing the quality of life, often become dangerous places in the night.

Fear reduces the quality of life also through reducing mutual trust among people. A certain level of mutual trust among people, especially neighbors, is important for maintaining the quality of social life. The mutual trust enables people to help each other. Mutual trust also builds a relaxed relationship among people, avoiding additional burdens of handling social life. Less mutual trust puts additional burdens on social relationships. Research suggests that there may be a tendency by victims to withdraw from public life and to become suspicious and distrustful of others as a result of their experiences ( LeJeune and Alex, 1973 ). People in high crime areas tend to withdraw psychologically, isolating themselves ( Kidd and Chayet, 1984 ). Fear as a dividing force hinders the interaction of people with each other and therefore reduces mutual understanding and trust.

I hypothesize that social solidarity improves the quality of life. Little research bears on this hypothesis; I suggest that social solidarity improves the quality of life because it promotes interaction among people, which is associated with socializing. In a high solidarity society, people visit their neighbors and friends often, they go out in the evening, and they enjoy social life. By same reason, social solidarity promotes mutual understanding and mutual trust, because it promotes social interaction. Through interaction, people understand each other better, and are more willing to help each other, therefore enhance quality of life. Social solidarity also reduces psychological strain. The common commitment to their community and shared culture provides social support to the members of society. In the face of crisis, people know that their neighbors and friend who are committed to the community would provide help and moral support that will reduces the difficulty and the psychological strain.

## 2. Socioeconomic Resource Level

Crime can cause changes in social structure. The socioeconomic level of communities in a society is an important aspect of a social structure. Based on the general theoretical model(Figure III. 1), five hypotheses involve socioeconomic resources:

II. 1. Crime reduces socioeconomic resources.

II. 2. Crime does not directly reduce socioeconomic resources in the area.

II. 3. Fear directly reduces socioeconomic resources in the area.

II. 4. Fear mediates the effect of crime on socioeconomic resources.

II. 5. Social solidarity increases socioeconomic resources.

The hypotheses emphasize that the fear mediates the effect of crime. Crime does not directly affect socioeconomic resources. Fear and social solidarity directly affect socioeconomic resources, and they have opposite effects on socioeconomic resources. Fear reduces socioeconomic resources, while social solidarity improves socioeconomic resources.

There are several ways in which fear reduces socioeconomic resources. First, fear pushes people with resources to migrate away from an area. This results in less business in the area, less job opportunities for people, and less tax revenue for the local government. Second, fear of violent crime also discourages outside potential investors and customers. Only those people with low social economic resources stay because of lack of resources to move, thus contributing to the concentration of the poor and problems in the adjoining communities.

There is supporting evidence that crime has the effect of driving people out of places(Smith, 1988; Kasl and Harburg, 1972; Droettboom et al. 1971). Sampson and Wooldredge (1986) test a hypothesis that high crime rates contribute to outmigration from central cities. They examined the population change in 55 large cities in the United States from 1970 – 1980 and net migration for 1975 – 1980. Their results show that crime rates have a relatively large impact on the decline of central city populations, both black and white after controls for the effects of northern location, tax rates, racial and age composition, employment, manufacturing base, and population density. Most researchers find that current residents of higher-risk city neighborhoods are more likely to express a strong desire to move somewhere else. Droettboom et al. (1971) found that respondents in a national survey who felt that crime and violence were significant problems in their communities were more dissatisfied with their neighborhood and were more likely to indicate that they wanted to move. Kasl and Harburg(1972) surveyed residents of high and low status neighborhoods in both black and white areas of Detroit. They found that residents of high crime areas were preoccupied with crime, thought their chances of being robbed were high, and desired to move out. Research also suggests that families and members of the middle class tend to leave first, often to be replaced by unattached and transient individuals(Stark, 1987; Frey, 1980; Duncan and Newman, 1976). Frey(1979) and Marshall(1979) in their analysis of 1965 – 1970 population shifts in large SMSAs, found that the impact of crime on the shift of households in the direction of the suburbs was substantial. Research by Price and Clay(1980) suggests that rapid immigration of urbanites may cause structural disturbances in rural communities.

a) There are also some studies reporting that the very few people move to suburbs only because of fear of crime in central city. LEAA's city victimization surveys asked members of households that reported moving within the past five years about why they left their old neighborhoods. In the eight cities surveyed in 1973, only 3 percent of these household informants cited crime as an important reason for moving. Therefore the evidence of pressure of crime is inconsistent.

b) However, we can reasonably assume that people with resources are not willing to move into neighborhoods where serious crime is believed to occur very often. There has been little investigation on this. People consider crime when they choose places to live and establish businesses. The reluctance to move into certain places because of fear of crime affects the formation and change of the socioeconomic resources. So we can still justify our hypothesis that fear of crime leads to the concentration of the poor. In sum, fear affects socioeconomic resources of communities.

I propose that social solidarity improves socioeconomic resources. Though there is no research bearing on this hypothesis, it seems reasonable. In a community with high social solidarity, people think of the community as their home, not just as a place to live. It is a place with which their life is associated and with which their social economic development is associated. With their commitment and the sense of responsibility for the community, people invest in the community, develop their business and property. Business and economy thus stabilize and develop. So social solidarity improves and stabilizes community's economic resources.

## 3. People's Pro-government Attitudes

I argue that crime affects people's political pro-government attitudes. Based on the general theoretical model( Figure III. 1 ), five hypotheses involve political pro-government attitudes:

III. 1.　Crime reduces people's pro-government attitudes.

III. 2.　crime does not directly reduce people's pro-government attitudes.

III. 3.　Fear directly reduces people's pro-government attitudes.

III. 4.　Fear mediates the effect of crime on pro-government attitudes.

III. 5.  Social solidarity increases people's pro-government attitudes.

The hypotheses emphasize that the fear mediates the effect of crime. Crime does not directly affect pro-government attitudes. Fear and social solidarity directly affect pro-government attitudes, and they have opposite effects on pro-government attitudes. Fear reduces pro-government attitudes, while social solidarity improves pro-government attitudes.

Fear of crime leads to negative attitudes toward government. This is because crime is supposed to be controlled by the government. The normal reaction of citizens to crime is to resort to the police. This is supposed to be the major way to get protection, to reduce fear, and to increase the sense of safety. Fear of crime makes people think that police are not capable of handling crime; this leads to citizens' loss of this fundamental way of fear reduction. We often notice that victims are not only angry with the offender, but also are angry with the police and government. People are disappointed with the police and government when they and their friends become victims of crime. A high fear level in a community not only provokes disappointment towards police and government, but also provokes the suspicion of the police and government's willingness to protect common people. These readily extend to criticism of the government on other issues, such as corruption, discrimination, and incompetence in general. This leads to general negative, even hostile, political attitudes.

Little research bears on this hypothesis. Stinchcombe et al. ( 1978 ) suggests a distinctive attribute of crime that causes fear is the feeling of our inability to do much about it. The feeling of an inability to do anything often follows the failure of the police to provide help. It is associated with negative attitudes towards the government and the police. Studies show that a high rate of victimization is experienced by the lower social economic status. Lower class people may perceive that the rich are protected better by government. Research documents the existence of hostile attitudes of lower class and minority ethnic groups towards police and government agency ( e. g. : Thornberry, 1979; Dannefer and Schutt, 1987 etc. ).

Through these linkages, fear affects the political attitudes.

Social solidarity improves government attitudes and attitudes toward the police. Social solidarity promotes the common anger against crime. It promotes collective cooperation with the police and the government. This interaction with government and the police facilitates mutual understanding between people and the government and the police. Research suggests that a high solidarity community develops more cooperative anticrime programs and they work better ( Skogan, 1990). Cohn et al. (1978) found that participants in organizations doing something concerning crime were more likely to believe that police can reduce crime. Through cooperation with the police and government, people may better understand the difficulties and problems of the police and the government. They may be better able to distinguish individual corruption from that of a government as a whole. This may reduce the negative attitude towards the government. To the contrary, the lower the social solidarity, the less mutual understanding between the community and the government, and the more likely a hostile attitude towards the government.

## 4. Community Decline

By community decline, I refer to the overall direction of change in the social economic conditions of a community. Toward which direction a community is changing reflects the future of a community. These changes are in many aspects of the community: social, economic, residential, demographic, appearances, and reputation.

Most communities are fairly stable although changes always happen. Business and residents move in and out, but a stable community reproduces itself. A declining community is the community that lost the capability to reproduce itself. In a declining community, the social and economic conditions deteriorate. Deterioration in residential housing is often most apparent; housing prices decrease; landlords and homeowners are not willing to repair and rehabilitate their buildings; mortgaging institutions refuse to make loans. Economically, business loses customers and profits. The deterioration of economic conditions of the community is an important part of the process, but is not the only aspect of it. Declining communities usually show more and more run down appearances and develop worsening reputation. Widespread "incivilities" or "disorders" (Hope, and Hough, 1988; Skogan, 1990) signify a community's decline. The ailment appearance include widespread junk and trash in vacant lots, decaying homes, abandoned buildings, the vandalism of public and private property, graffiti, bands of teenagers congregating on street corners, the presence of prostitutes etc. Based on the general theoretical model (Figure III. 1), five hypotheses involve community decline:

IV. 1. Crime increases community decline.

IV. 2. Crime does not directly increase community decline.

IV. 3. Fear directly increases community decline.

IV. 4. Fear mediates the effect of crime on community decline.

IV. 5. Social solidarity reduces community decline.

Although community decline is often associated with crime, the hypotheses emphasize that fear mediates the effect of crime. Crime does not directly affect community decline. Fear and social solidarity directly affect community decline, and they have opposite effects on community decline. Fear reduces community decline, while social solidarity improves community from decline.

Fear affects community decline. Fear of crime makes a community an undesirable place to live and to do business, thereby affecting the price of land and home. Fear also drives customers and potential customers out of the area, so businesses lose their profits. Fear discourages anticrime faith and activity. Outsider trouble makers are attracted in and crime-pro elements become concentrated because of the suitable atmosphere and opportunities for crime. Some studies suggest that fear and crime problems are divisive forces, destroying the capacity of communities to mount collective effort around almost any local problem (Lewis, 1979; Conklin, 1975). Disorder spreads; community declines.

I suggest that social solidarity reduces community decline. There is little research on this. People committed to the community will try to prevent the community from declining. Social solidarity combines individuals together to protest against unwanted changes in their community. People with commitment to their community tend to help each other, defend their home, and business. Social solidarity functions to maintain the social order. In a community with high social solidarity, people have a strong sense of responsibility for the community, and they organize themselves to watch for unwanted elements, to discourage unwanted elements, to take and keep control over what happens to the community, and to keep their community's social and economic condition from declining.

## 5. Summary

To address the basic questions from the research agenda, I propose a general theoretical model. The model suggests four consequences of crime (among possibly many others). Crime influences the quality of life, socioeconomic resources, government attitudes, and community decline. The theoretical model argues that two variables are important in explaining the consequences of crime: fear and social solidarity. The model proposes a causal structure among crime, fear, social solidarity, and consequences.

The model explains a central question of the field: how crime, fear, and social solidarity affect these consequences. The model suggests that fear and social solidarity directly affect social consequences; crime directly affects fear and social solidarity; crime does not directly affect social consequences; and fear and solidarity mediate the effects of crime on social consequences. Based on this theoretical model, I explicitly propose only five hypotheses for each consequence. The hypotheses address the theoretical questions that past research tested little or did not tested. The fear literature mostly treats fear of crime as a dependent variable, and has consistently demonstrated that fear is the major reaction to crime. So for each of the social consequences included in the theoretical model, I mainly use the existing literature to explain how and why fear and social solidarity affects these consequences.

In next section, I will address a controversy between the functions of crime literature, supporting Durkheim's thesis that crime increases solidarity, and the fear literature, reporting that fear decreases social solidarity.

## C. Crime and Social Solidarity

Durkheim argues that crime performs a positive function of increasing social solidarity. He explains that crime brings together upright consciences and concentrates them; this intensified social interaction thereby increases social solidarity. Erickson argues that the excitement generated by the crime, in other words, quickens the tempo of interaction in the group. In general, functionalists suggest that the outrage produced by crime draws people together, increases social interaction, and reminds them what they have in common, thereby increasing social solidarity. Within that tradition, most research supports the Durhkeim's argument that crime increases social solidarity. However while the research provides interpretative accounts of historical instances of the process, it provides few tests of the hypothesis. The hypothesis requires further rigorous testing.

In contrast, the literature on the fear of crime generally suggests that rather than drawing people together, crime causes fear, which in turn restricts people's daily behavior, drives people apart, reduces social interaction, and thereby decreases social solidarity ( Hartnagel, 1979; Goodstein and Shotland, 1980; Conklin, 1975 ). Studies on the fear of crime offer evidence that people limit the ir activities to safe areas during safe times because of their fear of crime, and that people unable to avoid living in unsafe neighborhoods often become prisoners in their own homes( Skogan and Maxfield, 1981; Garofalo, 1979; Clarke and Lewis, 1982; Yin, 1985; and Liska, Sanchirico, and Reed, 1988 ). Although most studies are at the individual rather than the societal level, their findings are clearly relevant

153

to this work. At the societal level, Liska and Warner's ( 1991 ) recent paper demonstrates that as robbery increases so does fear of crime which constrains social interaction, possibly undermining social solidarity. In general, the fear research literature suggests that crime, through fear, decreases social interaction, thereby decreasing social solidarity.

Clearly, the functionalist's hypothesis and the fear of crime research make very different predictions regarding the effects of crime on social solidarity. Durkheim suggests that crime increases social solidarity; in contrast, the fear research suggests that crime causes fear, and drives people apart, thereby decreasing social solidarity. While the fear of crime research generates consistent results, the functionalist hypothesis has not been directly tested by quantitative research.

However, the issue is theoretically important and therefore requires further consideration and rigorous testing. The major question is: Docesrimes really increase social solidarity? In real life, we do have situations where crime stimulates social solidarity. For example, a study by Hourihan( 1987 ) suggests that the effect of crime is complicated. Serious crime deters involvement in neighborhood watches, while victimization of some offenses results in a greater willingness to join neighborhood watches. A close look at the processes studied by Hourihan suggests they are not totally the same as the traditional functionalist account of the process which suggests that crime increases solidarity because of offending the collective conscience and draws people together. This suggests the original Durkheim's hypothesis should be elaborated to be able to apply to modern society and be tested using modern data.

I think that in modern society, social solidarity are organic as Durkheim suggested, and rational choice elements play more roles. In processes studied by Hourihan, decisions on participating in neighborhood watches are influenced by both the collective conscience and the assessment of the interests in avoiding victimization, which also are the shared interests of the community. When fear of crime overrides the collective conscience, people choose not to participate. When perceiving the shared interest is better realized by collective action, people participate.

I suggest that solidarity has two components, the cultural component, which is the collective conscience, and the structural component, which involves shared interests. Because of the organic element of modern solidarity, tests that based on the modern data require elaboration of the Durkheim's thesis: the social solidarity includes, probably dominated by the structural element of common interests.

In modern society, the process by which crime probably increases solidarity is mostly by reminding individuals to protect their shared interest. Crime may mostly increase organic solidarity. The process by which crime drives people apart through fear and the process by which crime stimulate people to organize together has one thing in common; both involving personal interests consideration. When the crime is violent and serious, people do not believe the collective action can do much, they are driven apart as the fear literature reports. When crime is nonserious, people are not too fearful, their collective conscience become dominant and they dare to protect their collective interests; so crime can stimulate solidarity.

I suggest that past research treats crime homogeneously. It ignores the important distinction between violent and nonviolent crime. It alsotreats the traditional concept of solidarity, which predominantly mechanic, the same as modern social solidarity, which are perhaps predominantly, of organic nature: mostly shared interests. I suggest that in modern society, violent crime and nonviolent crime have different effects. Violent crime causes fear, which drives people apart and constrains people's interaction/activities, thereby reducing social solidarity, while non-violent crime plays a function of stimulating social interaction, thereby increasing social solidarity. Based on my elaboration, Reformulating Durkheim's theoretical hypothesis for nonviolent crime, I distinguish between violent and nonviolent crime in their effects on social solidarity. I emphasize organic solidarity in modern society, and directly test hypothesis on the functionality of crime for increasing social solidarity in modern society. My explanation consists of following hypotheses:

V. 1. Violent crime produces fear.

V. 2. Nonviolent crime does not directly produce fear.

V. 3. Violent crime reduces social solidarity.

V. 4. Nonviolent crime increases social solidarity.

There are a few studies bearing on these hypotheses. Stinchcombe et al. ( 1978 ) suggest the distinctive attributes of crime that provoke fear: its concentration in space, its association with signs of danger, and our inability to do much about it. Wolfgang found that physical injury and the use of a weapon by far overshadow virtually all levels of financial loss when people evaluate the seriousness of crime ( Wolfgang, 1978 ). These studies suggest that it is reasonable to hypothesize that violent crimes are different from nonviolent crimes in causing fear.

In sum, Durkheim argues that crime performs a positive function of increasing social solidarity. Function of crime research suggests that the outrage produced by crime draws people together, increases social interaction, and reminds them what they have in common, thereby increasing social solidarity. In contrast, the literature on fear of crime generally suggests that rather than drawing people together, crime causes fear, which in turn restricts people's daily behavior, drives people apart, reduces social interaction, and thereby decreases social solidarity. I suggest that social solidarity includes cultural element and structural element. In modern society, the structural element becomes dominant and violent crime and nonviolent crime has different effects. Violent crime causes fear, which drives people apart and constrains people's interaction/activities, thereby reducing social solidarity, while non-violent crime plays a function of stimulating social interaction, thereby increasing social solidarity.

# D. Relationship between Fear and Solidarity

In recent years, fear research has developed a focus on conditions and characteristics of neighborhoods, particularly the causal relation between fear and neighborhood cohesion. Some research reports that fear reduces neighborhood cohesion; others report that neighborhood cohesion reduces fear.

On one hand, research reports that fear reduces neighborhood cohesion. For example, Conklin (1975) reports that a predominate individual reaction to fear is reducing contact with other people, especially strangers. This suggests a reduction of social solidarity. Some research argues that fear constrains people's behavior (e. g. Liska and Warner, 1991); therefore it reduces social interaction, thus reducing social solidarity.

On the other hand, research reports that social solidarity reduces fear. Research suggests that neighborhood disorganization and lack of social cohesion are the conditions that lead to a high level of fear of crime (Skogan and Maxfield, 1981; Hunter and Baumer, 1982; Skogan, 1990). Lack of cohesion increases fear (Fowler and Mangione, 1982). People expect that social support may relieve people from anxiety and fear. People also expect that individuals more committed to their neighborhood may interpret and react to the same situation more positively than those with less commitment.

Although both sides report a negative relationship between fear and solidarity, there is considerable disagreement about which is the cause. Some argue that a lack of social cohesion is the consequence of fear (Conklin, 1975; Yin, 1980). Fear of violent crime constrains people's daily behavior, drives people apart, and reduces social interaction (Hartnagel, 1979; Gookstein and Shotland, 1980; Conklin, 1975). Others argue that neighborhood disorganization and the lack of social cohesion lead to high levels of fear of crime (Skogan and Maxfield, 1981; Hunter and Baumer, 1982; Skogan, 1990). Some research proposes that fear is part of a psychological syndrome of anxiety, worry, and nervousness, termed "urban unease", associated with social disorganization and the physical and social disabilities of contemporary urban life. Cohn et al. (1978), for example, found that people who were involved in community organizations felt more control over crime and reported less fear of crime than did nonparticipants. They also discovered that women who took a self defense training course gained a greater sense of control over events and reported less fear of crime as a result. Therefore, increasing social solidarity reduces fear.

Based on this idea, many fear reduction public programs are developed. These programs design ways to increase interactions among individuals and to increase individuals' commitment to their neighborhood in the hopes for reducing crime and fear.

I think that the controversy suggests that there can be a possible reciprocal relation between fear and solidarity. While fear affects solidarity, solidarity also affects fear. That is, for the relationship between fear and solidarity, I hypothesize that:

VI. 1.　Fear reduces social solidarity.

VI. 2.　social solidarity reduces fear.

To solve the controversy, we should estimate a nonrecursive model in which fear affects solidarity and the solidarity affects fear.

In sum, research suggests and tests either the effect of fear on solidarity or the effect of solidarity on fear. Most suggest a negative unidirectional relation between fear and social solidarity, but disagree on which is the cause. I propose that a reciprocal relationship exists between fear and solidarity.

# E. Summary

In this chapter, I propose a general theoretical model to answer the basic questions from the research agenda. The model suggests four consequences of crime

( among possible many more others ). Crime influences the quality of life, socioeconomic resources, the government attitudes, and community decline. The theoretical model argues that two variables are important in explaining the consequences of crime: fear and social solidarity. The model proposes a causal structure among crime, fear, social solidarity, and consequences. The model explains three theoretically important issues. One, the model explains a central question of the field: how crime, fear, and social solidarity affect concequences. Two, the model addresses a controversy between the findings of the functions of crime research supporting Durhkeimian thesis and the findings of fear research in examining how crime affects social solidarity by elaborating the Durhkeimian idea and the concept of solidarity. Three, the model addresses a controversy on the causal relationship between fear and solidarity. The model suggests a reciprocal relationship between fear and social solidarity ( Figure III. 1 ).

In explaining the first issue, how crime, fear, and social solidarity affect consequences, the theoretical model argues that two variables are important in explaining the consequences of crime: fear and solidarity. The theoretical model suggests that fear and social solidarity directly affect social consequences; crime directly affects fear and social solidarity; and crime does not directly affect social consequences. Fear and solidarity mediate the effects of crime on social consequences.

The fear literature mostly treats fear of crime as a dependent variable, and has consistently demonstrated that fear is the major reaction to crime. For each of the social consequences included in the theoretical model, I explain how and why fear and social solidarity affect these consequences.

The second issue is a controversy between the functions of crime research supporting the Durhkeimian thesis and the fear research. Durkheim argues that crime performs a positive function of increasing social solidarity. Functions of crime research suggests that the outrage produced by crime draws people together, increases social interaction, and reminds them what they have in common, thereby increasing social solidarity. In contrast, the literature on fear of crime generally suggests that rather than drawing people together, crime causes fear, which in turn restricts people's daily behavior, drives people apart, reduces social interaction, and thereby decreases social solidarity. I suggest that social solidarity has cultural and structural elements. In modern society, violent crime and nonviolent crime have different effects. Violent crime causes fear, which drives people apart and constrains people's interaction/activities, thereby reducing social solidarity, while non-violent crime plays a function of stimulating social interaction, thereby increasing social solidarity.

Third, the model addresses a controversy on the causal relationship between fear and solidarity. Research suggests and tests either the effect of fear in reducing solidarity or the effect of solidarity in reducing fear. Most studies suggest a negative unidirectional relation between fear and social solidarity, but disagree on which is the cause. I propose that a reciprocal relationship exists between fear and solidarity. While fear affects solidarity, solidarity also affects fear.

The following chapters discuss and report the tests of the general theoretical model. I discuss methodological issues, perform univariate and bivariate analyses, build and test measurement models. I test hypotheses how crime, fear, and solidarity influencing social consequences, test hypotheses that address the controversy between Durkheim's thesis that crime increases social solidarity and the fear research, which reports that crime decreases social solidarity. I test a nonrecursive model to address the controversy on causal relationship between fear and solidarity. The last chapter summarizes the conclusions from the model testing and discusses these conclusions and relevant issues.

# Chapter IV. Methodology

## A. Data

The data were collected in Minneapolis and St. Paul by Marlys McPherson, Glenn Silloway, and David Frey in July, 1983 for their project titled "Crime, Fear, and Control in Neighborhood Commercial Center" ( ICPSR 8167 ). The data were collected in two stages. During the first stage, a survey of 93 commercial centers in Minneapolis and St. Paul was conducted. Each center contained an average of about 20 stores depending on the size of the area and was surrounded by the residential neighborhood within a radius of approximately 3 mile. The data includes crime data obtained from the Minneapolis and St. Paul police department, and demographic data obtained from the Minneapolis and St. Paul city assessors' offices, R. L. Polk and Company, and U. S. census reports. In the second stage of the study, 24 commercial centers were selected from the original sample. A telephone survey of 870 residents and in-person interviews of 213 business persons for each commercial center were conducted for the 24 selected areas.

Measures for present research are taken from the two files: the resident survey, and the business survey. The individual responses are aggregated for the 24 neighborhoods ( commercial centers ). For each question in the resident and business survey, the mean values of the answers from all the respondents from the same area are calculated and used as the values of that question for the area. Then, the two aggregated files are converged into a single file for the analysis. So the sample size for present research is 24 cases. Although these data were not collected for the present purpose, most information necessary for this research is available.

# B. Analysis

The choice of the analytical methods and procedures is determined by the particular theoretical issues and difficulties related to the research topic. Two issues are particularly important for this research. One is the measurement of theoretical concepts, and the other is the small sample. In attempting to propose a theoretical model and to test it, present research faces difficulties measuring the major theoretical concepts, such as solidarity and fear. Historically, solidarity has been recognized as a ambiguous concept and criticized for being difficult to measure. Durkheim himself realized this. Reliability and validity problems are raised. Also, fear as an emotional state obviously faces the same measurement problem. It can be easily demonstrated mathematically that in regression analysis, when an explanatory variable is measured with error, the OLS estimator will yield a biased and inconsistent estimate ( Hanushek and Jackson, 1977 ). Traditional approaches to these issues can not solve these problems satisfactorily.

Structural equation modeling methods have particular strengths in solving these problems; they can be used to estimate models where important conceptual variables are difficult to define and are inaccurately measured; thus they are used as primary methods for present research. The structural equation modeling methods use latent variables to represent theoretical concepts, and use multiple indicators to measure abstract theoretical concepts. This measurement approach has the advantage of allowing us to model structural relationships without assuming that measures of the concepts are perfect, which most of time is untenable.

Typical structural equation models include two parts: the measurement models and the structural models. The measurement models include theoretical concepts and their indicators. Each theoretical concept is measured by several indicators. The measurement errors of each indicator are explicitly modeled. Also, the errors do not have to be randomly distributed. The results, so called factor loadings, that we obtain from these analyses reflect the net part of the theoretical concept which each indicator measures. Thus constructed factors or latent variables are used to estimate the structural relationships between theoretical concepts. This process explicitly models the measurement error and thus can give us confidence that the structural parameters are not distorted by the measurement errors.

The most commonly used estimation technique in structural equation modeling is the Maximum likelihood ( ML ) estimation ( Bollen, 1989 ) , which is the default estimates in the two most popular computer programs for structure equation modeling, EQS and LISREL. The essence of the method is to choose the underlying parameters of a distribution maximizing the likelihood of yielding the observed sample. Under broad conditions, the maximum likelihood method estimators are consistent, asymptotically unbiased, and asymptotically efficient ( Bentler, 1989; Bollen, 1989 ). In a small sample situation, we may accept an estimator that may be biased in small samples, rather than to use one that is an inconsistent estimator, that is, one that does not converge on the population parameter even when the sample size is arbitrarily large( Bollen, 1989 ). Empirical research also suggests that ML estimates are robust, that is, they tend to hold up well as the model and data deviate from the underlying assumptions( Bollen, 1989 ). In the following analyses, the maximum likelihood estimation is used to estimate the structural coefficients.

The asymmetrical properties of the maximum likelihood estimator require that sample size is large relative to the number of free parameters to be estimated. Regarding what is considered a large sample, Bentler proposes a guideline: the ratio of sample size to number of free parameters to be estimated can go as low as 5 :1 ( Bentler 1989 ). For smaller samples, the properties of ML are not well known.

That is, while asymptotically unbiased, the properties of small sample estimates are not well known. So we are less confident of the estimates when small samples are used.

To address the small sample issue, the analytical procedure is divided into two stages to reduce the size of the model for estimations. I first estimate the measurement model, and then estimate the structural model. In the first step, I build measurement models for each of the theoretical concepts, select from all variables the potentially plausible measures for each theoretical concept, and conduct all possible confirmatory factor analyses to locate the measurement models that are theoretically meaningful and empirically well fitting. Then I use the measurement coefficients to construct the composite indexes for each of the theoretical concepts. The composite indexes are calculated by summing all the measures, using factor loadings as weights for each measure. That is: the composite index for a concept = $b_1 X_1 + b_2 X V_2 + b_3 X_3 + \cdots$, where b's are factor loadings.

In the second step, the testing of the structural model, the hypotheses and their tests are divided into three groups. Each group mainly addresses one of the three theoretical issue discussed in last chapter. The three issues are: crime, fear, and solidarity influencing consequences; crime influencing solidarity; and the relationship between fear and solidarity. I first test a recursive model ( Figure IV. 1 ), which is mainly relevant to the first issue involving hypotheses of crime, fear, and solidarity influencing consequences. Later, I test a nonrecursive model, which resolves the issue of the causal relationship between fear and solidarity and which confirms the results for the hypotheses of crime, fear, and solidarity influencing consequences.

In the test of recursive model, I decompose the general model into four submodels, each having only one consequence ( see Figures IV. 1. 1, IV. 1. 2, IV. 1. 3, and IV. 1. 4 ). There are four structural models in total, each model for one social consequence of crime. I test only these submodels to estimate a few parameters at a time, to avoid estimating too many parameters at the same time, and

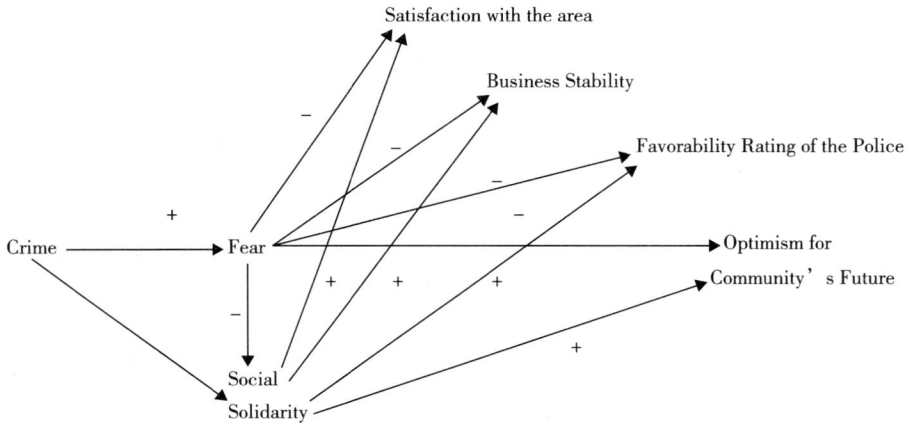

**Figure IV. 1    General Recursive Model**

to keep the number of estimated parameters at a minimum. I also reestimate the models with different measures of crime and social solidarity to check and confirm the stability of the models, as if doing replicated research.

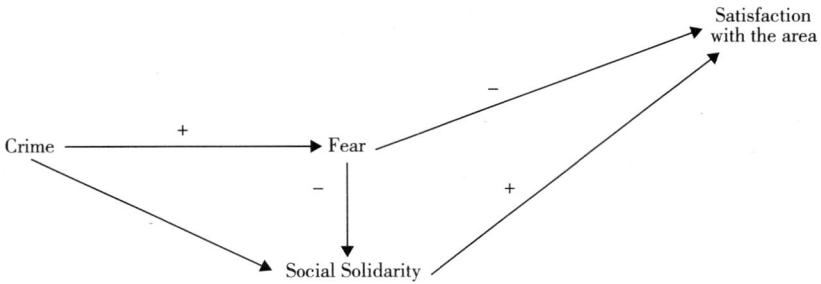

**Figure IV. 1. 1    Satisfaction Model**

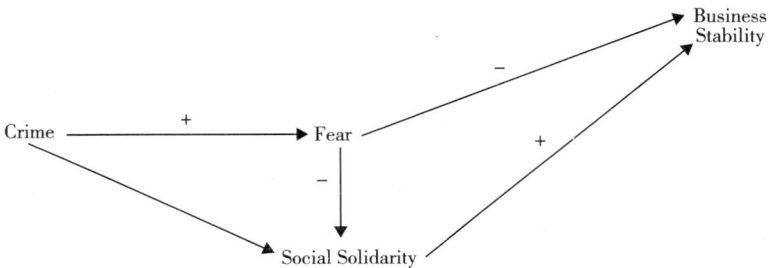

**Figure IV. 1. 2    Business Stability Model**

165

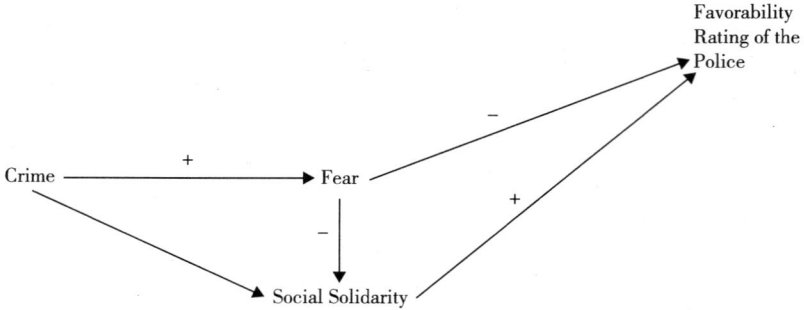

**Figure IV. 1. 3　Favorability Rating of Police Model**

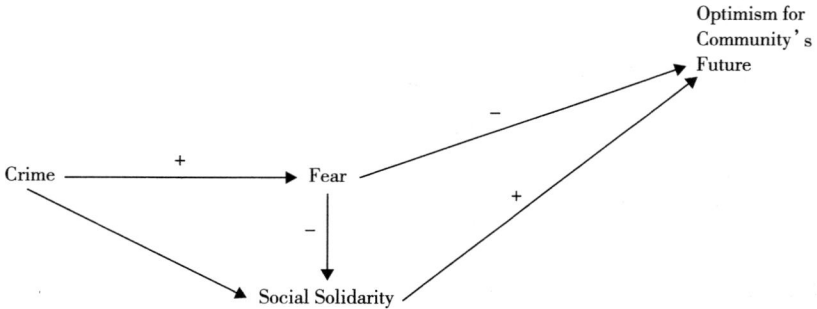

**Figure IV. 1. 4　Optimism for Community's Future Model**

# C. Operationalization and hypotheses

The theoretical concepts included in the theoretical model are: the quality of life, socioeconomic resources, government attitudes, community decline, fear, social solidarity, violent crime, nonviolent crime. When a concept is operationalized in term of a composite measure of several items, the construction process and the details of the items are reported in the chapter VI on measurement models.

*The quality of life* is opperationalized in terms of a composite measure of satisfaction with living and doing business in an area. It includes three items.

*Socioeconomic Resource Level* is opperationalized in terms of a composite measure of business stability with living and doing business in an area. It includes three items.

*Pro-government and the Police Attitudes* is opperationalized in terms of a composite measure of favorability rating of the police. It includes four items.

*Community Decline* is measured by a composite measure of optimism of a community's future. It includes three items. The composite measure uses items that ask people to assess whether their community's social and economic condition is getting better off or is declining. Notice that the measure is constructed so that the lower the value, the more decline.

*Fear of Crime* is operationalized in terms of a composite measure of fear. It includes five items.

*Social Solidarity* is operationalized in terms of three composite measures for three different dimensions of social solidarity. As discussed before, solidarity includes both a cultural component and a structural component. That is, it includes both collective conscience and shared interests. The first composite measure (SOL1) reflects residents' commitment to their neighborhood; it includes three items. The second(SOL2) measures residents' sense of responsibility for their neighborhood; it includes six items. The third(SOL3) measures business people's sense of responsibility for the shopping centers in the area; it includes three items. The third (SOL3) more reflects the perceived shared interests among business people.

*Violent personal crime* is measured by a question asking residents: About how often are people in your neighborhood threatened, beaten up, or anything of that sort? Would you say: almost never $\cdots 0$; once in a while $\cdots 1$; often $\cdots 2$; very often $\cdots 3$.

*Nonviolent crime* is measured by a question on shoplifting. The question asks business people: Since August, 1981, has anyone been observed shoplifting from your business? Yes $\cdots 1$; no $\cdots 0$; after aggregating to the neighborhood level, the measure becomes a continuous variable.

The operationalized general model is presented in Figure IV. 2; it consists of a series of hypotheses. In addressing the questions about how crime, fear, and social solidarity affect the social consequences, the model examines the four social consequences of crime: satisfaction with living and doing business in a area, business stability, favorability ratings of the police, and optimism of a community's future(see the operationalized general model Figure IV. 2).

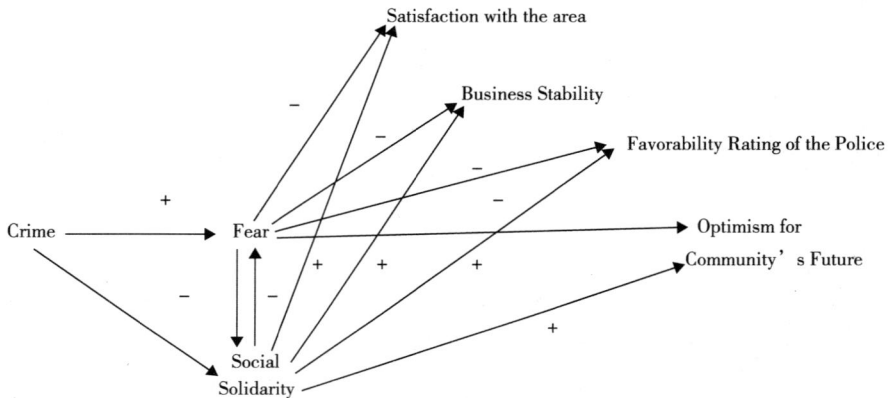

**Figure IV. 2　Operationalized General Model**

Relevant hypotheses are grouped around the different consequences. For satisfaction, the hypotheses are:

I. 1.　Crime reduces people's satisfaction with life and doing business in the area.

I. 2.　Crime does not directly reduce satisfaction.

I. 3.　Fear directly reduces satisfaction.

I. 4.　Fear mediates the effect of crime on satisfaction.

I. 5.　Social solidarity increases satisfaction with life and doing business in the area.

For business stability, the hypotheses are:

II. 1.　Crime reduces business stability in the area.

II. 2.　Crime does not directly reduce business stability in the area.

II. 3 .　Fear directly reduces business stability in the area.

II. 4.　Fear mediates the effect of crime on business stability.

II. 5.  Social business solidarity increases stability.

For people's favorability rating of the police, hypotheses are:

III. 1.  Crime reduces people's favorability rating of the police.

III. 2.  Crime does not directly reduce people's favorability rating of the police.

III. 3.  Fear directly reduces people's favorability rating of the police.

III. 4.  Fear mediates the effect of crime on favorability rating of the police.

III. 5.  Social solidarity increases people's favorability rating of the police.

For people's optimism of the community's future, the hypotheses are:

IV. 1.  Crime reduces people's optimism of the community's future.

IV. 2.  Crime does not directly reduce people's optimism of the community's future.

IV. 3.  Fear directly reduces people's optimism of the community's future.

IV. 4.  Fear mediates the effect of crime on optimism of the community's future.

IV. 5.  Social solidarity increases optimism of the community's future.

In addressing the issue of how crimes influence social solidarity, I elaborate the relevant part of the model, and examine the direct effects of different crimes. I suggest:

V. 1.  Violent crime produces fear.

V. 2.  Nonviolent crime does not directly affect fear.

V. 3.  Violent crime reduces social solidarity.

V. 4.  Nonviolent crime increases social solidarity.

In addressing the issue of the causal relationship between fear and solidarity, the hypotheses are:

VI. 1.  Fear reduces social solidarity.

VI. 2.  Social solidarity reduces fear.

# Chapter V. Univariate and Bivariate Analyses

The data analyses precede in three steps. The first step is the univariate and bivariate analyses; the second is the confirmatory factor analyses for building the measurement models; and the third estimates the structural parameters of the general models and tests the theoretical hypotheses.

Theoretically, ML estimates require a multinormal variable distribution, though the estimates usually checking are robust when the distribution is skewed. The multinormality of variables is a complex task, and still has not been fully resolved, but checking the univariate distributions of the variables can help find violations of the multinormal distribution assumptions. This is one of the major purpose of the univariate analysis.

I listed all the values for all variables for all 24 areas, and checked the frequencies for all the variables. The variable BEATVIC ( get beat ) was the only variable found to have excessive skewness ( Coefficient of skewness = 2. 1 ) in the survey data. The original question for BEATVIC is: please think back over the last year, say between August 1981 and now. Have you been held up on the street, threatened, beat up, or anything of that sort ( yes = 1; no = 0 )? The metric is arbitrary, so I took the square root of this variable to transform it, and the new variable, SBEATIC = Square root of BEATVIC, has only a skewness of 0. 2.

The other task in univariate ·analysis is to identify outliers. Combining information from the listing of the values of all the variables, the frequencies, the stem-leaf and box plots; I identified one area (number 830) as an outlier. It has extreme values on many variables. I went back to the original files of the resident survey and the business survey at the individual level, listed and checked all the cases on crime, fear, social solidarity, and some of the consequence variables. No errors were found. In general, this area has the highest value on almost all the crime variables; it has the highest values on almost all the fear measures; and it also has the lowest values on most of the social solidarity variables. The pattern is reasonable. In the factor analyses, I have conducted the analyses with this area in and with this area out. In general, no substantial differences in coefficients were found, but the fit of the models to the data was generally better when the area 830 was taken out.

In bivariate analysis, I mainly check two things. One, I compared the correlations between the major variables with past research. Two, I checked the plausibility of my hypothesized measurement model for each theoretical latent variable.

As discussed in the literature review earlier, there is little quantitative research examining the relationships among the major theoretical concepts in my theoretical models. A major relevant work is Liska and Warner's (1991) on the functions of crime. This work involves the relationship between crime, fear, and constrained social interaction, which my work also considers. Their sample is composed of the 26 cities of the National crime Survey (NCS), conducted by the National Institute of Justice and the Bureau of the Census. The NCS sampled about 10, 000 households and interviewed about 20,000 respondents ages 12 or older from each of 26 cities during 1973 and 1974. This research reports that the correlation between robbery (violent personal crime) and the index of fear is. 60; my data show that the correlation between the violent personal crime measure and measures of fear ranges from. 418 to. 847. The direction is the same; the size is comparable. Liska and Warner's (1991) research also reports the correlation between the two latent variables, fear during the day and fear during the night, and the constrained social interaction measured by self-reports of social interaction during the evening and self-reports of changed or limited social interaction because of crime, is. 88. In my data, there are no measures of social interaction or constrained social interaction, but there are items that can be used as measures of social solidarity. The index of fear constructed from five measures of fear correlates − . 384, −. 456, −. 206, with three indexes of solidarity respectively. The direction of the correlation between fear and solidarity is the same as that reported in Liska and Warner's research because using constrained social interaction as a measure of social solidarity, the sign of the correlation will be opposite. The difference in the size of the correlation is due to the difference in the contents of the measure.

Second, I checked whether the correlations between the indicators of the same theoretical concept can reasonably be considered measures of same latent variables. Indicators which are very weakly correlated to each other can not be indicators of a same latent variable empirically.

Thus, the bivariate analysis helps to classify and group variables, select variables for factors, and identify possible theoretical factors. The measures that constitute the composite measures for different theoretical variables are finally selected from the analyses for measurement models, which are reported in next section. It turns out that the correlations among measures of the same theoretical concept are all moderately strong or strong. For example, the correlations between the measures of fear range from. 419 to. 847.

# Chapter VI. Measurement models

The purpose of these analyses is to build measurement models which are theoretically meaningful and empirically well fitting, so they measure the theoretical concepts by fully utilizing all the information in the data. Building good measurement models for each theoretical concept is a crucial step for a solid test of the structural model. Estimating measurement models which explicitly model measurement error, the effects of measurement error for the tests of structural coefficients are taken care of, and thus the structural coefficients will better reflect the true population parameters.

First, I use theoretical and empirical criteria to select and classify all the variables that can be potentially used as measures of the theoretical concepts. The theoretical criterion is that the candidate measures must have face validity for the theoretical concepts. The empirical criterion is that the candidate measures for the same theoretical concept must be at least moderately correlated. A total of 87 variables are selected as potential candidates from the aggregated data file to form measurement models for each theoretical concept. The distributional statistics of the selected variables are reported in Table VI. 1.

### Table VI. 1　Frequency Distributions of variables

| | Mean | Std dev | Kurtosis | Skewess | Maximum | Minimum |
|---|---|---|---|---|---|---|
| PEOPBEAT | .455 | .219 | .668 | .826 | 1.000 | .118 |
| CRIMEAMT | 1.036 | .417 | .246 | 1.008 | 1.917 | .500 |
| SHOPLIFT | .318 | .221 | .171 | .444 | .857 | .000 |
| ARBSBROK | .886 | .341 | .388 | -.527 | 1.556 | .125 |
| BUSBROK | 1.160 | .416 | 3.622 | 1.602 | 2.500 | .625 |
| YOURBSBU | .245 | .141 | -.296 | .578 | .556 | .000 |
| FEAR31 | 1.660 | .327 | .192 | .275 | 2.432 | 1.057 |
| FEAR32 | 1.173 | .352 | .813 | 1.317 | 2.053 | .800 |
| POSSBEAT | 1.196 | .158 | 2.060 | 1.344 | 1.605 | .970 |
| SPOSBEAT | .977 | .156 | .335 | .830 | 1.342 | .706 |
| FEAR4 | 1.402 | .650 | .881 | .835 | 3.143 | .429 |
| RESYEAR | 13.420 | 3.575 | 1.928 | -1.163 | 18.588 | 3.471 |
| OPINEIBO | 1.777 | .103 | .015 | -.746 | 1.914 | 1.541 |
| COMNEIBO | 2.467 | .166 | .302 | .304 | 2.853 | 2.153 |
| LOTTOSAY | 3.277 | .305 | 5.527 | -1.966 | 3.686 | 2.216 |
| FEELRESP | 3.272 | .321 | 3.568 | -1.570 | 3.714 | 2.270 |
| TELLSTRG | 3.581 | .219 | -.091 | -.923 | 3.829 | 3.054 |
| BLOTOSAY | 2.085 | .195 | 1.878 | -1.238 | 2.412 | 1.528 |
| BFELRESP | 2.237 | .223 | .845 | -1.005 | 2.600 | 1.649 |
| BTELSTRG | 2.932 | .314 | -.198 | -.726 | 3.314 | 2.194 |
| BLOTOSA2 | 2.774 | .363 | -1.080 | .213 | 3.375 | 2.250 |
| BFELRES2 | 2.795 | .383 | .165 | -.353 | 3.667 | 2.000 |
| BTELSTR2 | 3.211 | .383 | .474 | -.353 | 4.000 | 2.333 |
| RATELIVE | 3.264 | .327 | 1.370 | -1.276 | 3.800 | 2.432 |
| AREARATE | 2.715 | .447 | -.314 | .009 | 3.714 | 2.000 |
| INVEHOME | .831 | .186 | 1.318 | -1.309 | 1.000 | .333 |
| ECOSTABL | 3.336 | .475 | -.561 | -.613 | 4.000 | 2.286 |
| OUTPLAN | .094 | .132 | .954 | 1.295 | .444 | .000 |
| LIKEMOVE2 | .699 | 2.540 | -.376 | -.662 | 3.000 | 2.125 |
| POLIWALK | .311 | .357 | 2.423 | 1.690 | 1.286 | .000 |
| POLICHAT | .350 | .377 | 1.866 | 1.526 | 1.400 | .000 |
| RATEPOLI | 2.623 | .433 | .608 | .774 | 3.714 | 1.889 |
| POLITRET | 2.457 | .433 | .608 | .774 | 3.714 | 1.889 |

continued

|  | Mean | Std dev | Kurtosis | Skewess | Maximum | Minimum |
|---|---|---|---|---|---|---|
| ECOTREND | 2. 058 | . 212 | 1. 979 | 1. 439 | 2. 618 | 1. 793 |
| ECOFUTUR | 2. 204 | . 415 | . 680 | −. 489 | 2. 889 | 1. 143 |
| ECOTRED2 | 2. 093 | . 360 | −. 788 | −. 068 | 2. 667 | 1. 429 |

For these selected variables, I performed a series of confirmatory factor analyses for each concept. I choose to use confirmatory factor analysis rather than exploratory factor analysis for selecting variables for two reasons. One, exploratory factor analysis has its limitations in accommodating our theoretical and substantive knowledge. It makes decisions purely based on arbitrary statistical criteria. Two, exploratory factor analysis does not allow correlated errors of measurement. It assumes the errors are purely random, which in our case is a hypothesis to be tested rather than an assumption. Confirmatory factor analysis overcomes these shortcomings. It allows us to specify models based on our substantive knowledge, and it does not make unrealistic assumptions about measurement errors.

To draw out all the strengths of the data, I exhaust all the possible alternative combinations of the 87 measures to locate the best factor models which are theoretically meaningful and statistically well fitting. In the factor analyses, items with much lower measurement coefficients in comparison with the others can not belong to a same latent variable. They are dropped, and the models are reestimated.

The analyses of the measurement model also test the hypothesis that measurement errors are purely random. This was done through two steps. First, I estimate the models restricting all measurement errors of the indicators to be uncorrelated to each other. Then, I estimate the models allowing some of the measurement errors to be correlated to improve the fit of the model to the data. By comparing the estimates with and without measurement errors correlated and examining the improvement of the model fit to the data, I can accept or reject the hypothesis. In the cases when allowing some the measurement errors to correlate significantly improves the estimates and the model fit, the hypothesis that measurement errors are purely random is rejected.

For each theoretical concept a one factor model is estimated. The estimates of the factor loadings(standardized ML estimates)are reported in Table VI. 2. Each column reports the factor loadings of one theoretical concept. Commercial burglary is denoted as COM, solidarity is denoted SOL, etc. (see note at the bottom of the table). X1, to X6 denotes different indicators for each of the factors; the specification of the indicator varies for different factors. For example, fear has six indicators; commercial burglary( COM ) has three indicators; and so on so forth. Results show that some of the measurement models have low loadings; the measurement model is thus not ideal. For example, for model for SOL2, all the loadings are around. 2. This indicates the measures used reflect only a small part of the variance of the theoretical concept SOL2. However, measurement model enables us to use this small part to reflect the theoretical concept and overcome the distortion of the structural coefficient which could have happened without using measurement model.

**Table VI. 2　Measurement Models**

( Standardized ML Estimates )

|  | FEAR | COM | SOL1 | SOL2 | SOL3 | SAT | BST | POL | OPT |
|---|---|---|---|---|---|---|---|---|---|
| X1 | . 856 | . 689 | . 680 | . 293 | . 734 | . 812 | . 582 | . 516 | . 825 |
| X2 | . 859 | . 747 | . 768 | . 302 | . 866 | . 658 | −. 588 | . 649 | . 861 |
| X3 | . 946 | . 645 | . 668 | . 182 | . 654 | . 739 | . 848 | . 714 | . 931 |
| X4 | . 902 | | | . 152 | | | | . 810 | |
| X5 | . 677 | | | . 178 | | | | | |
| X6 | | | | . 226 | | | | | |
| Chi-Squ | 4. 378 | 0 | 0 | 6. 419 | 0 | 0 | 0 | . 188 | 0 |
| df | 5 | 1 | 1 | 7 | 1 | 1 | 1 | 1 | 1 |
| p | . 49 | . 99 | . 98 | . 49 | . 99 | . 99 | . 99 | . 66 | . 99 |

continued

| | FEAR | COM | SOL1 | SOL2 | SOL3 | SAT | BST | POL | OPT |
|---|---|---|---|---|---|---|---|---|---|
| BBNFI | .95 | 1.00 | 1.00 | .95 | 1.00 | 1.00 | 1.00 | .99 | 1.00 |
| BBNNFI | 1.01 | 1.28 | 1.13 | 1.01 | 1.61 | 1.13 | 1.28 | 1.19 | 1.28 |
| CFI | 1.00 | 1.00 | 1.00 | 1.00 | 1.00 | 1.00 | 1.00 | 1.00 | 1.00 |

Note: Row titles denote different index. X1, X2, ⋯X6 denote different indicators for each index. For example, Fear has 5 indicators(X1, ⋯X5) that are different from the 3 indicators(X1, ⋯X3) for Commercial burglary(COM).

COM = Commercial Burglary
SOL1 = Residents' commitment to neighborhoods
SOL2 = Residents' sense of responsibility for the neighborhoods
SOL3 = Business people's sense of responsibility for the shopping centers in the neighborhoods.
SAT = satisfaction with life and doing business in the area.
BST = Business stability
POL = Favorability ratings of the police
OPT = The optimism of community's future
df = Degree of freedom
BBNFI = Bentler-Bonett normed fit index
BBNNFI = Bentler-Bonett nonnormed fit index
CFI = Comparative fit index

# A. Measurement Model for Satisfaction with Area

Table VI. 2 shows that the measurement model for satisfaction with the area (SAT) has three indicators. The factorloading(see the column with heading SAT) for the first indicator is .812; for the second is .658; and for the third is .739. The one factor model is exactly identified, and Chi-square = 0. In order to be able to assess the fitness of the model to the data, I fix one of the factor loadings estimated from the exactly identified model, so the model becomes overidentified, and the df = 1. I reestimate the model, and the model fits very well; p<.99; the Bentler-Bonett Normed fit index = 1.00; the Bentler-Bonett Nonnormed fit Index = 1.138; and the comparative fit Index = 1.000.

The first measure asks residents: Taking everything together, how would you rate this neighborhood as a place to live? Excellent⋯4; good⋯3; fair⋯2; poor⋯

1. The second measure asks businessmen: Overall, how would you rate this shopping area as a place to do business? Is it: excellent···4; good···3; fair···2; poor···1. The third measure asks businessmen: For someone considering buying a home in this neighborhood, would you recommend it as a good investment or would they be better off investing in another neighborhood? Good investment···2; better off in another neighborhood ··· 1. Overall, the factor reflects people's satisfaction with the area for living and doing business.

## B. Measurement Model for Business Stability

Table VI. 2 shows that the measurement model for business stability has three measures. The model is exactly identified, and Chi-square = 0. In order to be able to assess the fitness of the model to the data, I fix one of the factor loading estimated from the exactly identified model, so the model becomes overidentified, and the df = 1. I reestimate the model, and the model fits very well; $p < .99$; the Bentler-Bonett Normed fit index = 1. 00; the Bentler-Bonett Nonnormed fit Index = 1. 289; and the comparative fit Index = 1. 000.

The first measure is: In terms of business turnover, how stable is this shopping area? Is it: very stable···4; somewhat stable···3; somewhat unstable···2; very unstable ··· 1. The second measure is: Do you have any plans to relocate your establishment to another area? Yes···1; no···0. The third measure is: How much would you like to move your establishment to another location? Not at all···3; a little···2; very much···1.

The factor reflects the likelihood that business people will move their business to other places. The composite index constructed from this model reflects the stability of business; a high score means businesses stay in the area; and a low score means businesses migrate out of the area.

# C. Measurement Model for Favorability Ratings of Police

Table VI. 2 shows that the measurement model for favorability ratings of the police has four measures. The model fits very well, with a chi-square = . 188; df = 1; p < . 66; the Bentler-Bonett Normed fit index = . 994; the Bentler Bonett Nonnormed fit Index = 1. 191; and the comparative fit Index = 1. 000;

The four measures are: About how often do police just walk through this center, that you know of? Rarely or never···0; once or twice a month···1; once or twice a week···2; almost every day···3. How often do the police drop in to chat with you at work or just to see how you are doing? Rarely or never···0; once or twice a month···1; once or twice a week···2; almost every day···3. Overall, how would you rate the job the police are doing in providing security for this shopping area? Would you say: excellent···4; good···3; fair···2; poor···1. How well do the police usually treat people in this neighborhood? Do they treat them: very well···3; well enough···2; not so well···1; not well at all···0. The factor reflects the assessment and the attitude of people toward police.

# D. Measurement Model for Optimism of A community's Future

Table VI. 2 shows that the measurement model for optimism of a community's future has three measures. The model is exactly identified, and Chi-square = 0. In order to be able to assess the fitness of the model to the data, I fix one of the factor loadings estimated from the exactly identified model, so the model becomes overidentified, and the df = 1. I reestimate the model, and the model fits very well; p < . 99; the Bentler-Bonett Normed fit index = 1. 00; the Bentler-Bonett Nonnormed fit Index = 1. 289; and the comparative fit Index = 1. 000. The parameters change only very slightly.

The first measure asks residents: From what you have seen, do you think that in the next few years this shopping area will become economically better off, go along about the same, or will it decline economically? Economically better off⋯3; about the same 2; decline ⋯ 1. The other two measures ask business persons: From what you have seen, do you think that in the next few years this shopping area will become economically better off, go along about the same, or will it decline economically? Economically better off⋯3; about the same 2; decline⋯1. Have the general economic and social conditions in the neighborhood around your business improved, remained about the same, or declined in the past few years? Improved ⋯3; remained the same 2; declined⋯1. The factor reflects the people's perception the overall economic and social conditional trend in their area.

# E. Measurement Model for Fear of Crime

Table VI. 2 shows the results of the measurement models. The resulting measurement model for fear has five measures; the names of the items areFEAR31, FEAR32, POSSBEAT, SPOSBEAT, and FEAR4. The model fits very well, with chi-square = 4.378; df = 5; p<.49; Bentler-Bonett Normed fit index = .955; Bentler Bonett Nonnormed fit Index = 1.014; comparative fit Index = 1.000;

The measure FEAR31 is a summary of five questions: 1. I'm often a little worried that I will be the victim of a crime in my neighborhood. 2. I would not be afraid if a stranger stopped me at night in my neighborhood to ask for directions. 3. I worry about the safety of people close to me while they are in the neighborhood. 4. When I have to be away from home for a long time, I worry that someone might try to break in. 5. When I hear footsteps behind me at night in my neighborhood, it makes me feel uneasy. The answers are "mostly true" and "mostly false". For an individual respondent, the summary measures ranges from 5 for highest level of fear to 0 for lowest level of fear. FEAR32, FEAR4 use same set of questions. For FEAR32 residents were asked about the shopping areas in the neighborhoods; for FEAR4 business persons were asked about the shopping areas in the neighborhoods. The values for FEAR32 and FEAR4 are calculated in the same way as for FEAR31.

The question for POSSBEAT is: What would you say is the likelihood that you will be held up on the street, threatened, beaten up, or anything of that sort in your neighborhood? Would you say there is, no chance at all $\cdots$ 0; a slight chance $\cdots$ 1; a fair chance $\cdots$ 2; a good chance 3. The question for SPOSBEAT is the same as for POSSBEAT, asking about the shopping area in the neighborhoods.

## F. Measurement Model for Social Solidarity

The analyses result in three measurement models for social solidarity (Table VI. 2). The first solidarity factor has three measures. The model is exactly identified, and Chi-square = 0. In order to be able to assess the fitness of the model to the data, I fix one of the factor loading estimated from the exactly identified model, so the model becomes overidentified, and the df = 1. I reestimate the model. The model fits very well; p < . 98; the Bentler-Bonett Normed fit index = 1. 00; the Bentler Bonett Nonnormed fit Index = 1. 133; and the comparative fit Index = 1. 000.

The first measure is: how long have you lived at your current address (Number of years)? The second measure is: Some people feel their neighborhood is a real home to them, a place where they have roots. Other people think of their neighborhood as just a place where they happen to be living. Which one of these comes closest to the way you consider your neighborhood? A real home $\cdots$ 2; just a place to live $\cdots$ 1. The third measure is: Some people are strongly committed to their neighborhood and others are not. When you think of your commitment to this neighborhood, are you strongly committed, undecided, or not committed. Strongly committed $\cdots$ 3; undecided $\cdots$ 2; not committed $\cdots$ 1. The solidarity factor measured by these indicators reflects one dimension of social solidarity, that is, the resident's commitment to their neighborhood.

The second solidarity model has six measures. The model fits very well; the chi-square = 6. 419; p < . 49; the Bentler-Bonett Normed fit index = . 958; the Bentler-Bonett Nonnormed fit Index = 1. 009; and the comparative fit Index = 1. 000. However, although indicators are carefully selected, the loadings are low. This also demonstrates the necessity of constructing measurement models to take into account measurement errors rather than simply assuming measures are good as in regression analysis.

The first three measures are three statements for one question, asking residents to choose from four choices ranging from agree strongly ( coded 4 ) to disagree strongly( coded 1 ). The question is: First, let's consider the area right around your home, such as right outside your front or back door. This would include the hallway if you live in anapartment or the sidewalk or alley right next to your house. Thinking about these areas, please tell me if you agree or disagree with the following statements: a. I have a lot to say about what goes on. b. I feel personally responsible for what goes on. c. I can tell people who belong there from outsiders.

The second three measures are three statements for one question, using the same format and choices. The question is: Now let's consider the rest of the block where you live. Tell me whether you agree or disagree with each statement I read as it applies to the block where you live. a. I have a lot to say about what goes on. b. I feel personally responsible for what goes on. c. I can tell people who belong there from outsiders. This factor reflects another dimension of social solidarity, that is, the sense of residents' responsibility for the neighborhoods.

The third solidarity factor has three measures. The model is exactly identified, and Chi-square = 0. In order to be able to assess the fitness of the model to the data, I fix one of the factor loading estimated from the exactly identified model, so the model becomes overidentified, and the df = 1. I reestimate the model, and the model fits very well; p < . 99; the Bentler-Bonett Normed fit index = 1. 00; the

Bentler-Bonett Nonnormed fit Index = 1. 61; and the comparative fit Index = 1. 000.

The three measures are three statements for one question, asking business people to choose from the four choices ranging from agree strongly ( coded 4 ) to disagree strongly ( coded 1 ). The question is: Now let's consider the sidewalk in front of your establishment or the parking lot next to it. Tell me how much you agree or disagree with each statement I read as it applies to theses areas. a. I have a lot to say about what goes on. b. I feel personally responsible for what goes on. c. I can tell people who belong there from outsiders. This solidarity factor reflects the sense of business people's responsibility for the shopping areas in the neighborhoods.

## G. Measurement Model for Crimes

I examine four types of crimes in the general model: violent personal crime, nonviolent property crime, general crime level, and serious property crime. Because not many measures exist in the data or no well fitting factor models can be located for the violent personal crime, general crime level, and nonviolent crime, they are measured using individual measures rather than a summary composite measure.

Violent personal crime is measured by a question asking residents: about how often are people in your neighborhood threatened, beaten up, or anything of that sort? Would you say: almost never $\cdots 0$; once in a while $\cdots 1$; often $\cdots 2$; very often $\cdots 3$.

Nonviolent crime is measured by a question on shoplifting. The question asks business people: since August, 1981, has anyone been observed shoplifting from your business? Yes $\cdots 1$; no $\cdots 0$; after aggregating to the neighborhood level, the measure becomes a continuous variable.

General crime level is measured by a question asking business people about crime problem in the neighborhood. The question is: Regarding crime in general in this neighborhood, would you say that there is a lot of crime, quite a bit of crime, some crime, or almost no crime? A lot of crime $\cdots$ 3; quit a bit of crime $\cdots$ 2; some crime $\cdots$ 1; almost no crime $\cdots$ 0.

A factor model is developed for serious property crime, which includes three measures of commercial burglary. The model is exactly identified, and Chi-square = 0. In order to be able to assess the fitness of the model to the data, I fix one of the factor loading estimated from the exactly identified model, so the model becomes over identified, and the df = 1. I reestimate the model, and the model fits very well. p = .99; the Bentler-Bonett Normed fit index = 1.00; the Bentler-Bonett Nonnormed fit Index = 1.289; and the comparative fit Index = 1.000. One question for the factor model is: About how often are businesses in this shopping area held-up or broken into? Would you say: almost never $\cdots$ 0; once in a while $\cdots$ 1; often $\cdots$ 2; very often $\cdots$ 3. Another question is: What would you say is the likelihood that this establishment will be burglarized or broken into in the next year or so? No chance at all $\cdots$ 0; a slight chance $\cdots$ 1; a fair chance $\cdots$ 2; a good chance $\cdots$ 3. The other question is: since August, 1981, has your establishment been burglarized or broken into? Yes $\cdots$ 1; no $\cdots$ 0. The factor reflects the extent of commercial burglary crime.

In sum, the analyses for the measurement model build factors for fear of crime, social solidarity, satisfaction with living and doing business in a area, business stability, the favorability ratings of the police, and optimism of a community's future. These measurement models fit data well. Allowing the measurement errors to correlate for SOL2, fear, and POL does not significantly improve the estimates and the model fit. The hypothesis that measurement errors are purely random is confirmed. For other concept, allowing errors to correlate will under identify the models.

I developed the composite indexes for each of the theoretical concepts from the factor loadings of the measurement models, and they are to be used in the structural model analyses in the following chapters. In next three chapters, I report the results of the tests of the hypotheses for the three issues.

# Chapter VII. Results for the Recursive Model

## A. Issues in Testing the Recursive Models

The tests of the recursive models (Figure IV. 1) mainly address the issue of the consequences of crime, fear, and social solidarity. The relevant hypotheses are grouped around the different consequences. For satisfaction, the hypotheses are:

I. 1. Crime reduces people's satisfaction with life and doing business in the area.

I. 2. Crime does not directly reduce satisfaction.

I. 3. Fear directly reduces satisfaction.

I. 4. Fear mediates the effect of crime on satisfaction.

I. 5. Social solidarity increases satisfaction with life and doing business in the area.

For business stability, the hypotheses are:

II. 1. Crime reduces business stability in the area.

II. 2. Crime does not directly reduce business stability in the area.

II. 3. Fear directly reduces business stability in the area.

II. 4. Fear mediates the effect of crime on business stability.

II. 5.　Social solidarity increases business stability.

For people's favorability rating of the police, the hypotheses are:

III. 1.　Crime reduces people's favorability rating of the police.

III. 2.　Crime does not directly reduce people's favorability rating of the police.

III. 3.　Fear directly reduces people's favorability rating of the police.

III. 4.　Fear mediates the effect of crime on favorability rating of the police.

III. 5.　Social solidarity increases people's favorability rating of the police

For people's optimism of the community's future, the hypotheses are:

IV. 1.　Crime reduces people's optimism of the community's future.

IV. 2.　Crime does not directly reduce people's optimism of the community's future.

IV. 3.　Fear directly reduces people's optimism of the community's future.

IV. 4.　Fear mediates the effect of crime on optimism of the community's future.

IV. 5.　Social solidarity increases optimism of the community's future.

Three relevant issues are the test procedure, collinearity, and effects decomposition. Maximum Likelihood methods require appropriate test procedures to address the small sample issue. My analyses are designed to minimize the number of parameters estimated and at the same time to meet the Bentler guidelines (maximum parameter number is five). The design uses replicated tests for the same model to assess the stability of the coefficients and to test for the influence of multicollinearity.

First, I estimate a recursive model in which fear affects social solidarity, but solidarity does not affect fear (Figure IV. 1). The general recursive model is divided into four separate models; each of them has only one social consequence (see Figures IV. 1. 1, IV. 1. 2, IV. 1. 3, and IV. 1. 4). I only test the models with one consequence to estimate the basic models with a maximum of five parameters at a time, avoiding estimating too many parameters at the same time. The four models can be called the satisfaction model, the business stability model, the police rating model, and optimism of a community's future model.

Second, the factor analyses for the measurement models in last chapter result in one composite index for fear and one for each of the four social consequences, and three composite indexes for solidarity. In estimating each of the four structural models, rather than estimating models including different measures or indexes of theoretical concepts at same time, I estimate separate structural models for different measures. I put in only one measure or composite index of each theoretical concept at a time to keep the number of free parameters at its minimum. That is, I use different measures to retest the same model, so the same test for each consequence is replicated 12 times. For four consequences, and the corresponding four submodels, I test 48 replications. This design enables me to check and confirm the stability of the estimates in all situations through comparing all tests with different measures, replicating the research with different measures. For each of these 48 replications with different types of crime, solidarities, and social consequences, I estimate a model with a change in specification, that is, I allow crime to affect consequences directly. The change in specification allows the assessment of the hypotheses that crime does not directly affect consequences, and that fear mediates the effect of crime. It also shows the stability of the structural coefficients, and therefore provides an assessment of the influence of collinearity, which I will discuss shortly. Thus, I estimate a total of 96 models.

Third, based on the results of all the replications of the model with different measures of crime and solidarity, I select those measures of crime and solidarity that show significant effects in the tests, and test a model for each consequence with all these independent variables affecting the consequence simultaneously to assess the relative importance of the effect of each measures of crime and solidarity.

The influence of multicollinearity is always an issue that should be considered and examined in the tests of linear models. Multicollinearity is a problem of correlated independent variables in a sample. The standard errors of regression coefficient estimators increase as the correlations among the independent variables increase. Large standard errors for coefficient estimators are a major consequence of multicollinearity. When the independent variables in an equation are highly correlated, it is impossible to separate out the effect of the independent variables with any degree of precision; the coefficients are highly correlated to each other; and the coefficients become unstable, therefore untrustable. When high multicollinearity is present, switching samples, changing the indicator used to measure a variable in the model, deleting or adding a variable to the equation, or slightly changing the model specification all lead to dramatic changes in the coefficient estimates. Because independent variables are usually correlated to each other in a sample, multicollinearity is not something that either exists or does not exit; it exists in different degree. When multicollinearityis present in only a very small amount, there is little reason to be concerned about its impact, but as the degree of multicollinearity increases, its consequences become more pernicious.

The most commonly used test for multicollinearity is to inspect the correlation matrix, even though simple bivariate correlation by themselves are insufficient to diagnose collinearity problem. Typically, if no correlation between independent variables exceeds. 80, multicollinearity is not a problem ( Berry and Feldman, 1985). In the extreme case, when one of the independent variables is perfectly linearly related to one or more of the other independent variables in the same equation, perfect collinearity exists. So the most reasonable test for multicollinearity is to regress each independent variable in the equation on all other independent variables, and look at the R squares for these regressions; if any are close to 1. 00, there is a high degree of multicollinearity present( Berry and Feldman,1985). The fundamental way to assess the influence of multicollinearity is to replicate the model testing with slightly different measures or specification and assess the changes in the coefficients.

An examination of the correlation matrix ( Table VII. 1 ) reveals that some of the correlations between crime, fear and solidarity, which are the independent variables for the models, are higher than. 5. To make sure collinearity is not a problem in equations where crime, fear, and solidarity affect consequences, I regress one of them on the others; the R squares are reported in table VII. 2; no R square is beyond the traditional criterion. 75 (Fisher and Mason, 1981); and this indicates multicollinearity is generally not a problem except in one case, when regressing SOL1 and Fear on violent crime (Table VII. 2, model I. 1) the R square is. 742. This indicates a potential multicolinearity problem. But further, the coefficients across replications for the same model with different indicators are very stable. This confirms that multicollinearity is not a problem.

**Table VII. 1　Bivariate correlations Between Variables**

|  | VIOLENT | CRIMEAMT | COM | SHOPLIFT | FEAR | SOL1 |
|---|---|---|---|---|---|---|
| VIOLENT | 1. 0000 | . 6635 * * | . 1982 | . 2798 | . 7114 * * | −. 7220 * * |
| CRIMEAMT | . 6635 * * | 1. 0000 | . 6313 * * | . 2740 | . 8016 * | −. 5178 * * |
| COM | . 1982 | . 6313 * * | 1. 0000 | . 3914 | . 4469 * | −. 3177 |
| SHOPLIFT | . 2798 | . 2740 | . 3914 | 1. 0000 | . 3486 | −. 0928 |
| FEAR | . 7114 * * | . 8016 * * | . 4469 * | . 3486 | 1. 0000 | −. 3845 |
| SOL1 | −. 7220 * * | −. 5178 * * | −. 3177 | −. 0928 | −. 3845 | 1. 0000 |
| SOL2 | −. 7106 * * | −. 5338 * * | −. 2640 | −. 4174 * | −. 4564 * | . 6455 * * |
| SOL3 | −. 2178 | −. 1591 | −. 0067 | . 3222 | −. 2069 | . 2257 |
| SAT | −. 6617 * * | −. 6869 * * | −. 2630 | −. 1837 | −. 7120 * * | . 4050 * |
| STA | −. 5073 * | −. 4904 * | −. 0065 | . 1104 | −. 5615 * * | . 2923 |
| POL | −. 2214 | −. 4473 * | −. 1755 | . 1930 | −. 3887 | . 4104 * |
| OPT | . 3465 | . 1500 | . 0901 | . 1972 | . 0729 | −. 5135 * |

Note: VIOLENT = Violent personal crime

　　　CRIMEAMT = General Crime Level

　　　COM = Commercial Burglary

　　　SOL1 = Residents' commitment to neighborhoods

　　　SOL2 = Residents' sense of responsibility for the neighborhoods

　　　SOL3 = Business people's sense of responsibility for the shopping centers in the neighborhoods

　　　SAT = Satisfaction with life and doing business in the area

　　　BST = Business stability

　　　POL = Favorability ratings of the police

　　　OPT = The optimism of community's future

　　　* p<. 05, two-tailed test.

　　　* * p<. 01, two-tailed test.

continued

| | SOL2 | SOL3 | SAT | STA | POL | OPT |
|---|---|---|---|---|---|---|
| VIOLENT | −.7106** | −.2178 | −.6617** | −.5073* | −.2214 | .3465 |
| CRIMEAMT | −.5338** | −.1591 | −.6869** | −.4904* | −.4473* | .1500 |
| COM | −.2640 | −.0067 | −.2630 | −.0065 | −.1755 | .0901 |
| SHOPLIFT | −.4174* | .3222 | −.1837 | .1104 | .1930 | .1972 |
| FEAR | −.4564* | −.2069 | −.7120** | −.5615** | −.3887 | .0729 |
| SOL1 | .6455** | .2257 | .4050* | .2923 | .4104* | −.5135* |
| SOL2 | 1.0000 | .2296 | .4802* | .2386 | −.0099 | −.3898 |
| SOL3 | .2296 | 1.0000 | .2322 | .3679 | .2440 | −.1656 |
| SAT | .4802* | .2322 | 1.0000 | .6913** | .5573** | −.0136 |
| STA | .2386 | .3679 | .6913** | 1.0000 | .4336* | .1579 |
| POL | −.0099 | .2440 | .5573** | .4336* | 1.0000 | −.1249 |
| OPT | −.3898 | −.1656 | −.0136 | .1579 | −.1249 | 1.0000 |

Note: VIOLENT = Violent personal crime

CRIMEAMT = General Crime Level

COM = Commercial Burglary

SOL1 = Residents' commitment to neighborhoods

SOL2 = Residents' sense of responsibility for the neighborhoods

SOL3 = Business people's sense of responsibility for the shopping centers in the neighborhoods

SAT = Satisfaction with life and doing business in the area

BST = Business stability

POL = Favorability ratings of the police

OPT = The optimism of community's future

* p<.05, two-tailed test.

** p<.01, two-tailed test.

### Table VII. 2　Checking Multicollinearity

R squares for Regressing Independent Variables on

Independent Variables Influencing Consequences

| | | Model I. 1 | | |
|---|---|---|---|---|
| | | SOL1 | fear | Violent Crime |
| Fear | Violent Crime | .555 | | |
| SOL1 | Violent Crime | | .540 | |

continued

| | | SOL2 | fear | Violent Crime |
|---|---|---|---|---|
| SOL1 | Fear | | | .742 |
| | | **Model II. 1** | | |
| | | SOL2 | fear | Violent Crime |
| Fear | Violent Crime | .509 | | |
| SOL2 | Violent Crime | | .511 | |
| SOL2 | Fear | | | .694 |
| | | **Model III. 1** | | |
| | | SOL3 | fear | Violent Crime |
| Fear | Violent Crime | .052 | | |
| SOL3 | Violent Crime | | .508 | |
| SOL3 | Fear | | | .511 |
| | | **Model I. 2** | | |
| | | SOL1 | fear | General Crime |
| Fear | General Crime | .271 | | |
| SOL1 | General Crime | | .643 | |
| SOL1 | Fear | | | .694 |
| | | **Model II. 2** | | |
| | | SOL2 | fear | General Crime |
| Fear | General Crime | .287 | | |
| SOL2 | General Crime | | .643 | |
| SOL2 | Fear | | | .678 |
| | | **Model III. 2** | | |
| | | SOL3 | fear | General Burg |
| Fear | General Crime | .042 | | |
| SOL3 | General Crime | | .649 | |
| SOL3 | Fear | | | .642 |
| | | **Model I. 3** | | |
| | | SOL1 | fear | Commercial Burg |
| Fear | Commercial Burg | .174 | | |
| SOL1 | Commercial Burg | | .265 | |
| SOL1 | Fear | | | .224 |
| | | **Model II. 3** | | |
| | | SOL2 | fear | Commercial Burg |

continued

| | | | | |
|---|---|---|---|---|
| Fear | Commercial Burg | . 212 | | |
| SOL2 | Commercial Burg | | . 322 | |
| SOL2 | Fear | | | . 204 |

| | | Model III. 3 | | |
|---|---|---|---|---|
| | | SOL3 | fear | Commercial Burg |
| Fear | Commercial Burg | . 051 | | |
| SOL3 | Commercial Burg | | . 241 | |
| SOL3 | Fear | | | . 207 |

| | | Model I. 4 | | |
|---|---|---|---|---|
| | | SOL1 | fear | Shoplifting |
| Fear | Shoplifting | . 149 | | |
| SOL1 | Shoplifting | | . 246 | |
| SOL1 | Fear | | | . 124 |

| | | Model II. 4 | | |
|---|---|---|---|---|
| | | SOL2 | fear | Shoplifting |
| Fear | Shoplifting | . 284 | | |
| SOL2 | Shoplifting | | . 238 | |
| SOL2 | Fear | | | . 205 |

| | | Model III. 4 | | |
|---|---|---|---|---|
| | | SOL3 | fear | Shoplifting |
| Fear | Shoplifting | . 219 | | |
| SOL3 | Shoplifting | | . 235 | |
| SOL3 | Fear | | | . 283 |

Note: Violent Crime = Violent Personal Crime

General Crime = General Crime Level

Commercial Burg = Commercial Burglary

SOL1 = Residents' commitment to neighborhoods

SOL2 = Residents' sense of responsibility for the neighborhoods

SOL3 = Business people's sense of responsibility for the shopping centers in the neighborhoods

Model I, II, III denote for models using SOL1, SOL2, and SOL3; 1, 2, 3, and 4 denote for models using violent crime, general crime level, commercial burglary, and shoplifting for crime.

When testing hypotheses using estimates from a structural equation system, the calculations of total, direct and indirect effects and the discomposition of total effects is also an issue that should be discussed. To examine the effects of crime on consequences, the direct, indirect, and total effects should be examined. For example, the general model suggests that a change in crime results in changes in fear and solidarity, and changes in fear and solidarity in turn result in changes in the consequences. The total expected changes in the consequences include all the changes that result from the fear and solidarity brought about by crime. The total effect of crime on consequences can be decomposed into the direct effect of crime on consequences and the total indirect of crime on consequences. These indirect effects may either reinforce or negate the direct effects of crime, if there is any direct effect. The total indirect effect can again be decomposed into three indirect effects: 1. the indirect effect of crime on consequences mediated by fear; 2. the indirect effect of crime on consequences mediated by social solidarity; and 3. the indirect effect of crime on consequences mediated by fear and then solidarity ( crime → fear → solidarity → consequences ). The most important component for assessing the central hypotheses that fear mediates the effect of crime on consequences is the indirect effect of crime on consequences mediated by fear; therefore, I report the total effect of crime on a consequence, the total indirect effect ( that is, the total effect minus direct effect of crime on a consequence ), and the indirect effect of crime on a consequence mediated by fear ( calculated by the product of the direct effect of crime on fear and the direct effect of fear on a consequence ).

In the decomposition of total effect, we should keep in mind that there is an important difference between the decomposition for population data and for sample data. The interpretation of the relative size of an effect to the total effect estimated from a sample of data can be misleading. For population data, where the significance test is not an issue, all the coefficients reflect the real size of the effects. The decomposition of the total effect into direct effects and indirect effects allow us to calculate the proportion of a particular indirect effect to the total effect. We can calculate the percentage of an indirect effect through a particular path to the total effect, and this percentage informs us how much of the total effect is mediated by this path(Alwin and Hauser,1981). However,for a sample of data,a coefficient is an estimate of the population coefficient. Our focus has to be first of all on the significance test. If a indirect effect is not significant,that means that this effect is likely to be zero in the population,the calculation of the percentage of this effect in the total effect is meaningless because it is considered statistically to be zero in the population. The interpretation of this percentage as the proportion of the total effect mediated by the mediating variable is thus misleading. The important thing here is whether or not the indirect effect mediated by a mediating variable is significant. Only for those statistically significant direct and indirect effects,can we compare the relative importance of the effects.

# B. Hypotheses of Crime,Fear and Solidarity Influencing satisfaction

Figure IV. 1. 1 is the recursive model in which the satisfaction with living and doing business in the area is the social consequence to be examined. In this section,in order to concentrate on the hypotheses of how crime,fear and social solidarity affect satisfaction,I only report results for structural equations in which crime,fear and solidarity affect satisfaction. Table VII. 3 reports the structural coefficients estimated by ML methods.

**Table VII. 3　Effects of Crime,Fear,and Solidarity on Satisfaction**

(Standardized ML Estimates)

| Independent Variables | Models for Satisfaction | | | | | | | | | |
|---|---|---|---|---|---|---|---|---|---|---|
| | I | | | II | | | III | | | |
| | (a) | (b) | (c) | (a) | (b) | (c) | (a) | (b) | (c) | (d) |
| Fear | −.653** | −.483** | −.343** | −.623** | −.495** | −.352** | −.694** | −.482** | −.342** | |
| Violent Personal Crime | | −.334 | −.328* | | −.260 | −.402** | | −.305 | −.357** | −.662 |
| SOL1 | .154 | −.022 | | | | | | | | |

194

continued

| Independent Variables | Models for Satisfaction | | | | | | | | | |
|---|---|---|---|---|---|---|---|---|---|---|
| | I | | | II | | | III | | | |
| | (a) | (b) | (c) | (a) | (b) | (c) | (a) | (b) | (c) | (d) |
| SOL2 | | | | .196 | .069 | | | | | |
| SOL3 | | | | | | | .089 | .066 | | |
| Chi-square | 1.442 | | | 1.051 | | | 1.331 | | | |
| Fear | −.653** | −.459** | −.360** | −.623** | −.440** | −.353** | −.694** | −.431** | −.345** | |
| General Crime Level | | −.274 | −.413** | | −.259 | −.428** | | −.327 | −.360** | −.687 |
| SOL1 | .154 | .087 | | | | | | | | |
| SOL2 | | | | .196 | .141 | | | | | |
| SOL3 | | | | | | | .089 | .090 | | |
| Chi-square | 1.148 | | | 1.097 | | | 1.883 | | | |
| Fear | −.653** | −.691** | −.309** | −.623** | −.657** | −.294** | −.694** | −.772** | −.345** | |
| Commercial Burglary | | .100 | −.363** | | .084 | −.347** | | .060 | −.323** | −.263 |
| SOL1 | .154 | .171 | | | | | | | | |
| SOL2 | | | | .196 | .202 | | | | | |
| SOL3 | | | | | | .089 | .083 | | | |
| Chi-square | .381 | | | .282 | | | .716 | | | |
| Fear | −.653** | −.677** | −.236** | −.623** | −.651** | −.227** | −.694** | −.712** | −.248** | |
| Shoplifting | | .066 | −.250* | | .145 | −.329** | | .041 | −.225* | −.184 |
| SOL1 | .154 | .151 | | | | | | | | |
| SOL2 | | | | .196 | .243 | | | | | |
| SOL3 | | | | | | | .089 | .072 | | |
| Chi-square | .189 | | | .864 | | | .056 | | | |

Note: SOL 1 = Residents' commitment to neighborhoods

SOL 2 = Residents' sense of responsibility for the neighborhoods

SOL 3 = Business people's sense of responsibility for the shopping centers in the neighborhoods

Model I, II, and III are models with different types of solidarity used in the models

Column (c)s are the indirect effects for model (b)s. The first numbers in column (c)s are the indirect effects of crimes on satisfaction mediated by fear. The second number is the total indirect effect; it includes the effects of crime on satisfaction mediated by fear, by solidarity, and both by fear and then solidarity (see figure 5).

Column (d) is the total effects of crimes on satisfaction.

* p <. 10, one−tailed test.

** p <. 05, one−tailed test.

In the table VII. 3, the column headings, Model I, II and III, indicate that different types of social solidarity are used in the estimation. Model I uses the index of the residents' commitment to neighborhoods as the measure for solidarity (SOL1); model II uses the index of the residents' sense of responsibility for the neighborhoods as the measure for solidarity(SOL2); and model III uses the index of business people's sense of responsibility for the shopping centers in the neighborhoods as the measure for solidarity(SOL3).

Under each of the models, I, II, and III, column a reports a model where only fear and social solidarity affect satisfaction (Figure IV. 1. 1); crime does not directly affect satisfaction. In contrast, column b reports a model in which crime also affects satisfaction directly. This model only differs from the model a by adding a direct path from crime to satisfaction on model a(Figure IV. 1. 1 is model a). Therefore, each of the models I, II, and III includes two models, model a and model b; they are with and without the direct effect of crime on satisfaction. So altogether we have model Ia, Ib, IIa, IIb, IIIa and IIIb.

Column c and column d( the last column in the table) report indirect effects and the total effect of model bs to illustrate the decomposition of the total effect for model b. Column c reports two indirect effects of model b. The first number is the indirect effects of crime on satisfaction through fear; it is calculated from the products of the direct effect of crime on fear and the direct effects of fear on satisfaction( see Figure IV. 1. 1 adding a path from crime to satisfaction to get model b). The second number in column c is the total indirect effect of crime on satisfaction. It is the total effect of crime( reported in column d, the last column in the table) minus the direct effect of crime on satisfaction. It includes three indirect effects( see Figure IV. 1. 1 adding a path from crime to satisfaction for model b): 1. the effect of crime on satisfaction mediated by fear, 2. the effect of crime mediated by solidarity, and 3. the effect of crime mediated by both fear and solidarity. Because the theoretical interest is whether fear mediates the effect of crime on satisfaction, I only report these two indirect effects.

The row headings, the independent variables, indicate for each of the model Ia, Ib, IIa, IIb, IIIa, and IIIb, that four tests are performed using different crime measures: violent personal crime, general crime level, commercial burglary, and shoplifting. I will describe the results of model Ia, and model Ib, which are reported at the upper left hand of the table, to further explain the table.

For model Ia, in which SOL1 ( the index of the residents' commitment to neighborhoods) affects satisfaction and violent personal crime does not directly affect satisfaction, the effect of fear on satisfaction is $-.653$, with $t = -4.203$; it is statistically significant. The effect of solidarity on satisfaction is $.154$; it is not statistically significant. Because the direction of structural parameters is hypothesized, a one tailed test is performed to examine the statistical significance. When determining the significance of parameters in Table VII. 3, because the sample size is small, the critical value for the t ratio is adjusted for the degree of freedom, which is $df = 24 - k - 1 = 24 - k$, where k is the number of parameters estimated. In this case, k equals 2. The results suggest that fear reduces satisfaction. The Chi-square for this model is $1.442$; the model fits well.

For Model Ib, where fear and SOL1, as well as violent personal crime affect satisfaction, the effect of fear on satisfaction is $-.483$, with $t = -2.355$, remaining statistically significant, suggesting that fear reduces satisfaction. The effect of violent personal crime on satisfaction is $-.334$, with $t = -1.220$, not significant, suggesting that the direct effect of crime on satisfaction is insignificant. Also, the chi-square changes from $1.442$ for model a to 0 for model b. Column a and column b represent nested models; the chi-square change is insignificant at $p < .05$ level; so this confirms the result that direct effect of crime on satisfaction is insignificant. These results show that the hypothesis that crime does not directly affect satisfaction is confirmed. The effect of SOL1 on satisfaction is $-.022$, still not significant; indicating that SOL1 does not affect satisfaction. This disconfirms the hypothesis that social solidarity improves satisfaction.

Model b involves one more independent variable, namely violent personal crime. This complicates the picture of the effects and necessitates reporting the most theoretically important indirect effects and the total effect besides reporting direct effects. Column c reports two indirect effects of model b: the first number is the indirect effects of crime on satisfaction through fear; it is −. 343, and it is calculated as the products of direct effect of crime on fear and the direct effects of fear on satisfaction(see Figure IV. 1. 1, add one path from crime to satisfaction to get model Ib). Because both the direct effect of crime on fear and the direct effect of fear on satisfaction are significant, the product of them must be also significant; this confirms the hypothesis that fear mediates the effect of crime on satisfaction. The second number in column c is the total indirect effects of crime on satisfaction; it is .. 328; t = 1. 331; it is significant at p<. 10 for a one tailed test. The total indirect effect includes three indirect effects: 1, the indirect effect of crime on consequences mediated by fear; 2, the indirect effect of crime on consequences mediated by social solidarity; and 3, the indirect effect of crime on consequences mediated by fear and then solidarity( crime → fear → solidarity → satisfaction). Column d, the last column in Table, shows the total effects of crimes on satisfaction; it is−. 662. It is the sum of the direct effect and all the indirect effects of crime on satisfaction. The total effect shows that the effect of crime is to reduce satisfaction; this confirms the hypothesis that crime reduces people's satisfaction with life and doing business in the area.

As I substitute different types of crime and different types of social solidarity, the results show that the pattern remains virtually the same. For all 24 replications reported in table VII. 3, fear consistently affects satisfaction; the effects of social solidarity are consistently insignificant. When allowing crimes directly to affect satisfaction, the effects are insignificant.

To assess the relative importance of fear, crimes, and solidarity, I estimate equations with satisfaction as dependent variables ( table VII. 4 ). In the first equation, I put fear into the equations. I also put Sol 1 and personal violent crime and general crime level into the equation because in the replication tests ( Table

VII. 3) they generally show relatively stronger effects on satisfaction although the effects are not significant. In the other following equations I take away one at a time the least significant crime variable, then the other crime variable, and finally the solidarity variable to reestimate the model.

**Table VII. 4   Relative Importance of Variables Influencing Satisfaction**
( Standardized Maximum Likelihood Estimates )

|  | Satisfaction | | | |
| :---: | :---: | :---: | :---: | :---: |
|  | I | II | III | IV |
| Fear | −. 262 $^*$ | −. 483 $^{**}$ | −. 653 $^{**}$ | −. 712 $^{**}$ |
| SOL1 | . 107 | −. 022 | . 154 |  |
| Personal Violent Crime | −. 314 | −. 334 |  |  |
| General Crime Level | −. 294 |  |  |  |

Note: $^{**}$ p < . 05 , one−tailed test
$^*$ p < . 10 , one−tailed test

Table VII. 4 shows that the results are consistent with Table VII. 3. Fear significantly reduces satisfaction. Crimes do not directly affect satisfaction; the coefficients are insignificant. Solidarity does not directly affect satisfaction ( insignificant ). Fear is the most important variable in affecting satisfaction.

To summarize, the results show that the total effect of crime is to reduce satisfaction with living and doing business in the area; this confirms the hypothesis I. 1. Crime does not directly reduce people's satisfaction; this confirms the hypothesis I. 2. Fear directly reduces satisfaction; this confirms the hypothesis I. 3. Fear mediates the effect of crimes on satisfaction; this confirms the hypothesis I. 4. Allowing crime to directly affect satisfaction, the effect is insignificant. The corresponding chi-square change is also insignificant, and this confirms the conclusion that crime does not directly reduce satisfaction. Testing the model with different measures of crime and solidarity, the pattern stays same. The effects are quite stable. However, the effect of solidarity on satisfaction is consistently insignificant; hypothesis I. 5 is not confirmed.

## C. Hypotheses of Crime, Fear and Solidarity Influencing Business Stability

In the tests of the hypotheses II. 1, II. 2, II. 3, II. 4 and II. 5, namely, the hypotheses of crime, fear, and solidarity influencing business stability, the recusive model ( Figure IV. 1. 2 ) test is replicated with different measures of social solidarity, and different types of crime. Table VII. 5 reports the results. The organization of the table is the same as Table VII. 3. Model I, II, and III distinguish models with types of solidarity. Column a and b are models with and without crime directly affecting business stability.

**Table VII. 5   Effects of Crime, Fear, and Solidarity on Business Stability**
( Standardized ML Estimates )

| Independent Variables | Models for Business Stability | | | | | | | | | |
| | I | | | II | | | III | | | |
| | (a) | (b) | (c) | (a) | (b) | (c) | (a) | (b) | (c) | (d) |
|---|---|---|---|---|---|---|---|---|---|---|
| Fear | -.527** | -.393* | -.279* | -.572** | -.385* | -.273* | -.507** | -.360* | -.270* | |
| Violent Personal Crime | | -.263 | -.245 | | -.381 | -.126 | | -.183 | -.325* | -.507 |
| SOL1 | .090 | -.049 | | | | | | | | |
| SOL2 | | | | -.022 | -.208 | | | | | |
| SOL3 | | | | | | | .263* | .249* | | |
| Chi-square | .611 | | | 1.542 | | | .615 | | | |
| Fear | -.527** | -.477* | -.382* | -.572** | -.475* | -.381* | -.507** | -.412* | -.330* | |
| General Crime Level | | -.071 | -.420* | | -.137 | -.353* | | -.118 | -.471** | -.490 |
| SOL1 | .090 | .072 | | | | | | | | |
| SOL2 | | | | -.022 | -.051 | | | | | |
| SOL3 | | | | | | | .263* | .264* | | |
| Chi-square | .052 | | | .204 | | | .185 | | | |
| Fear | -.527** | -.654** | -.292** | -.572** | -.698** | -.312** | -.507** | -.637** | -.285** | |

continued

| Independent Variables | Models for Business Stability | | | | | | | | | |
|---|---|---|---|---|---|---|---|---|---|---|
| | I | | | II | | | III | | | |
| | (a) | (b) | (c) | (a) | (b) | (c) | (a) | (b) | (c) | (d) |
| Commercial Burglary | | .332** | −.286** | | .306* | −.312** | | .208* | −.218** | −.006 |
| SOL1 | .090 | .146 | | | | | | | | |
| SOL2 | | | | −.022 | .001 | | | | | |
| SOL3 | | | | | | | .263* | .238* | | |
| Chi-square | 3.103 | | | 2.643 | | | 2.435 | | | |
| Fear | −.527** | −.654** | −.228* | −.572** | −.647** | −.226* | −.507** | −.630** | −.220* | |
| Shoplifting | | .345** | −.235* | | .378** | −.268* | | .283* | −.172 | .110 |
| SOL1 | 0.090 | .073 | | | | | | | | |
| SOL2 | | | | −.022 | .101 | | | | | |
| SOL3 | | | | | | | .263* | .147 | | |
| Chi-square | 3.845 | | | 4.175 | | | 2.233 | | | |

Note : SOL1 = Residents' commitment to neighborhoods

SOL2 = Residents' sense of responsibility for the neighborhoods

SOL3 = Business people's sense of responsibility for the shopping centers in the neighborhoods

Model I, II, and III are models with different types of solidarity used in the models.

Column( c )s are the indirect effects for model( b )s. The first numbers in column( c )s are the indirect effects of crimes on business stability mediated by fear. The second number is the total indirect effect.

Column( d ) is the total effects of crimes on business stability.

* p < .10 , one-tailed test.

** p < .05 , one-tailed test.

Although the results across the models are mixed, some patterns exit. The effects of fear on business stability are consistently significant in both models where crime does not directly affect business stability( model a ) and where crime directly affects business stability ( model b ). The effect ranges from −.36 ( Model III. b ) to −.698 ( model II. b ). These results confirm the hypothesis that fears reduces business stability.

When allowing crime to directly affect business stability ( model b ) , violent personal crime and general crime level show very different effects than property crime, namely, than commercial burglary and shoplifting. The direct effects of violent personal crime and general crime are consistently insignificant, confirming the hypothesis that crime does not directly affect business stability. In contrast, the direct effects of property crime are consistently significant. The direct effect of commercial burglary ranges from .208 to .332; and the direct effect of shoplifting ranges from .283 to .378. The positive signs indicating surprisingly that the more burglary and shoplifting, the more business stability. These results suggest perhaps that the characteristics of different crimes have something to do with the causal relationships between crimes and business stability. But in general, the total effect (column d) of crime on business stability is negative, indicating that crime reduces business stability.

The effects of social solidarity on business stability depend on the types of solidarity. Comparing model III with model I and II, the results indicate that SOL3 (used only in model III) generally significantly affects business stability both in model a, where crime does not directly affect business stability, and in model b, where crime directly affect business stability. In contrast, under model I and II, all tests show that SOL1 and SOL2 do not have significant effects on business stability. Notice that SOL3 is the index of business people's sense of responsibility for the shopping areas in the neighborhoods. This suggests that business people's social solidarity does increase business stability.

To assess the relative importance of fear, crimes, and solidarity, I estimate equations with business stability as dependent variables. The results are reported in Table VII. 6. In the first equation, I only put into the equations those variables that have shown significant effects on business stability in any of the replication tests reported in Table VII. 5. The variables that have never shown any significant effect on business stability in all of the 12 replication tests of the model need not to be put in the equation. This way I keep the number of estimated parameters to minimum. In the following equations I try to see the stability of the effect of fear by deleting sequentially the least significant crime variables, then the other crime variable, and finally the solidarity measure and reestimate the model.

**Table VII. 6    Relative Importance of Variables Influencing Business Stability**

( Standardized Maximum Likelihood Estimates )

|  | Business Stability | | | |
|---|---|---|---|---|
|  | I | II | III | IV |
| Fear | −. 707 * * | −. 637 * * | −. 507 * * | −. 561 * * |
| SOL3 | . 152 | . 238 * | . 263 * |  |
| Commercial Burglary | . 224 | . 208 * |  |  |
| Shoplifting | . 220 |  |  |  |

Note: * * p <. 05 , one−tailed test

   * p <. 10 , one−tailed test

Table VII. 6 shows that fear significantly reduces business stability. Commercial burglary seems directly affect business stability . SOL 3 , the business people's responsibility for the shopping center, seems to increase business stability. Shoplifting is not significant, but compare to the size of the effects of SOL 3 and commercial burglary, it is a sizable effect. In general, the results are consistent with the replication test reported in table VII. 5 Fear is the most important variable affecting business stability.

To summarize, the results show that the total effect of crime is to reduce business stability; this confirms the hypothesis II. 1. Business stability, violent personal crime and general crime level show very different effects from that of property crimes. In general, violent personal crime and general crime level do not directly affect business stability; this is consistent with the hypothesis II. 2. However, commercial burglary and shoplift directly increase business stability; this is inconsistent with the hypothesis II. 2. These results are unexpected from my hypothesis. Fear directly reduces business stability; this confirms the hypothesis II. 3. Fear mediates the effects of crime on residents ' commitment and sense of responsibility for the neighborhood on business stability are insignificant, the effect of business people's responsibility for the shopping area on business stability is significant at p<. 10 level; this partially confirms the hypothesis II. 5. Testing the model with different measures of crime and solidarity, the patterns are quite similar.

# D. Hypotheses of Crime, Fear, and Solidarity Influencing Favorability Ratings of the Police

This section reports the results of the tests of the hypotheses III. 1, III. 2, III. 3, III. 4, and III. 5, namely, the hypotheses of crime, fear, and solidarity influencing favorability ratings of the police. The police model ( Figure IV. 1. 3 ) is tested with different business stability; this confirms the hypothesis II. 4. The effects of solidarity on business stability vary with different type of solidarity, while the effects of measures of social solidarity and different types of crime.

Table VII. 7 shows the results of the effects of crime, fear, and solidarity on people's favorability rating of the police. As before, model I, II, and III distinguish models with different types of solidarity in the model. Under each of the model I, II, and III, column a reports the effects of fear and solidarity on the favorability ratings of the police, and column b reports the results for the model when allowing crime to directly affect the favorability ratings of the police.

**Table VII. 7   Effects of Crime, Fear, and Solidarity on**
**Favorability Ratings of Police**

( Standardized ML Estimates )

| Independent Variables | Models for Favorability Ratings of Police | | | | | | | | | |
|---|---|---|---|---|---|---|---|---|---|---|
| | I | | | II | | | III | | | |
| | ( a ) | ( b ) | ( c ) | ( a ) | ( b ) | ( c ) | ( a ) | ( b ) | ( c ) | ( d ) |
| Fear | −. 271 * | −. 651 * * | −. 462 * * | −. 497 * * | −. 439 * | −. 312 * | −. 353 * * | −. 449 * | −. 319 * | |
| Violent Personal Crime | | . 746 * * | −. 968 * * | | −. 118 | −. 103 | | −. 138 | −. 359 * | −. 221 |

204

continued

| | Models for Favorability Ratings of Police | | | | | | | | | |
|---|---|---|---|---|---|---|---|---|---|---|
| | **I** | | | **II** | | | **III** | | | |
| SOL1 | .306* | .699** | | | | | | | | |
| SOL2 | | | | -.237 | -.294 | | | | | |
| SOL3 | | | | | | | .171 | .181 | | |
| Chi-square | 4.754 | | | .123 | | | .200 | | | |
| Fear | -.271* | -.106 | -.085 | -.497** | -.112 | -.090 | -.353** | -.046 | .036 | |
| General Crime Level | | -.234 | -.213 | | -.545 | .095 | | -.383 | -.064 | -.447 |
| SOL1 | .306* | .249 | | | | | | | | |
| SOL2 | | | | -.237 | -.352* | | | | | |
| SOL3 | | | | | | | .171 | .174 | | |
| Chi-square | .506 | | | 2.913 | | | 1.518 | | | |
| Fear | -.271* | -.292* | -.131* | -.497** | -.488** | -.218** | -.353** | -.344* | -.154* | |
| Commercial Burglary | | .055 | -.231* | | -.020 | -.155 | | -.021 | -.155 | -.176 |
| SOL1 | .306* | .316* | | | | | | | | |
| SOL2 | | | | -.237 | -.238 | | | | | |
| SOL3 | | | | | | | .171 | .173 | | |
| Chi-square | .071 | | | .009 | | | .010 | | | |
| Fear | -.271* | -.403** | -.141** | -.497** | -.564** | -.197** | -.353** | -.512** | -.179** | |
| Shoplifting | | .360** | -.167 | | .337* | -.144 | | .365** | -.172 | .193 |
| SOL1 | .306* | .289* | | | | | | | | |
| SOL2 | | | | -.237 | -.127 | | | | | |
| SOL3 | | | | | | | .171 | .021 | | |
| Chi-square | 3.685 | | | 2.729 | | | 2.836 | | | |

Note: SOL1 = Residents' commitment to neighborhoods

SOL2 = Residents' sense of responsibility for the neighborhoods

SOL3 = Business people's sense of responsibility for the shopping centers in the neighborhoods

Model I, II, and III are models with different types of solidarity used in the models.

Column(c)s are the indirect effects for model(b)s. The first numbers in column(c)s are the indirect effects of crimes on optimism for the favorability ratings of the police mediated by fear. The second number is the total indirect effect.

Column(d) is the total effects of crimes on the favorability ratings of the police.

* p <. 10, one-tailed test.

** p <:. 05, one-tailed test.

The results show that effects of fear on favorability ratings of the police are generally significant except in the models where general crime level is allowed to directly affect people's favorability rating of the police. The effect of fear on the police rating ranges from $-.271$ to $-.651$.

Results for the direct effects of crime on the favorability ratings of the police are mixed with only shoplifting consistently show clear significant effects. The effect ranges from $.337$ to $.365$, indicating surprisingly that shoplifting directly increases favorability ratings of the police, which is just opposite to my hypothesis. In one case, violent personal crime indicates a positive effect of $.746$ (model Ib); this can be an indication of multicollinearity because of the high correlation between fear and violent personal crime, which is $.71$. Regressing violent crime on SOL1 and fear, the R square is $.74$, which is very close to the traditional criterion $.75$ (Fisher and Mason, 1981); indicating possible multicollinearity problem and needs further confirmation. On the other hand, the total effects (column d) of general crime level and burglary on the favorability ratings of the police are negative; indicating these crimes reduces the favorability ratings of the police.

The effect of social solidarity on the favorability ratings of the police varies depending on different types of solidarity. The effects of SOL1 (model I) on the police ratings are generally significant, while the effects of SOL2 (model II), and SOL3 (model III) are generally insignificant. The hypothesis that solidarity increases the favorability ratings of the police is supported only when the index of residents' sense of commitment to the neighborhoods are used as the measure of social solidarity.

Table VII. 8 assesses the relative importance of fear, crimes, and solidarity on the favorability rating of the police, and also help to assess the stability of some coefficients. I put fear, SOL1, personal violent crime, and shoplifting into a equation and estimate equations from which I take away one at a time the least significant crime variable, and then finally the solidarity to see the stability of the effects.

**Table VII. 8  Relative Importance of Variables Influencing**
**Favorability Rating of the Police**

(Standardized Maximum Likelihood Estimates)

|  | Favorability Rating of the Police | | | |
|---|---|---|---|---|
|  | I | II | III | IV |
| Fear | −.734** | −.651** | −.271* | −.388* |
| SOL 1 | .649** | .699** | .306* |  |
| Personal Violent Crime | .680** | .746** |  |  |
| Shoplifting | .319* |  |  |  |

Note: ** p < .05, one-tailed test

* p < .10, one-tailed test

Generally consistent with the results from the replication tests reported in table VII. 7, table VII. 8 shows that fear significantly reduces the favorability rating of the police. The effect ranges from −.271 to −.734. Interestingly, personal violent crime and shoplifting directly increase the favorability rating of the police; this is in contrary to my hypotheses. Consistent with hypotheses, SOL1, residents' commitment to the neighborhoods, increases the favorability rating of the police. Fear is the most important variable affecting the favorability rating of the police.

To summarize, the results show that the total effect of crime is to reduce the favorability rating of the police; this confirms the hypothesis III. 1. In general, the general crime level and commercial burglary do not directly affect the favorability rating of the police; this is inconsistent with the hypothesis III. 2 and unexpected. Violent personal crime and shoplifting show some signs of directly increasing the favorability rating of the police; this is inconsistent with the hypothesis III. 2 and surprisingly, suggests the existence of different processes than hypothesized. Results also show that fear directly reduces the favorability rating of the police, this confirms hypothesis III. 3. Fear mediates the effects of crime on the favorability ratings of the police, this confirms hypothesis III. 4. The effects of social solidarity on the favorability rating of the police depend on types of solidarity. Residents' commitment to the neighborhood significantly increases the favorability rating of the police. But SOL2, residents' sense of responsibility for the neighborhood, and SOL 3, business people's sense of responsibility for the shopping area, do not significantly affect the favorability rating of the police, suggesting that different dimensions of solidarity have different effects on the favorability ratings of the police.

# E. Hypotheses of Crime, Fear, and Solidarity Influencing optimism of a community's Future

The tests of the hypotheses of crime, fear, and solidarity influencing optimism of a community's future, that is, hypotheses IV. 1, IV. 2, IV. 3, IV. 4, and IV. 5, are reported in this section. The optimism of a community's future model ( Figure IV. 1. 4 ) is tested by substituting different measures of social solidarity and different types of crime. Table VII. 9 shows the results from 24 replication tests. The headings and the organization are the same as before.

**Table VII. 9　Effects of Crime, Fear, and Solidarity on Optimism for Community's Future**

( Standardized ML Estimates )

| Independent Variables | Models for Optimism for Community's Future | | | | | | | | | |
| | I | | | II | | | III | | | |
| | ( a ) | ( b ) | ( c ) | ( a ) | ( b ) | ( c ) | ( a ) | ( b ) | ( c ) | ( d ) |
|---|---|---|---|---|---|---|---|---|---|---|
| Fear | -.146 | -.223 | -.159 | -.133 | -.326 | -.232 | .040 | -.364* | -.259 | |
| Violent Personal Crime | | .152 | .195 | | .395 | -.049 | | .580** | -.234 | .347 |
| SOL1 | -.570** | -.490** | | | | | | | | |
| SOL2 | | | | -.450** | -.258 | | | | | |
| SOL3 | | | | | | | -.157 | -.114 | | |
| Chi-square | 1.91 | | | 1.356 | | | 4.27 | | | |
| Fear | -.146 | -.082 | -.022 | -.133 | -.168 | -.135 | .040 | -.168 | -.135 | |

continued

| Independent Variables | Models for Optimism for Community's Future | | | | | | | | | |
|---|---|---|---|---|---|---|---|---|---|---|
| | I | | | II | | | III | | | |
| | (a) | (b) | (c) | (a) | (b) | (c) | (a) | (b) | (c) | (d) |
| General Crime Level | | −.091 | .241 | | .050 | .100 | | .259 | −.109 | .150 |
| SOL1 | −.570** | −.592** | | | | | | | | |
| SOL2 | | | | −.450** | −.440** | | | | | |
| SOL3 | | | | | | | −.157 | −.159 | | |
| Chi-square | .081 | | | .022 | | | .576 | | | |
| Fear | −.146 | −.134 | −.060 | −.133 | −.148 | −.066 | .040 | −.001 | −.0005 | |
| Commercial Burglary | | −.033 | .123 | | .038 | .052 | | .090 | .001 | .090 |
| SOL1 | −.570** | −.575** | | | | | | | | |
| SOL2 | | | | −.450** | −.447** | | | | | |
| SOL3 | | | | | | | −.157 | −.165 | | |
| Chi-square | .027 | | | .032 | | | .091 | | | |
| Fear | −.146 | −.228 | −.079 | −.133 | −.147 | −.051 | .040 | −.101 | −.035 | |
| Shoplifting | | .223 | −.026 | | .070 | .127 | | .326* | −.129 | .197 |
| SOL1 | −.570** | −.580** | | | | | | | | |
| SOL2 | | | | −.450** | −.428** | | | | | |
| SOL3 | | | | | | | −.157 | −.292 | | |
| Chi-square | 1.437 | | | .107 | | | 1.882 | | | |

Note: SOL1 = Residents' commitment to neighborhoods

SOL2 = Residents' sense of responsibility for the neighborhoods

SOL3 = Business people's sense of responsibility for the shopping centers in the neighborhoods

Model I, II, and III are models with different types of solidarity used in the models.

Column (c) s are the indirect effects for model (b) s. The first numbers in column (c) s are the indirect effects of crimes optimism for community's future on mediated by fear. The second number is the total indirect effect.

Column (d) is the total effects of crimes on optimism for community's future.

* p <. 10, one-tailed test.

** p <. 05, one-tailed test.

The results indicate that the effects of fear on the optimism of a community's future are negative; this is consistent with the hypothesis that fear reduces the optimism of a community's future. However, the effects are generally insignificant.

The hypothesis that fear reduces the optimism of a community's future is not strongly supported; indicating that contrary to the hypotheses, people's optimism may not directly affected very much by fear of crime.

The direct effect of crime on optimism of a community's future is generally insignificant. An exception is the model III b, where violent personal crime shows a significant positive effect of . 580. This single case may be abnormal. In general, the total effect(column d) of crime on optimism of a community's future is surprisingly positive; indicating that crime increases the optimism of a community's future.

Different from the hypotheses, the effects of social solidarity varies depending on the types of solidarity in the model. Contrary to hypotheses, SOL1, as measured by residents' commitment to neighborhoods, and SOL2, as measured by residents' sense of responsibility for the neighborhood, generally show a negative effect on the optimism of a community's future(model I); but the effects of SOL3 are all insignificant. The greater Sol 1 and Sol 2, the lower the optimism of the community's future.

Table VII. 10 reports the results for assessing the relative importance of fear, crimes, and solidarity on optimism of a community's future. The first equation includes fear, SOL1, SOL2, and personal violent crime as independent variables because these variables have shown significant effects on optimism of a community's future in the replication tests reported in Table VII. 9. In the following equations I keep fear in the equation, take away one at a time the least significant variable, and reestimate the model.

**Table VII. 10　Relative Importance of Variables Influencing**
**Optimism of A community's Future**

(Standardized Maximum Likelihood Estimates)

| | Optimism of A community's Future | | | |
| --- | --- | --- | --- | --- |
| | I | II | III | IV |
| Fear | −. 219 | −. 187 | −. 133 | . 073 |

continued

| | Optimism of A community's Future | | | |
|---|---|---|---|---|
| | I | II | III | IV |
| SOL1 | −. 450* | −. 478** | −. 450** | |
| SOL2 | −. 148 | −. 167 | | |
| Personal Violent Crime | . 072 | | | |

Note: ** p <. 05, one-tailed test

　　　* p <. 10, one-tailed test

Consistent with the results from the replication tests, table VII. 10 shows that the effect of fear on optimism of a community's future is insignificant. SOL1, residents' commitment to the neighborhoods, increases optimism of a community's future. Personal violent crime does not directly affect optimism of a community's future.

To summarize, the results show that the total effect of crime is to increase the optimism of a community's future; this disconfirms the hypothesis IV. 1. In general, crime does not directly affect the optimism of a community's future; this is consistent with the hypothesis IV. 2. Fear does not significantly reduces the optimism of a community's future; the hypothesis IV. 3 is not confirmed. So fear does not significantly mediate the effects of crime on the optimism of a community's future; the hypothesis IV. 4 is not confirmed. Residents' commitment to their neighborhood and their sense of responsibility for their neighborhood decrease optimism of a community's future; this disconfirms hypothesis IV. 5.

# F. Summary of Hypothesis Testing for Consequences of Crime

The results for the effects of crime on consequences confirm some hypotheses, are mixed for some hypotheses, and disconfirm some others. For some consequences, the results show some patterns; but for some others, the patterns are less clear.

The results for the satisfaction model are most clear. In general, four hypotheses are supported, and one is not. The results show that the total effect of crime is to reduce satisfaction with living and doing business in the area; this confirms the hypothesis I. 1. Crime does not directly reduce people's satisfaction; this confirms the hypothesis I. 2. Fear directly reduces satisfaction; this confirms the hypothesis I. 3. Fear mediates the effect of crimes on satisfaction; this confirms the hypothesis I. 4. Allowing crime to directly affect satisfaction, the effect is insignificant. The corresponding chi-square change is also insignificant, and this confirms the conclusion that crime does not directly reduce satisfaction. Testing the model with different measures of crime and solidarity, the pattern stays same; the effects are quite stable. However, the effect of solidarity on satisfaction is consistently insignificant; the hypothesis I. 5 is not confirmed.

For the business stability model, the patterns are more complex. The results show that the total effect of crime is to reduce business stability; this confirms the hypothesis II. 1. The direct effects on business stability, violent personal crime and general crime level show very different effects from that of property crimes. In general, violent personal crime and general crime level do not directly affect business stability. Surprisingly, commercial burglary and shoplift directly increase business stability; this is inconsistent with the hypothesis II. 2. Fear directly reduces business stability; this confirms the hypothesis II. 3. Fear mediates the effects of crime on business stability; this confirms the hypothesis II. 4. The effects of solidarity on business stability vary with different types of solidarity. While the effects of residents' commitment and sense of responsibility for the neighborhood on business stability are insignificant, the effect of business people's responsibility for the shopping areas on business stability is significant at $p < .10$ level; this is consistent with the hypothesis II. 5.

For the favorability rating of the police model, the patterns are less clear than the satisfaction and business stability models. The results show that the total effect of crime is to reduce the favorability rating of the police; this confirms the hypothesis III. 1. In general, the general crime level and commercial burglary do not directly affect the favorability rating of the police; this is consistent with the hypothesis III. 2. While the effects of crime are mixed, shoplifting show some signs of directly increasing the favorability rating of the police; this is contrary to the hypothesis III. 2. Fear directly reduces the favorability rating of the police; this confirms the hypothesis III. 3. Fear mediates the effects of crime on favorability rating of the police; this confirms the hypothesis III. 4. The effects of social solidarity on the favorability rating of the police depend on type of solidarity. Residents' commitment to the neighborhood significantly increases the favorability rating of the police. SOL2, residents'sense of responsibility for the neighborhood, and SOL3, business people's sense of responsibility for the shopping area, do not significantly affect the favorability rating of the police. Fear is the most important variable affecting the favorability rating of the police.

The patterns for the optimism of a community's future model are the most unexpected. Most hypotheses are not supported. The results show that the total effect of crime is to increase the optimism of a community's future; this disconfirms the hypothesis IV. 1. In general, crime does not directly affect the optimism of a community's future; this is consistent with the hypothesis IV. 2. Fear does not significantly reduce the optimism of a community's future; the hypothesis IV. 3 are not confirmed. So Fear does not significantly mediate the effects of crime on the optimism of a community's future; the hypothesis IV. 4 is not confirmed. Residents' commitment to their neighborhood and their sense of responsibility for their neighborhood decrease optimism of a community's future; this is opposite to the hypothesis IV. 5.

To compare results across different consequence models, the results show that the effects of fear and solidarity vary, and some patterns seem to appear. As expected, fear significantly reduces satisfaction, the business stability, and the favorability ratings of the police. But its effect on the optimism of the community's future is insignificant; this is unexpected. The effects of solidarity on different consequences is mixed; most of them are not significant, indicating that solidarity, in most situations, does not affect consequences as expected, except in a few situations. SOL1, the residents' commitment to the neighborhood, significantly increase the favorability ratings of the police; SOL3, the sense of the business people's responsibility, significantly increases business stability. However, in contrary to the hypotheses, SOL1 significantly reduces the optimism of the community's future; and SOL2, the sense of residents' responsibility for the neighborhood, significantly reduces the optimism for the community's future.

# Chapter VIII. Results for Crime Influencing Solidarity

Durkheim proposes that crime increases social solidarity while fear research consistently reports that crime produces fear which directly or indirectly decreases solidarity. To resolve the contradictory arguments on whether crime increases or decreases social solidarity, I suggest that we must consider the structural component of solidarity, the shared interests, and we should distinguish and test the relative effect of different types of crimes. The direct effects of violent crime and nonviolent crime are different. I propose several hypotheses:

V. 1. Violent crime produces fear.

V. 2. Nonviolent crime does not directly affect fear.

V. 3. Violent crime reduces social solidarity.

V. 4. Nonviolent crime increases social solidarity.

I estimate the effects of violent and nonviolent crime on fear, and the effects of violent and nonviolent crime on each of the three different types of social solidarity. Among the four measures of crime that are included in our data ( violent personal crime, general crime level, commercial burglary, and shoplifting) , violent personal crime is the most reasonable measure for violent crime, and shoplifting is the most reasonable measure for nonviolent crime. So we examine how violent

215

personal crime affects fear and solidarity, and how shoplifting affects fear and solidarity.

Table VIII. 1 reports the effects of violent personal crime, general crime level, commercial burglary, and shoplifting on fear. I first regress fear on all the crimes, and then take away one at a time the one variable with the least effect. The results show that personal violent crime significantly produces fear ( . 286 to. 330 ) ; this confirms the hypothesis V. 1. The direct effect of shoplifting on fear is insignificant ( . 118, t = . 927 ) ; this confirms the hypothesis V. 2. Also, the results show that the general crime level has significant effects on fear ( Table VIII. 1 ) ; this indicates that if no distinction between violent and nonviolent crime is made, crime in general will produce fear, as the fear of crime literature suggests.

**Table VIII. 1   Effects of Crimes on Fear**

( Standardized ML Estimates )

| Crime | Fear | | |
|---|---|---|---|
| | I | II | III |
| Violent Personal Crime | . 286 * <br> ( 1. 695 ) | . 330 * * <br> ( 1. 998 ) | . 321 * * <br> ( 2. 101 ) |
| General Crime Level | . 603 * * <br> ( 2. 898 ) | . 569 * * <br> ( 2. 728 ) | . 589 * * <br> ( 3. 858 ) |
| Commercial Burglary | −. 036 <br> ( −. 214 ) | . 023 <br> ( . 143 ) | |
| Shoplifting | . 118 <br> ( . 927 ) | | |

Note: * * p <. 05, one-tailed test

     * p <. 10, one-tailed test

To test hypothesis V. 3 that violent crime reduces social solidarity and hypothesis V. 4 that nonviolent crime increases social solidarity, I regress different types of social solidarity on the different types of crime and fear. For each type of solidarity, I first let fear and all crimes affect solidarity, then take away, one at a time, the least significant or least important crime, and reestimate the model. The results are reported in Table VIII. 2 , VIII. 3 and VIII. 4.

### Table VIII. 2   Effects of Crimes and Fear on Social Solidarity

(Standardized ML Estimates)

|  | SOL1 | | |
|---|---|---|---|
|  | I | II | III |
| Fear | .461* | .446** | .466** |
| Violent Personal Crime | −1.004** | −1.014** | −.988** |
| Commercial Burglary | −.374* | −.389** | −.330** |
| Shoplifting | .183 | .188 | |
| General Crime Level | −.036 | | |

Note: ** p <.05 , one-tailed test

      * p <.10 , one-tailed test

### Table VIII. 3   Effects of Crimes and Fear on Social Solidarity

(Standardized ML Estimates)

|  | SOL2 | | |
|---|---|---|---|
|  | I | II | III |
| Fear | .347 | .374 | .180 |
| Violent Personal Crime | −.712** | −.709** | −.764** |
| Shoplifting | −.269* | −.270* | −.266* |
| General Crime Level | −.284 | −.289 | |
| Commercial Burglary | −.005 | | |

Note: ** p <.05 , one-tailed test

      * p <.10 , one-tailed test

### Table VIII. 4   Effects of Crimes and Fear on Social Solidarity

(Standardized ML Estimates)

|  | SOL3 | | |
|---|---|---|---|
|  | I | II | III |
| Fear | −.301 | −.293 | −.243 |
| Violent Personal Crime | −.249 | −.186 | −.172 |

continued

| | SOL3 | | |
|---|---|---|---|
| | I | II | III |
| Shoplifting | . 498 * * | . 456 * * | . 455 * * |
| General Crime Level | . 203 | . 074 | |
| Commercial Burglary | −. 146 | | |

Note: * * p <. 05 , one-tailed test

* p <. 10 , one-tailed test

For SOL1 ( residents' commitment to their neighborhood ) , the results ( Table VIII. 2 ) show that for three models, I, II, and III, coefficients of violent personal crime on SOL1 are − 1, − 1, and − . 98 respectively. These indicate possible multicollinearity problems caused by high correlation between violent crime and fear, which has been discussed before. But the coefficients in all three equations consistently show the same direction and similar magnitude; this reflects some stability. So with caution in mind, I tentatively conclude that violent crime reduces SOL1; this is consistent with hypothesis V. 3. The results show that shoplifting does not significantly affect SOL1; the hypothesis V. 4 is not confirmed, suggesting the theoretical idea is not supported.

For SOL2 ( residents' sense of responsibility for their neighborhood ) , the results ( Table VIII. 3 ) show that violent personal crime significantly reduces SOL2; the hypothesis V. 3 is confirmed. The results show that shoplifting significantly reduces SOL2; the hypothesis V. 4 is rejected, suggesting the theoretical idea could be incorrect.

For SOL3 ( the sense of responsibility of business people for the shopping area ) , the results ( Table VIII. 4 ) show that violent personal crime does not significantly reduces SOL3; the hypothesis V. 3 is not confirmed. The results show that shoplifting significantly increases SOL3; the hypothesis V. 4 is confirmed. Considering that SOL3 only asks questions from business people about the shopping area and it does not indicate a community wide solidarity, this result only shows that shoplifting reminds business people's of their shared interests and stimulates their sense of responsibility for the shopping areas, that is, shoplifting mainly stimulates the structural element of solidarity.

To summarize, violent personal crime increases fear as hypothesized; shoplifting does not significantly affect fear as hypothesized. When we do not make distinctions between violent and nonviolent crime, the results suggest that the general crime increase fear as the fear literature suggests. The effects of fear and crimes on social solidarity vary for different types of social solidarity. In general, hypothesis V. 3, that violent crime (measured as resident reported violent personal crime) reduces social solidarity is supported but the effect is not significant for business solidarity. The results for hypothesis V. 4, that nonviolent crime (shoplifting) increase solidarity is not supported when measures of solidarity for residents are used; however, the results show that shoplifting significantly increases SOL3, the sense of responsibility of business people for the shopping area, so hypothesis V. 4 is confirmed for business people. These results suggest that the measures of solidarity are taping different aspects of solidarity; they reflect the different dimensions of solidarity which respond differently to fear and crime.

# Chapter IX. Nonrecursive model

## A. Theoretical Exploration of Nonrecursive Models

The fear literature, though not conclusive, mostly reports that fear is negatively related to social cohesion. As discussed in Chapter III, there is a controversy as to the causal relationship between fear and social solidarity. Some research suggests fear reduces solidarity; some suggests social solidarity reduces fear. Although both sides suggest a negative unidirectional relation between fear and social solidarity, they disagree on which is the cause and which is the consequence.

The controversy suggests that there can be a possible reciprocal relation between fear and solidarity. While fear affects solidarity, as the recursive theoretical model suggests, solidarity could also affect fear. To solve the controversy, we should estimate a nonrecursive model in which the effect of fear on solidarity and the effect of solidarity on fear are estimated simultaneously.

Also, it can be worthwhile to explore the possibility of reciprocal effects between solidarity and the consequences, to see if there are effects of satisfaction on social solidarity, of business stability on social solidarity, of the favorability rating of the police on social solidarity, and of optimism of a community's future on social solidarity.

Unfortunately, as stated before, there are very few studies at the aggregate level involving theoretical concepts such as fear, social solidarity, satisfaction with life and doing business in an area, business stability, the favorability rating of the police, and optimism of the community's future. No suitable data set is available to test the nonrecursive model, which requires that the number of parameters to be estimated simultaneously to at least ten. That is, in addition to the six structural parameters, at least two instrumental variables are needed for the estimation of the reciprocal effect. This adds four more parameters to the estimation (one direct effect from each of the two instruments and one variance for each of the two instrumental variables) (See Figure IX.1). The asymptotic properties of the ML estimators require that the sample size is large relative to the number of free parameters to be estimated. According to Bentler guideline, for ML estimator, the ratio of the sample size to the number of free parameters to be estimated can go as low as 5:1 (Bentler 1989).

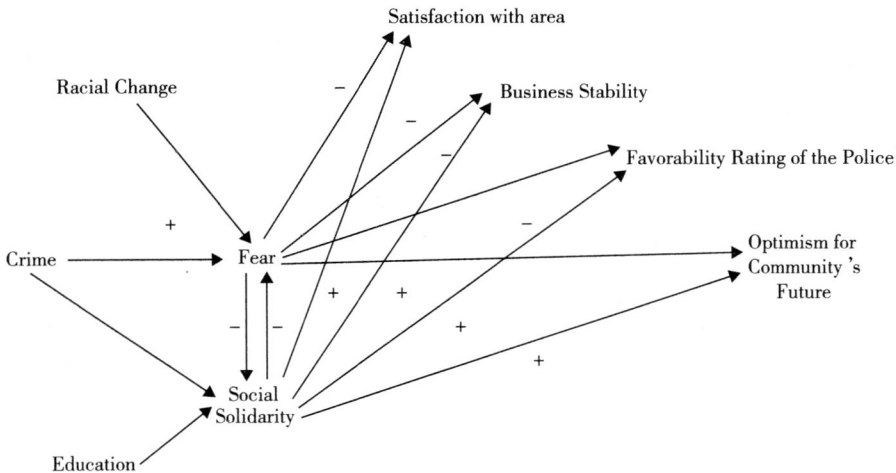

**Figure IX. 1　Estimating the Nonrecursive Model**

Because no adequate data set is available for a confident testing of the nonrecursive model, we are facing a situation that we either do some explorative work with caution to try to increase our understanding of the causal relationship, or

221

do nothing but wait for the emergence of a suitable data set. These data sets are unlikely to become available in the near future, because most data sets at the aggregate levels are very unlikely to include variables such as fear and solidarity. Also, it is very expensive to collect data at the individual level from very many geographic aggregates or communities. Only with data collected from very many different geographic aggregate units, such as cities and communities, can we aggregate the individual data to the aggregate level to acquire a large number of cases. In any case, explorative work is always valuable; it can contribute ideas to future research. For example, the theoretical discussion on adequate instrumental variables will contribute ideas to future research in selecting instrumental variables for further possible surveys.

For these reasons, I will try some very preliminary tests with the data set. Also, because of the very small sample size, namely, because of the extremely low ratio between the parameters that have to be estimated to the number of the cases in the sample, the statistical power of the test may be too low to pick up effects. It is expected that sizable effects may be insignificant.

To estimate the reciprocal effect between two variables, instrumental variables are needed for each of the two variables affecting each other. To estimate the reciprocal effects between fear and solidarity, I need to have at least one instrumental variable for fear, and at least one instrumental variable for social solidarity. An instrumental variable for fear should cause fear and not cause solidarity. Similarly, an instrumental variable for social solidarity should cause social solidarity and not cause fear. Often it is difficult to find instruments that empirically fit these requirements because of the idiosyncratic nature of data sets, although theoretically some variables were thought to fit. This often makes estimating reciprocal relationship difficult empirically. So from a practical point of view, we can start by examining the correlation matrix, looking for potential candidates for instrumental variables. The candidate instrumental variable for fear should be highly and significantly correlated with fears, therefore possibly a cause of fear. But its correlation with solidarity should be statistically insignificant so that it can not be a cause of solidarity. The candidate instrumental variable for social solidarity should be highly and significantly correlated with social solidarity but insignificantly correlated with fear so that it can be a cause of solidarity but not a cause of fear. These are the variables that are most likely to empirically fit the definition of the instrument variables.

I started from theoretical considerations and then checked the correlations to look for instrumental variables for fear. Considerable research has been focused on the characteristics indicative of individual vulnerability to crime. With a few exceptions ( e. g. Lebowitz, 1975 ) , research at the individual level consistently finds that sex and age are strongly related to fear of crime ( Clemente and Kleiman, 1977 ; Baumer, 1978 ; Skogan and Maxfield, 1981 ; stafford and Galle, 1984 ; Van der Wurff, Adri et. al. , 1989 ; Parker, and Ray, 1990 ; Parker, 1988 ; Sharp, and Dodder, 1985 ; LaGrange, and Ferraro, 1987 ; Liska, Sanchirco, and Reed, 1988 etc. ). Women and the elderly are more fearful because they are more vulnerable. Some research also finds that the socially vulnerable groups, such as the poor and the nonwhites, have higher fear than others ( Skogan and Maxfield, 1981 ; Clemente and Keiman, 1977 ; Yin, 1985 ; Kennedy and Silverman, 1985 ; Miethe and Lee, 1984 ; Baumer, 1985 etc. ).

Despite these conclusions at the individual level, however, in our data set at the aggregate level, gender, age, and race are not highly correlated with fear. The correlation between gender and the composite measure of fear is $-.16$; it is not statistically significant. So gender cannot be used as an instrumental variable for fear. In the current data set, the correlation between age and the composite measure of fear is $.34$; and it is not significant. This indicates that age can not be used as an instrumental variable for fear.

Some research also finds that the socially vulnerable groups, such as the nonwhites, have higher fear than others. In the current data set, the correlation between race and fear is $.01$. It is also insignificant. It shows that in this survey, the proportion of minority in a neighborhood dose not strongly correlate with fear at a neighborhood level. Race is also not highly correlated with any dimension of social solidarity; the correlation of race with resident's commitment to the community is .02, the correlation of race with residents' sense of responsibility is .19, and the correlation of race with business people's sense of responsibility is .14. None of them is statistically significant. Because race is neither significantly correlated with fear nor solidarity, it can not be used as an adequate instrumental variable for fear or solidarity.

The data set offers only one variable that can be used as an instrumental variable forfear that is racial change. A high level of fear is reported in the places where racial change and racial conflict occur rather than in stabilized communities. The survey question for racial change asks residents: How has the racial composition of this neighborhood changed in the past two years or so? Would you say there has been a: large decrease in minorities···1; small decrease···2; stayed the same···3; small increase···4; large increase in minorities···5. The correlation of racial change with the composite index of fear is .44, and it is significant. On the other hand, racial change is not highly correlated with any dimension of social solidarity; the correlation of racial change with resident's commitment to the community is .09, with residents' sense of responsibility is .01, and with business people's sense of responsibility significant. is −.14. None of them is statistically significant.

In sum, the theoretical consideration and empirical data offer us one possible instrumental variable for fear in the test of the reciprocal relationship between fear and social solidarity, which is racial change in a community.

To test the reciprocal relationship between fear and social solidarity, we also need instrumental variables for social solidarity. As discussed before, empirically the variables should be significantly correlated with social solidarity but only weakly correlated with fear. In looking for instrumental variables for social solidarity, we have little research to turn to for suggestions. There are quite a few studies on the causal relationships between fear and solidarity, but little research suggests variables which cause solidarity, but not fear.

Outside of fear research, we can argue that social disorganization theories are related to the concept of social solidarity. We can recognize that among them there are some important commonalities. Both are concerned about a particular state of the community: social integration. The concept of disorganization can be considered similar to the destruction of social integration. But most variables that cause social disorganization are very likely to also cause crime and fear. This suggests that it can be difficult to find instrumental variables for solidarity based on disorganization theory. So the research on testing the reciprocal effect between social solidarity and fear could have a special empirical difficulty. There are two variables included in the current data set that can be used as poverty measures, one is house type, and the other is employment. The house type is both highly correlated with fear and solidarity; and employment is both weekly correlated with fear and solidarity, and the correlations are insignificant. This hinders the variables from being used as instrumental variables.

However, in the current data set I have a variable, education, that is not suggested by theoretical considerations, but empirically, has a moderate correlation with SOL1 ( $-.47$ ), the resident's commitment to the community. It is weakly correlated with fear( $-.15$ ) ; the correlation is not significant; therefore, it is not a cause of fear. So although theoretically not very clear, for an exploratory purpose, I use it as an instrumental variable for SOL1, and perform an exploratory test for the relationship between fear and SOL1.

In sum, the only possible instrumental variable for fear is racial change. In searching for instrumental variables for solidarity, the data provide no adequate instrumental variables that are theoretically clear. However, the data set does provide one variable that is empirically promises to be an instrument of SOL1; it is educational level. In this explorative test, general crime level is used as the measure of crime, because it best reflects crime in general. I also use personal violent crime as the measure of crime to retest the model and to check the stability of the coefficients. The nonrecursive model is diagramed in Figure IX. 1.

## B. Model Identification

To estimate structural equation models, identification of the model must be first established. The estimation process is a process by which we reach a solution for the unknown parameters of the structural equation models. We must establish whether unique values exist for these unknown parameters of the structural equation models before estimation.

Identification is demonstrated by showing that the unknown parameters are functions only of the identified parameters and that these functions lead to unique solutions. If this can be done, the unknown parameters are identified; otherwise, one or more parameters are unidentified. To demonstrate identification of a structural equation model is to demonstrate that a unique solution exists for the unknown parameters in terms of the known parameters, such as variances and covariance of the observed variables, for which consistent sample estimators are readily available.

Identification is not a problem of the sample and not a problem of too few cases. It is defined in terms of the population parameters. The population covariance matrix is the source of identified information. The parameters refer to population, not sample values. An unidentified model can not have a unique solution for the unknown parameters, no matter how big the sample. So the issue has nothing to do with sample size. Model identification sometimes can be very easily established, but sometime it can be complex. For nonrecursive models, the order condition and rank conditions are most widely used to establish model identification. Our nonrecursive model to be tested is a multiequation system consisting of three equations:

$$Y1 = 0 \quad + \quad b12Y2 \quad + \quad 0 \quad + \quad r11X1 \quad + \quad r12X2 \quad + \quad 0 \quad + \quad D1$$

$$Y2 = b21\,Y1 + \quad 0 \quad + \quad 0 \quad + \quad r21\,X1 \quad + \quad 0 \quad + \quad r23\,X3 \quad + \quad D2$$

$$Y3 = b31\,Y1 + \quad b32\,Y2 \quad + \quad 0 \quad + \quad 0 \quad + \quad 0 \quad + \quad 0 \quad + \quad D3$$

In matrix form, the equation system is written as:

$$\begin{bmatrix} Y1 \\ Y2 \\ Y3 \end{bmatrix} = \begin{bmatrix} 0 & b12 & 0 \\ b21 & 0 & 0 \\ b31 & b12 & 0 \end{bmatrix} \begin{bmatrix} Y1 \\ Y2 \\ Y3 \end{bmatrix} + \begin{bmatrix} r11 & r12 & 0 \\ r21 & 0 & r23 \\ 0 & 0 & 0 \end{bmatrix} \begin{bmatrix} X1 \\ X1 \\ X1 \end{bmatrix} + \begin{bmatrix} D1 \\ D1 \\ D1 \end{bmatrix}$$

$$c = \left[ \begin{array}{ccc|ccc} 0 & -b12 & 0 & -r11 & -r12 & 0 \\ -b21 & 0 & 0 & -r21 & 0 & -r23 \\ -b31 & -b12 & 0 & 0 & 0 & 0 \end{array} \right]$$

The order condition can be stated as: A necessary condition for an equation to be identified is that the number of variables excluded from the equation be at least p−1, where p is the number of dependent variable Y's in the model ( Bollen, 1989 ). If all the equations in the model are identified, then the model is identified. For the nonrecursive model under testing, the p, number of Y's is 3; p−1 = 2. The first row of C has 3 zeros; that is more than 2; it meets the order condition; so the first equation in the system is identified. The second row has 3 zeros; that is more than 2; it meets the order condition; so the second equation in the system is identified. The third row has 4 zeros; that is more than 2; it meets the order condition; so the third equation in the system is also identified. Since all the equations are identified, the model can be identified. The application of the order condition gives us a quick check of the identification status of the model, but the order condition is a necessary condition. For a model to be identified, it must satisfy the necessary condition. I apply the rank condition to further ensure the identification status of the nonrecursive model.

The rank condition starts with $C = [ ( I - B ) \mid - R ]$ also. To check the identification of the ith equation, I delete all columns of C that do not have zeros in the ith row of C, and use the remaining columns to form a new matrix, Ci. The rank condition states that a necessary and sufficient condition for the identification of the ith equation is that the rank of Ci equals( p−1 ) ( Bollen, 1989 ). To examine the identification of the first equation, we form the matrix C1 from C by deleting all columns of C that do not have zeros in the first row of C. Similarly, we form the matrix C2 from C by deleting all columns of C that do not have zeros in the second row of C. We form the matrix C3 from C by deleting all columns of C that do not have zeros in the third row of C. So the C1, C2, and C3 are:

$$c1 = \begin{bmatrix} 0 & 0 \\ 0 & -r23 \\ 1 & 0 \end{bmatrix}$$

$$c2 = \begin{bmatrix} 0 & -r12 \\ 0 & 0 \\ 1 & 0 \end{bmatrix}$$

$$c3 = \begin{bmatrix} -r11 & -r12 & 0 \\ -r21 & 0 & -r23 \\ 0 & 0 & 0 \end{bmatrix}$$

The rank of a matrix or vector is the number of independent rows and columns. The ranks of C1, C2, and C3 all equal 2. For the nonrecursive model under testing, the p, number of Y's is 3; $P-1=2$. The rank condition for the ith equation is that the rank of Ci equals $(p-1)$, we have the rank of each $ci = p-1 = 2$. So all the equations in the system are identified.

In sum, I applied the order condition and the rank condition to our nonrecursive model, and the identification status of the model is demonstrated.

# C. Results and Conclusion

The nonrecursive model tested is shown in Figure IX. 1. The model includes four submodels for each of the consequences: satisfaction, business stability, the favorability rating of the police, and optimism of the community's future. Table IX. 1 shows the results of the analyses of each of these four models. Each of the four models is a simultaneous equation system composed of three equations; one equation in which fear is the dependent variable, one equation in which solidarity is the dependent variable, and the other in which one of the four social consequences are the dependent variables.

**Table IX. 1  Nonrecursive Model**

(Standardized ML Estimates)

| | | | Nonrecursive Models | | | |
|---|---|---|---|---|---|---|
| | | | I | II | III | IV |
| | FEAR | SOL1 | SAT | BST | PLO | OPT |
| Fear | | -. 777 | -. 653 | -. 527 | -. 271 | -. 146 |
| | | -1. 317 | -4. 246 | -2. 863 | -1. 382 | -. 772 |
| Solidarity | . 405 | | . 154 | . 090 | . 306 | -. 570 |
| | 1. 156 | | . 986 | . 479 | 1. 537 | -2. 959 |
| General Crime | 1. 007 | . 134 | | | | |
| | 4. 524 | . 266 | | | | |
| Racial Change | . 002 | | | | | |
| | . 014 | | | | | |
| Education | | -. 600 | | | | |
| | | -3. 012 | | | | |
| Chi-square | | | 12. 25 | 8. 795 | 7. 893 | 9. 239 |
| df | | | 6 | 6 | 6 | 6 |
| p | | | . 057 | . 185 | . 246 | . 161 |
| BBNFI | | | . 840 | . 865 | . 871 | . 856 |
| BBNNFI | | | . 747 | . 860 | . 897 | . 835 |
| CFI | | | . 899 | . 944 | . 959 | . 934 |

Note: SAT = satisfaction with life and doing business in the area

　　　BST = Business stability

　　　POL = Favorability ratings of the police

　　　OPT = The optimism of a community's future

　　　SOLI = Residents' commitment to the neighborhoods

　　　df = Degree of freedom

　　　BBNFI = Bentler-Bonett normed fit index

　　　BBNNFI = Bentler-Bonett nonnormed fit index

　　　CFI = Comparative fit index

In each submodel, which includes one social consequence as dependent variable, I allow fear to affect solidarity, and allow solidarity to affect fear; using racial change as the instrumental variable for fear and using education as the instrumental variable for solidarity(see Table IX. 1). The remaining part of the model is the same as the recusive models that we tested before.

The results indicate that fear reduces solidarity; this is consistent with the theoretical hypothesis. The standardized coefficient is $-.777$; $t = -1.317$. For a one tailed test with the degree of freedom $= n - 3 - 1 = 4$, the critical t value for the significant test at $p < .10$ is 1.325. So the effect is almost significant. Considering that the sample is extreme small with a ratio of cases to the number of parameter about 2 : 1; we can expected that a big effect of $-.777$ may still fail to be significant.

In the recusive models, the hypothesis that fear reduces social solidarity is inconclusive. In the tests using SOL1 as dependent variable, the hypothesis is rejected; the coefficient for the effect of fear on SOL1 is about. 45(Table VIII. 2). Comparing the coefficients obtained from the recusive model, about. 45, and the nonrecusive model, $-.777$, we can see that the effect changes dramatically.

The results also indicate a sizeable effect of solidarity on fear; the coefficient is. 405. Contrary to my hypothesis, the result shows that social solidarity increases fear, rather than reduces fear as the unidirectional research has suggested. Again, although the effect size is moderate, the t (1.156) fails to be statistically significant. Considering the extremely small sample, this is expected.

In Table IX. 1, two values need attention. One, the effect of general crime on fear is 1.007; a standardized coefficient exceeding 1 often signifies multicollinearity problem. If that is the case, the coefficients could be unstable and untrustworthy. Two, the effect of racial change on fear is. 002, insignificant. Racial change is the instrument of fear; it is expected to have a sizable effect on fear. These results call for further checking on the stability and robustness of the results.

In sum, the models fit the data. The results are consistent with the hypothesis that fear reduces solidarity. Different from past research on the causal relationship between fear and solidarity, the results report that solidarity positively affects fear; other parts of the model show the same pattern as for the recursive model. Crime produces fear, fear negatively affects all the consequences; the coefficients stay the same, and the t values change slightly. Solidarity has the same effects on the consequences as in the recursive model, and the t values change slightly. However, to increase confidence in the results, further checks of the stability of the results are called for.

To further check the stability of the results, I changed some measures in the model, and retested the model. The only possible change the data allows is to change the measure of crime, because we have only one measure of solidarity which has only one available instrument, one available instrument for fear, and one composite index for satisfaction, business stability, the favorability rating of the police, and optimism of a community's future.

I changed the measure of crime from general crime to violent personal crime, and retested the same four nonrecursive models. The results are presented in Table IX. 2. The results indicate that fear reduces solidarity; this is consistent with the theoretical hypothesis and consistent with the model and results in Table IX. 1. The standardized coefficient is $-.264$; $t = -.693$; it fails to be significant.

**Table IX. 2 Checking Stability of theNonrecursive Model**

( Standardized ML Estimates )

| | | | Nonrecursive Models | | | |
|---|---|---|---|---|---|---|
| | | | I | II | III | IV |
| | FEAR | SOL1 | SAT | BST | PLO | OPT |
| Fear | | $-.264$ | $-.653$ | $-.527$ | $-.271$ | $-.146$ |
| | | $-.693$ | $-4.185$ | $-2.821$ | $-1.362$ | $-.760$ |
| Solidarity | .352 | | .154 | .090 | .306 | $-.570$ |
| | 1.035 | | .948 | .461 | 1.478 | $-2.847$ |

continued

| | | | Nonrecursive Models | | | |
|---|---|---|---|---|---|---|
| | | I | II | III | IV |
| | FEAR | SOL1 | SAT | BST | PLO | OPT |
| Violent Personal Crime | .919 | -.446 | | | | |
| | 3.652 | -1.501 | | | | |
| Racial Change | .255 | | | | | |
| | 1.843 | | | | | |
| Education | | -.417 | | | | |
| | | -2.552 | | | | |
| Chi-square | | | 10.54 | 7.143 | 9.534 | 7.233 |
| df | | | 6 | 6 | 6 | 6 |
| p | | | .104 | .307 | .145 | .299 |
| BBNFI | | | .867 | .894 | .858 | .891 |
| BBNNFI | | | .823 | .946 | .830 | .940 |
| CFI | | | .929 | .978 | .932 | .976 |

Note: SAT = satisfaction with life and doing business in the area

BST = Business stability

POL = Favorability ratings of the police

OPT = The optimism of a community's future

SOL1 = Residents' commitment to the neighborhoods

df = Degree of freedom

BBNFI = Bentler-Bonett normed fit index

BBNNFI = Bentler-Bonett nonnormed fit index

CFI = Comparative fit index

The results also indicate a sizeable effect of solidarity on fear; the coefficient is .352; showing that social solidarity increases fear, rather than reduces fear as the unidirectional research suggests. Again, although the effect size is moderate, the t (1.035) fails to be statistically significant. Considering the extremely small sample, this is expected.

Other coefficients generally follow the same pattern as the results from the analyses of the recursive models and from the original nonrecursive model in Table

IX. 1. The effect of crime on fear is positive, high and significant.

In sum, the models for the stability test fit the data (Table IX. 2). The results reveal the same pattern as the test results in Table IX. 1. Fear negatively affects solidarity; solidarity positively affects fear; fear negatively affects all the consequences, the coefficients stay the same, and the t values change slightly; solidarity has the same effects on the consequences as before, and the t value changes slightly; violent crime produces fear and reduces solidarity. The results are generally stable.

To conclude, I find that when estimating the causal relationship from fear to solidarity and solidarity to fear, simultaneously, the results indicate a negative effect of fear on solidarity. This is consistent with past research. However, the results also indicate a sizable positive effect of solidarity on fear. After changing the measure of crime and retest the model, the results reveal the same pattern. Past research has not tested the reciprocal effect.

Past research reports that solidarity reduces fear and the lack of cohesion increases fear; therefore, increasing people's commitment to their neighborhood can be an important way of reducing fear. Many public fear reduction programs are designed to increase interactions among individuals and to increase individuals' commitment to the neighborhood in the hopes for reducing crime and fear.

My results from the nonrecursive model here suggest the opposite conclusion: the residents' commitment to their neighborhood increases their fear. This is theoretically interesting and has important policy implications.

I speculate that perhaps this is because those who have higher levels of commitment to their neighborhood are more sensitive to and stronger in their reactions to crime problems. The more committed to the neighborhoods they are, the more they care for the community; and the more sensitive they are to crime problem, the more fearful they are. Also, the higher the social solidarity, the more frequent the social interactions among people, the more widely and quickly the fearful crime stories spread. Research has suggested that news paper coverage increases fear (Liska, 1990), because news coverage widely and quickly spreads fearful crime stories. This is consistent with the reasoning here.

I term this effect a "sensitive reaction effect". In today's urban American neighborhoods, solidarity reduces fear, for example, high social support related to commitment to neighborhoods may be able to reduce some fear; but not be able to balance the "sensitive reaction" effects. So paradoxically, when more committed to their neighborhood, people become more fearful.

Great caution has to be taken, however, in viewing these results, because the sample is small and the instruments are not ideal. Further research based on a larger sample and more theoretically reasonable and empirically sound instruments is needed to reach a higher confidence in the results.

# Chapter X. Conclusion and Discussion

## A. The Problems and the Methods

The function of crime is a long standing classic issue in sociology. Durkheim proposes that crime is an important social fact that affects social order and social organization. Different from mainstream modern criminological study, where crime is mostly considered an abnormality of society, Durkheim argues about the normality of crime. Durkheim argues that crime "plays a normal role in social life" (1982, p. 102) and that "crime is necessary" (1982, p. 101). Modern mainstream criminology mostly focuses on criminal events and individuals involved in crime. In contrast, Durkheim examines the functions of crime for society, and his research focuses on society. Durkheim's work suggests that the functions of crime are a theoretically important topic. His work implies a different direction for modern criminology. However, this implication of his work is largely ignored by modern criminological research.

Also, research regarding the Durkheimian thesis of the functions of crime has been very limited and has involved only a few issues. The concerns and foci of the research on the functions of crime have been very loosely organized without systematic direction. The research is isolated from other research areas in criminology. Research on functions of crime can be grouped roughly around four related issues: social solidarity, repressive justice, boundary maintenance, and the stability of punishments. Most studies are historical and field observational ( Erikson, 1966; Scott, 1976; Connor, 1972; Ben-Yehuda, 1980; Dentler and Erikson, 1959). A few of them are theory testing( Lauderdale, 1976; Lauderdale et al. , 1984 ). Despite some criticism, the research generally supports Durkheim's hypothesis that crime is functional in increasing social solidarity.

Summarizing Durkheim's arguments on the functions of crime, I think that he asks two questions about crime: One, what is the role that crime plays in a social system? Two, how does crime play its role?

In answering the first question, he suggests that crime has an important function for maintaining the social order. Durkheim proposes the functionality of crime in increasing social solidarity. In explaining how crime plays its role for increasing social solidarity, Durkheim states: " Crime brings together upright consciences and concentrates them. We have only to notice what happens, particularly in a small town, when some scandal has just been committed. They stop each other on the street, they visit each other, they seek to come together to talk of the event and to wax indignant in common" ( 1933, p. 102).

Considering that crime has other functions or consequences beyond increasing solidarity, I suggest that we should expand the two questions into two similar questions: What are the functions of crime? How does crime play its role in realizing its functions or consequences? This expansion develops the topic. The first question ask us to examine systematically the functions or consequences of crime on every social process and every institution. The second question concerns the explanation of the functions or consequences of crime. It requires us first to find important variables influencing the social processes whereby crime plays its roles; and then to answer questions about the causal relationships among these variables, that is, to propose theories about the functions of crime. Finally, we will also ask: what are the policy implications of the theory? These questions suggest a new research agenda for the field.

In this work I propose a general theoretical model to answer the basic questions. The model suggests four consequences of crime ( among many possible others ). Crime influences the quality of life, socioeconomic resources, pro-government attitudes, and community decline. The theoretical model argues that two variables are important in explaining the consequences of crime: fear and social solidarity. The model proposes a causal structure among crime, fear, social solidarity, and these consequences. The model addresses three theoretical important issues. One, the model explains the central question of the field: how crime, fear, and social solidarity affect consequences. Two, the model addresses a controversy on how crime affects social solidarity. Three, the model addresses a controversy on the causal relationship between fear and solidarity, suggesting a reciprocal relationship between fear and social solidarity( Figure III. 1, theoretical model).

In explaining the first issue on how crime, fear, and social solidarity affect consequences, the theoretical model suggests that fear and social solidarity directly affect social consequences, that crime directly affects fear and social solidarity, and that crime does not directly affect social consequences. Fear and solidarity mediate the effects of crime on social consequences.

The second issue is a controversy between the functions of crime research supporting the Durhkeimian thesis and the fear research. Durkheim argues that crime performs a positive function of increasing social solidarity. Function of crime research suggests that the outrage produced by crime draws people together, increases social interaction, and reminds them of what they have in common, thereby increasing social solidarity. In contrast, the contemporary fear of crime literature generally suggests that rather than drawing people together, crime causes fear, which in turn restricts people's daily behavior, drives people apart, reduces social interaction, and thereby decreases social solidarity. I suggest that violent crime and nonviolent crime have different effects in modern society. Violent crime causes fear, which drives people apart and constrains people's interaction/

activities. It reduces social solidarity. Non-violent crime does not cause fear but stimulates social interaction, thereby increasing social solidarity.

Third, the model addresses a controversy on the causal relationship between fear and solidarity. Some past research reports that fear reduces solidarity by driving people apart. Research also suggests that lack of cohesion increases fear ( Fowler and Mangione, 1982 ). Researchers argue that neighborhood disorganization and lack of social cohesion lead to high levels of fear of crime ( Skogan and Maxfield, 1981; Hunter and Baumer, 1982; Skogan, 1990 ). Therefore, increasing people's commitment to their neighborhood can be an important way of reducing fear. Based on this assumption, many fear reduction programs design ways to increase interactions among individuals and to increase individuals' commitment to the neighborhood, hoping to reduce crime and fear.

Studies test either the effect of fear in reducing solidarity or the effect of solidarity in reducing fear. Most suggest a negative unidirectional relation between fear and social solidarity, but disagree on which is the cause. I propose a reciprocal relation between fear and solidarity. While fear affects solidarity, solidarity also affects fear. The data were collected in Minneapolis and St. Paul by Marlys McPherson, Glenn Silloway, and David Frey in July, 1983 for their project titled "Crime, Fear, and Control in Neighborhood Commercial Center" ( ICPSR 8167 ). The data were collected in two stages. During the first stage, a survey of 93 commercial centers in Minneapolis and St. Paul was conducted. In the second stage of the study, 24 commercial centers were selected from the original sample. A telephone survey of 870 residents and in-person interviews of 213 business persons for each commercial center were conducted for the 24 selected areas.

Measures for the present research are taken from the two files: the resident survey, and the business survey. The individual responses are aggregated for the 24 neighborhoods ( commercial centers ). For each question in the resident and business survey, the mean values of the answers from all the respondents from the same area are calculated and used as the values of that question for the area. Then, the two aggregated files are converged into a single file for the analysis. So the sample size for the present research is 24 cases. Although these data were not collected for the present purpose, most information necessary for this research is a-vailable.

Two issues are particularly important for this research. One is the measurement of the theoretical concepts, and the other is the small sample issue. Present research faces difficulties measuring the major theoretical concepts, such as solidarity and fear. Historically, solidarity has been recognized as an ambiguous concept and criticized for being difficult to measure. Durkheim himself realized this. Reliability and validity problems are raised, especially when regression analysis methods are used. Traditional approaches to these issues can not solve these problems. Structural equation modeling methods have particular strengths in solving these problems; thus they are used as primary methods for the present research.

The other analysis issue is the small sample. The most common and most wildly available estimation technique for structural modeling is Maximum Likelihood ( ML ). It is sensitive to sample size. That is, while asymptotically unbiased, the properties of ML estimates for small sample are not well known. So we are less confident of the estimates when small samples are used. To address this issue, I divide the model testing into two stages to reduce the size of the model for estimations. I first test the measurement model, and then test the structural model. In the first step, I build well fitting measurement models for each of the theoretical concepts, select from all the variables the potentially plausible measures for each theoretical concept, and conduct all possible confirmatory factor analyses to locate the measurement models that are theoretically meaningful and empirically well fitting. Then I use the resulting estimates to construct the composite indexes for each of the theoretical concepts. In the second step, the testing of the structural model, I first test a recursive model ( Figure IV. 1 ) ; then test the nonrecursive model. I decompose the recursive model into four submodels, each having only one consequence( see Figure IV. 1. 1 , IV. 1. 2 , IV. 1. 3 , and IV. 1. 4 ). There are four structural models in total, each model for one social consequence of crime. I test these submodels to estimate only a few parameters at a time, to avoid estimating too many parameters at the same time, and to keep the numbers of estimated parameters at its minimum. To be confident in the estimates, I reestimate the models with different measures of crime and social solidarity to check and confirm the stability of the models, replicating the model tests.

More specifically, I test the following hypotheses. They are grouped into six groups; the first four groups examine effects of crime, fear, and solidarity on consequences.

For satisfaction, the hypotheses are:

I. 1. Crime reduces people's satisfaction with life and doing business in the area.

I. 2. Crime does not directly reduces satisfaction.

I. 3. Fear directly reduces satisfaction.

I. 4. Fear mediates the effect of crime on satisfaction.

I. 5. Social solidarity increases satisfaction with life and doing business in the area.

For business stability, the hypotheses are:

II. 1. Crime reduces business stability in the area.

II. 2. Crime does not directly reduce business stability in the area.

II. 3. Fear directly reduces business stability in the area.

II. 4. Fear mediates the effect of crime on business stability.

II. 5. Social solidarity increases business stability.

For people's favorability rating of the police, hypotheses are:

III. 1. Crime reduces people's favorability rating of the police.

III. 2. Crime does not directly reduce people's favorability rating of the police.

III. 3. Fear directly reduces people's favorability rating of the police.

III. 4. Fear mediates the effect of crime on favorability rating of the police.

III. 5. Social solidarity increases people's favorability rating of the police.

For people's optimism of the community's future, hypotheses are:

IV. 1. Crime reduces people's optimism of the community's future.

IV. 2. Crime does not directly reduce people's optimism of the community's future.

IV. 3. Fear directly reduces people's optimism of the community's future.

IV. 4. Fear mediates the effect of crime on optimism of the community's future.

IV. 5. Social solidarity increases optimism of the community's future.

For crimes influence fear and solidarity, I examine the direct effects of different crimes. I suggest:

V. 1. Violent crime produces fear.

V. 2. Nonviolent crime does not directly affect fear.

V. 3. Violent crime reduces social solidarity.

V. 4. Nonviolent crime increases social solidarity.

For the relationship between fear and solidarity, the hypotheses are:

VI. 1. Fear reduces social solidarity.

VI. 2. Social solidarity reduces fear.

In sum, Durkheim's work implies that an important direction of criminology is to examine the function or consequences of crime for society. However, although modern criminological theory and research draw much from his work, this important implication is largely ignored. Research in functions of crime has been limited to a few issues and has been isolated from mainstream criminology. I suggest the main questions for the field are implied by Durkheim. We should examine systematically the consequences of crime. We should explain how important social variables affect the consequences of crime, and explain the causal relationship among these variables. I propose a theoretical model to explain how fear and social solidarity affect satisfaction, business stability, progovernmental attitudes, and community decline. I address the controversy between the functions of crime research

241

supporting the Durhkeimian thesis and the fear research to examine how crime affects social solidarity. I address the controversy on the causal relationship between fear and solidarity. I suggest a reciprocal relationship between fear and social solidarity.

# B. The Findings: the Reshaping of Ideas

For each of the three issues, the results are mixed. Some of the hypotheses are confirmed, and some are disconfirmed. For the issue of how crime, fear, and solidarity affect consequences of crime, which is the central issue of the work, the situation differs for different consequences. The unexpected results reshape my ideas in several ways.

Most hypotheses for satisfaction model are supported. The results show that total effect of crime is to reduce satisfaction with living and doing business in the area. Crime directly produces fear; fear directly reduces people's satisfaction. Allowing crime to directly affect satisfaction, the effect is insignificant. This confirms the hypothesis that crime does not directly reduce people's satisfaction. Fear mediates the effects of crimes on satisfaction and the mediating effect is significant.

However, the effects of solidarity on satisfaction are consistently insignificant. This reshapes my idea about how solidarity affects consequence. I speculate that modern American society is very much an individualistic society, and in such a type of society, satisfaction mostly comes from success in individual life and individual feelings of the life. Collective characteristics like social solidarity, therefore, may not affect personal satisfaction. I expect significant effects of solidarity on satisfaction from societies that emphasize collectivism.

For the business stability model, the same is true as in the satisfaction model. The results confirm some hypotheses, but some others are unexpected and interesting. The results, as expected, show that the total effect of crime is to reduce business stability. The results show that crime directly produces fear, and fear reduces business stability. Fear mediates the effect of crime on business stability; the mediating effect is significant. These findings are consistent with the hypotheses. However, when examining the direct effects of crime on business stability, violent personal crime and general crime show a different pattern than property crimes. In general, violent personal crime and general crime do not directly affect business stability, but surprisingly, commercial burglary and shoplifting directly increase business stability. The result shows that in addition to the mediating effect of fear through which property crime affects business stability, property crime, such as burglary and shoplifting, also directly affects business stability.

This unexpected finding reshapes my understanding of the effects of crime on business stability. It suggests that the causal relationship has to do with the characteristics of crimes. Property crimes are committed mostly for profit. Violent crime and general crime drives business out of area, while property crimes do not. Businesses concentrate properties and this maximizes the opportunities for criminals to realize their purpose.

I speculate that the causal direction between the property crime and business stability is opposite to what I have hypothesized. The major purpose of businesses is to profit. The more profit in an area, the higher the businesses stability. The more stable, the businesses in an area, the more property crimes, because they offer more opportunity for property crime to profit. Criminals get familiar with surrounding situations of stable businesses easier than with unstable businesses, so business stability increases property crimes. Opportunity theory (Cohen and Felson, 1979) suggests that suitable targets are one of the three components for the opportunity for crime.

I hypothesize that solidarity increase business stability. However, the results show that the effects of solidarity on business stability vary with different types of solidarity. While the effects of residents' commitment ( SOL1 ) and sense of responsibility(SOL2) for the neighborhood on business stability are insignificant, the effect of business people's responsibility for the shopping area (SOL3) on business stability is significant. These results indicate that residents' solidarity (SOL1 and SOL2) and business people's solidarity (SOL3) are very different in their effects on business stability. Business people's solidarity does increase business solidarity as theoretically hypothesized; I assume that dominant part of the solidarity is organic; reflecting the shared interests of business people. The effects of residents' solidarity on businesses stability are not significant. This indicates the activities of residents and businesses belong to different domains.

For the favorability rating of the police model, the results are more mixed. Consistent with expectation, the total effect of crime is to reduce the favorability rating of the police. In general, crime directly produces fear; fear directly reduces the favorability rating of the police; fear mediates the effects of crime on favorability ratings of the police; and the mediating effects are statistically significant.

Concerning the direct effect of crime on the favorability rating of the police, results show that general crime level and commercial burglary do not directly affect the favorability rating of the police; the direct effects are statistically insignificant. These are consistent with the hypotheses. However, contrary to the hypotheses, shoplifting seems to directly increase the favorability rating of the police; so does violent crime. This is unexpected and reshapes my understanding of the causal processes.

Perhaps the responses of the police to the report of shoplifting satisfy people; this in turn increases the favorability ratings of the police. UCR consistently reports high clearance rates on theft, this perhaps supports my speculation. For example, in 1991, the theft clearance rate is 21%; in cities, it is 25%. They are higher than the overall property crime clearance rate of 18%, and much higher than the burglary clearance rate 13% (Uniform Crime Report, FBI, 1991). In comparison, burglary perhaps is harder to handle than shoplifting, and less imminent in terms of the priority of policing. This perhaps is why business burglary does not have positive direct effects on the favorability rating of the police. By the same reason, police usually give violent crime priority to handle. In 1991, for example, the homicide clearance rate is 67% (Uniform Crime Report, FBI, 1991). This perhaps is why violent crime also leads to increases of the police ratings.

I hypothesize that solidarity directly increase the favorability rating of the police. Results are mixed for this hypothesis. The effects of social solidarity on the favorability rating of the police vary depending on the types of solidarity. Residents' commitment to the neighborhood (SOL1) significantly increases the favorability rating of the police. Residents' sense of responsibility for the neighborhood (SOL2), and business people's sense of responsibility for the shopping area (SOL3), does not significantly affect the favorability rating of the police. There seems to be a difference between commitment and sense of responsibility in their effects on the favorability rating of the police. Residents' commitment may affect the favorability rating of the police as theoretically hypothesized because it increases cooperation and interaction with the police, and an understanding of the police. The sense of responsibility (SOL2, SOL3) differs from commitment; it reflects the sense of control by people over their neighborhood and the business in the area. It perhaps reflects a type of control independent of police activity and relies less on the police activity; therefore it does not significantly affect favorability ratings of the police.

For the optimism of the community's future model, most hypotheses are not confirmed, and the patterns are the least clear. Results show that fear does not significantly reduce the optimism of the community's future, although the signs of the coefficients are correct. Fear does not significantly mediate the effect of crime on the optimism of a community's future; crime does not directly affect people's optimism of the community's future. This perhaps indicates that people's optimism of the community's future is mostly determined by other factors that are not included in the model. For example, government policy for a community can increase the optimism of the community's future. Results also show that residents' commitment to their neighborhood and their sense of responsibility for their neighborhood decrease optimism of a community's future. Perhaps this is because the stronger the commitment and sense of responsibility, the higher the expectation of the community's future, therefore, the less optimistic people are in their assessment of a community's future.

The second issue addressed is whether or not crime increases social solidarity. As expected, violent crime measured by violent personal crime significantly affects fear; nonviolent crime measured as shoplifting does not have a significant effect on fear. Concerning the effects of violent crime and nonviolent crime on solidarity, the results are mixed, and showing some interesting patterns: the effects vary for different types of social solidarity.

The effects of violent crime on SOL1, measured by resident's commitment to the neighborhood, and on SOL2, measured by resident's sense of responsibility, as expected, are negative and significant; however, the effect of violent crime on SOL 3, measured by business people's sense of responsibility is not significant. These results suggest that residents and business people respond to violent crime in a different fashion. Violent crime reduces residents' solidarity, but does not significantly affect business people's solidarity. Perhaps business people will feel responsible for the shopping area because their profits require the responsibility whether or not violent crime occurs.

The effects of nonviolent crime, measured by shoplifting, on solidarity are also mixed, varying with types of solidarity used in the model. Only for SOL3, business people's sense of responsibility, nonviolent crime increases solidarity as expected. It should be recognized that the concept of solidarity here is predominantly organic solidarity in modern society, the shared interests among business people. The hypothesis is derived from Durkheim's idea for traditional society. For resident's solidarity, the results are mixed. For SOL1, residents' commitment to the neighborhoods, the effects are positive, as expected, but not significant. For SOL2, the resident's sense of responsibility, the effects are negative and significant. Why this is the case is hard for me to understand.

The third issue is the causal relationship between fear and solidarity. When estimating the causal relationship from fear to solidarity and solidarity to fear simultaneously, the results indicate a negative effect from fear to solidarity. This is consistent with past research. However, the results also indicate a sizable positive effect of solidarity on fear: the residents' commitment to their neighborhood increases their fear. This is theoretically interesting and has important policy implications.

I speculate that perhaps this is because those who have higher levels of commitment to their neighborhood are more sensitive to crime and stronger in their reactions to crime problem. The more committed to the neighborhoods they are, the more they care for the community; and the more sensitive they are to the crime problem, the more fearful they are. Also, the higher the social solidarity, the more frequent the social interactions among people and thus the more widely and quickly fearful crime stories spread. Research has suggested that newspaper coverage increases fear (Liska, 1990), because news coverage widely and quickly spreads the fearful crime stories. I term this effect a "sensitive reaction effect". In today's urban American neighborhoods, although solidarity may have an effect in reducing fear, it is unable to balance the "sensitive reaction" effects; so paradoxically, when more committed to their neighborhood, people become more fearful.

## C. Policy Implications

The findings for each of the three issues have their policy implications. The three issues are integrated in the general theoretical model around fear. In examining how crime, fear, and solidarity affect the consequences, the findings suggest that fear mediates the effects of crime on the consequences. In general, the results suggest that fear is the key variable in the process by which crimes affect

247

the consequences. This provides the most important policy implication for present work. To control social consequences, we must control fear.

In dealing with the second issue, the Durkheimian issues that crime increases solidarity, the tests suggest that violent crime increases fear. This suggests that violent crime is more salient in causing social consequences. The policy implication is that the controlling violent crime is most important in controlling the social consequences of crime.

The third issue tests the relationship between fear and solidarity, suggesting that paradoxically, increasing social solidarity may increase fear because increases in social interaction may facilitate the spread of fear. Perhaps social interaction among people has two opposite effects; on the one hand, it provides social support which reduces fear, on the other hand, it spreads fearful stories. If the social interaction spreads more fear than it provides social support, then solidarity increases fear. From a policy making point of view, therefore, a fear reduction program cannot accomplish its goal only by increasing social interaction in general. The fear reduction program has to be designed to control the mechanism of social interaction so that it increases social support and reduces the spread of fear. This makes the design of a fear reduction program difficult task; it needs thoughtful efforts and the further knowledge of the conditions that affect the social support and fear spreading processes.

In conclusion, functions of crime are an important area that emphasizes and focuses on society rather than on criminal events and individuals. Different from mainstream criminology, which focuses on criminal events and individuals, I suggest that focusing on society is an important direction for criminology. I develop and test a theoretical model in an attempt to answer the theoretical important questions about what are the functions or consequences of crime, and how crime plays its roles in affecting social consequences. I examine the causal relationship among theoretically important variables and try to solve theoretically important issues regarding how crime affects social solidarity, and causal relationships between fear and social solidarity. Some of the findings support the hypotheses; some reshape the understanding of the causal relationships. The findings suggest important policy implications.

## D. Limitations of Present Work

The present work has several limitations. The data do not include variables that probably affect both social consequences and causal variables included in the model and therefore should be controlled in assessing the effect of model variables on social consequences.

For business stability model, government's performance probably affects both business stability and social solidarity. If local governments are capable of developing an area, business may be more stable and people may be more confident and more committed to the area. Therefore, when assessing the effect of solidarity on business stability, government performance should be controlled.

For the favorability rating of the police model, police resources affect police performance and therefore their favorability rating and crime. It is reasonable to assume that more resources the police have, the lower the crime, and higher the favorability rating. When assessing the direct effect of crime on the favorability rating of the police, the police resources should be controlled.

For the optimism of a community's future model, the effects of governmental development programs should be considered. If there are effective governmental programs supporting an area's development and growth, people probably would hold an optimistic view for the community's future, and they probably would care more about the community, leading to higher social solidarity. So governmental programs should be controlled to assess the effects of solidarity on people's optimism of a community's future.

Also, the data do not allow us to examine possible reciprocal relationships from consequences to crime because of the lack of appropriate instruments. I hypothesize that social solidarity improves satisfaction with living and doing business in an area, but it is also possible that satisfaction improves social solidarity as well. Satisfaction may strengthen people's commitment to the community. The theoretical model hypothesizes that fear affects the favorability rating of the police. It is possible that the favorability rating of the police also affects fear. The favorability rating of the police reflects confidence in the capability the police in capturing and punishing the criminals. This confidence would give people a feeling that things are under control, therefore, feeling less fearful.

Another limitation is that the sample size is small. With the small sample, the results have to be viewed with caution. It is preferable to replicate the tests with a larger sample.

In sum, I suggest that the data does not include some variables that should be controlled because they affect social consequences and other variables in the model. I also suggest that the data does not include instrumental variables for testing possible reciprocal effects. Even if the data would have these variables, the small sample size would limit our ability to perform desirable tests. Thus, the results should be viewed with great caution. These limitations call for future research.

# E. Future Research

The previous section discussed many limitations of this study, pointing out that future research should overcome these limitations. As far as this study is concerned, future work should first of all collect a larger sample to retest the theoretical model. We would want to collect larger sample of societies, such as neighborhoods, communities, cities, nations. As important as to collecting a larger sample, future study should include the variables that are not included in the data set, as suggested in the previous section.

Ideally, a longitudinal design should be considered to further develop the theoretical model. We should collect data at several time points if possible, for example, collect data every six month for a few years. With data at several time points, we can test not only the hypotheses proposed in the theoretical model, but also test new hypotheses concerning how the causal relationships operate in the process. Perhaps the effect of crime on different consequences takes different time lengths to realize; perhaps the different crimes take different lengths of time to realize their effects on same consequences; perhaps the same crime has different effects on the same consequence during different time period. For example, violent crime may have a little effect on business stability until the violent crime rates are consistently high. These hypotheses are theoretically interesting and important in terms of improving our understanding of the social process by which crime affects the consequences studied in this work.

However, the most important task for future research is to go beyond this work to develop research on the functions of crime and develop a new direction of criminology. We should examine a broader range of consequences of crime in much more depth and detail. I argue that Durkheim's work implies that society is an important logical starting point and should be an important focus for criminology. This implication of his work is largely ignored by modern criminological research. We should develop a new focus in criminology on what are the functions or consequences of crime for social processes and social institutions, and how crime affects these social consequences and social institutions.

In a new research agenda, we should examine what social processes and institutions are affected by crimes, and in what way they are affected. To stimulate the thinking on the functions or consequences of crime, I would like to propose some more possible consequences of crime for society, and to suggest new research topics or general directions.

I suggest that crime affects the social economy. There are at least several ways this would happen. The investment behavior of industrial and business institutions has important impacts on the economy of communities. The behavior of financial institutions, such as banks and loan institutions, consider the effect of crime on

251

property values. Housing values, for example, are clearly affected by crime. Insurance companies consider crime when making policies because of the possibility of lost of life and property.

Crime affects population distributions. Research suggests that crime plays a role in the suburbanization of the metropolis(Skogan and Maxfield,1981). This has important consequences for many social processes and institutions. A change in the population distribution can have many repercussions. It can contribute to the concentration of the poor in the central city, and to racial residential and school segregation, because it affects the migration of different social groups with different resources, and this affects the distribution of different population groups in different areas.

Crime also affects the behavior of governmental agencies. For example, urban planning agencies probably consider the fact that building a park in an area may draw crimes and disorder to the area. Most city governments facing problems in rebuilding declining urban neighborhoods; thus they have to respond to crime. Crime probably affects the organization of justice systems such as police organization. These systems probably change their forms and behavior in response to crime in different time and across places.

crime has consequences for social norms, customers, and people's life style. People living in high crime areas probably are more afraid of helping strangers because they have to be more cautious. People who often hear of gang crime stories probably are less tolerant of some behavior, such as juvenile's drinking and noise, considering these as cues of disorder and crime. Crime affects people's leisure activity because parks often become dangerous places. Routine activity theory suggests that the changes in life style contribute to the increasing crime rate; but crime contributes to the life style of people as well. In inner city areas with high crime, people avoid going out in the night, and people living in suburbs may be afraid of going into cities in the night to use the entertainment facilities.

We know little about whether crime indeed has these suggested consequences, and if so, we know little on how these consequences occur. Many more questions can be asked regarding the functions or consequences of crime to suggest possible areas of research, even though I can not formulate the ideas and the answers. For example, crime should have consequences for neighborhood organizations. In high crime neighborhoods, dealing with crime often becomes the major task of neighborhood organizations. Crime should have consequences for families. To the least, many crimes occur within family, and they affect them. We know little about how families are affected by crime outside families and within families. Does crime contribute to the change in family structure in society? We know little about whether educational institutions are affected by crime, and in what way. Does the change in juvenile crime lead to some changes in schools? If so, what are the implications of these effects?

In sum, once we turn to this new direction of criminology, we will find that many possible functions or consequences of crime should be examined, and that many questions should be asked and answered. Research on functions of crime faces great challenges and a promising future.

# References

Alwin, Duane F. and Robert M. Hauser ( 1981 ). *The Decomposition of Effects in Path Analysis* in Linear Models in Social Research, edited by Peter v. Marsden Sage Publications Beverly Hills, London.

Balkin, Steven ( 1979 ). *Victimization Rates, Safety and Fear of Crime.* Social-Problems, 26, 3, Feb, 343 − 358.

Baumer, Terry L( 1985 ). *Testing a general model of fear of crime.* Journal of Research on Crime and Delinquency, 22, 239 − 56.

Ben-Yehuda, N ( 1980 ). *The European witch Craze of the 14th to 17th Centuries: A Sociologist's Perspective.* American Journal of Sociology, 86, 1 − 31.

Bentler, Peter M( 1989 ). *EQS: Structural Equations Program Manual.* BMDP Statistical Software, Inc. Los Angeles.

Biderman, A. D. , L. A. Johnson, J. McIntyre, and A. W. Weir( 1967 ). Report on a pilot Study in the District of Columbia on victimization and Attitudes toward Law Enforcement, Field Surveys I. Washington, DC: Government printing Office.

Blumstein, Alfred and Jacqueline Cohen ( 1973 ). *A theory of the stability of punishment.* Journal of criminal Law and criminology, 64, 198 − 207.

Blumstein, Alfred and Soumyo Moitra( 1979 ). *An analysis of the time series of theunited States.* Journal of Criminal Law and Criminology, 70, 376 − 90.

Blumstein, Alfred, Jacqueline Cohen, and Daniel Nagin (1977). *The dynamics of a homeostatic punishment process.* Journal of Criminal Law and Criminology, 67, 317 – 34.

Bollen, Kenneth A. (1989). *Structural Equations with Latent Variables.* Wiley-Interscience Publication, John wiley & Sons, New York.

Boorman, Scott A. and Harrison C. White (1976). *Social structure from multiple networks II: role structure.* American Journal of Sociology, 81, 1384 – 1446.

Bursik, Robert J., Jr. (1986). *Ecological stability and the Dynamics of Delinquency, pp. 35 – 66. In Albert J. Reiss, Jr., and Michael Tony, eds.* Communities and Crime, Chicago: University of Chicago Press.

Cahalan, Margaret (1979). *Trends in incarceration in the United States since 1880.* Crime and Delinquency, 25, 9 – 14.

Clarke, Alan and Margaret J. Lewis (1982). *Fear of Crime Among the Elderly: An Exploratory Study.* British Journal of criminology, 22, 49 – 62.

Cloward, Richard and Lloyd Ohlin (1960). *Delinquency and Opportunity,* Free Press, New York.

Cohen, Albert (1955). *Delinquent Boys,* Free Press, New York Cohen. Albert and James Short (1958). *Research on Delinquent Subcultures.* Journal of Social Issues, 14, 20.

Cohn, E. S. Lo Kidder, and J. Harvey (1978). *Crime prevention vs. victimization: the psychology of two different reactions.* Victimology 3, 3 – 4: 285 – 296.

Conklin, John E. (1975). *The Impact of Crime.* New York: MacMillan.

Connor, W. D. (1972). *The Manufacture of Deviance: The Case of the Soviet Purge,* 1936 – 1938. American sociological Review, 37, 403 – 13.

Crutchfield, Robert D., Geerken, Michael R. and Gove, Walter R. (1982). *Crime Rate and Social Integration: The Impact of Metropolitan Mobility,* Criminology 20, Nov, 467 – 478.

Dannefer and Schutt (1987). *Race and juvenile justice processing in court and police agencies.* Crime and Delinquency,33,224 - 58.

Dentler,R. A. and Kai T. Erikson ( 1959 ). *The Functions of Deviance in Groups.* Social Problems,7,98 - 107.

Donnelly,Patrick G. ( 1989 ). *Individual and Neighborhood Influences on Fear of Crime.* Sociological Focus,22,Feb,69 - 85.

Droettboom,T. , McAllister,R. J. , Kaiser,E. J. , and Butler,E. W. ( 1971 ) . *Urban violence and residential mobility.* Journal of the American Institute of Planners,37,319 - 25.

Droettboom,T. , R. J. Mcallister,E. J. Kaiser,and E. W. Butler( 1971 ). *Urban violence and residential mobility.* J. of the Amer. Institute of Planners,37,319 - 325.

Dubow,F. ( 1979 ). *Reactions to Crime*: *A critical Review of the Literature.* Washington,DC: Government Printing Office.

Duncan,G. ,and Newman,S. ( 1976 ). *Expected and actual residential moves.* Journal of the American Institute of Planners,42,174 - 86.

Durkheim,Emile( 1982 ). *The Rules of Sociological Method*,*and selected texts on sociology and its method*, Edited with an Introduction by Steven Lukes, Translated by W. D. Halls,Macmillan Press Ltd.

Durkheim,Emile( 1984 ). *The Division of Labor in Society*,with an introduction by Lewis Coser,Translated by W. D. Halls,Macmillan Publishers Ltd.

Erikson,Kai T. ( 1966 ). *Wayward Puritans*:*A Study in the Sociology of Deviance.* John Wiley & Sons,Inc.

Federal Bureau of Investigation( 1991 ). *Crime in the United States*: *Uniform crime Report.* Washington,D. C: U. S. Government Printing Office.

Ferraro,Kenneth and LaGrange Randy ( 1987 ). *The measurement of fear of crime.* Sociological Inquiry,57,1:70 - 101.

Fisher,Joseph. E. and Robert L. Mason( 1981 ). *The analysis of multicollinear data in criminology.* pp. 99 - 125,in Methods in Quantitative Criminology,edited by Janes A. Fox,New York Academic Press.

Frey,W. H. ( 1979 ). *Central city white flight*: *racial and non-racial causes.* American sociological Review, 44, 425 – 448.

Frey, W. H. ( 1980 ). *Black in-migration of metropolitan whites and blacks and the structure of demographic change in large central cities.* American Sociological Review, 49, 803 – 27.

Friedmann, Robert R. and Sherer, Moshe ( 1984 ). *Community Reaction to Crime.* Crime and Social Deviance, 12, 87 – 93.

Furstenberg, F. F. Jr. ( 1971 ). *Public Reaction to crime in the Streets.* The American Scholar, 40, autumn, 601 – 610.

Garofalo, James ( 1979 ) *victimization and the fear of crime.* Journal of Research in crime and Delinquency, 16, 80 – 97.

Gibbons, Don C. and Jones, Joseph F. ( 1975 ). *The Study of Deviance.* Englewood Cliffs, N. J. : Prentice Hall.

Gordon, M. T. , S. Riger, R. K. LeBailly, and L. Heath ( 1980 ). *Crime women, and the quality of urban life.* Signs 5 ( spring ), 144 – 160.

Gordon, Margaret T. and Linda Heath ( 1981 ). *The news business, crime, and fear.* In Reactions to Crime, ed. Dan A. Lewis. Beverly Hills, Calif. : Sage.

Gove, Walter R. , Michael Hughes, and Michael Geerken ( 1985 ). *Are Uniform Crime reports a Valid Indicator of the Index Crime? An Affirmative Answer with Minor Qualifications.* Criminology, 23, 451 – 501.

Hanushek, Eric and John E. Jackson ( 1971 ). *statistical Methods for Social Scientists,* Academic Press.

Harrison, White, Scott Boorman and Ronald Breiger ( 1976 ). *Social structure from multiple networks I. : block models of roles and positions.* American Journal of sociology, 81, 730 – 80.

Hartnagel, Timothy F. ( 1979 ). *The perception and fear of crime: implications for neighborhood cohesion, social activity and community affect.* Social Forces, 58, 176 – 93.

Heitgerd, Janet L. and Bursik, Robert J. ( 1987 ). *Extracommunity Dynamics and the Ecology of Delinquency.* American Journal of Sociology, 92, 775 – 87.

Hindelang, M. J. ( 1978 ). *Race and involvement in crimes.* American sociological Review, 43, 93 – 109.

Hope, T. and Hough, M. ( 1988 ). *Area, crime, and incivility: a profile from the British Crime Survey.* In Hope, T. and Shaw, M. ( Eds. ), Communities and Crime Reduction. London: Her Majesty's stationery Office, 30 – 47.

Hough, M. and P. Mayhew ( 1985 ). *Taking Account of Crime: Key Findings* From the British Crime Survey. London: HMSO.

Hourihan, Kevin ( 1987 ). *Local community Involvement and Participating in Neighborhood Watch: A Case study inCork, Ireland.* Urban studies, 24, Apr, 129 – 136.

Joreskog, Karl G. and Dag Sorbom ( 1989 ). *LISREL 7: A Guide to the Program and Applications* 2nd Edition, SPSS Inc.

Kail, Barbara Lynn and Kleinman, Paula Holzman ( 1985 ). *Fear, Crime, community organization, and Limitations on Daily Routines.* Urban Affairs Quarterly, March, 400 – 408.

Kasl, S. V. and Harburg, E. W. ( 1972 ). *Perceptions of the neighborhood and the desire to move out.* Journal of the American Institute of Planners, 38, 318 – 24.

Kasl, S. V. and E. Harburg ( 1972 ). *Perceptions of the neighborhood and the desire to move out.* J. of the Amer. Institute of Planners, 38, 318 – 324.

Kennedy, Leslie W. and Robert A. Silverman ( 1985 ). *Significant others and fear of crime among the elderly.* Journal of Aging and Human Development, 20, 241 – 56.

Kidd R. F. and Chayet, A. F. ( 1984 ). *Why do victims fail to report: the psychology of criminal victimization.* Journal of Social Issues, 40, 39 – 50.

Kornhauser, Ruth ( 1978 ). *Social Sources of Delinquency.* Chicago: University of Chicago Press.

Krohn, Marvin D. ( 1986 ). *The web of conformity: a network approach to the explanation of delinquent behavior.* Social Problems, 33, 581 – 93.

Krohn, Marvin D. ( 1991 ). *Delinquent Behavior.* 5th edition. Englewood Cliffs, N. J. : Prentice Hall.

Lauderdale, P. , J. Parker, P. Smith-Cunnien and J. Inverarity ( 1984 ). *External*

*Threat and the Definition of Deviance.* Journal of Personality and social Psychology, 46,1058 – 68.

Lauderdale, Pat ( 1976 ) . *Deviance and Moral Boundaries.* American Sociological Review,41,660 – 676.

Laumann,Edward O. ( 1973 ). *Bonds of Pluralism.* New York: Wiley.

Lavrakas,P. J. ( 1981 ). *On households. In Lewis*, D. A. ( Ed. ) , *Reactions to Crime*,Newbury Park,CA:Sage Publications,67 – 68.

Lawton,M. P. , L. Nahemow, S. Yaffe, and S. Feldman ( 1976 ). *Psychological aspects of crime and fear of crime.* in J. Goldsmith and S. Goldsmith ( eds. ) crime and the Elderly. Lexington,MA: D. C. Heath.

LeJeune,R. and N. Alex. ( 1973 ). *On being mugged: the event and its aftermath.* Urban Life and culture 2 ( October ) ,259 – 287.

Lewis,D. A. ( 1979 ). *Design problems in public policy development: the case of the community anti-crime program.* Criminology,17,172 – 183.

Lewis,Dan A. and Maxfield,Michael G. ( 1980 ). *Fear in the neighborhoods: An Investigation of the Impact of crime.* Journal of Research in crime and Delinquency,July,160 – 189.

Liska, Allen E. ( 1987 ). *Perspectives on Deviance* 2nd edition. Englewood Cliffs,N. J. : Prentice Hall.

Liska, Allen E. and Warner, Barbara ( 1991 ). *Functions of crime: A paradoxical process.* American Journal of Sociology,96,1441 – 63.

Liska,Allen E. and William Baccaglini ( 1990 ). *Feeling safe by comparison: crime in the newspapers.* Social Problems,37,360 – 74.

Liska,Allen E. ,Andrew Sanchirico,and Mark D. Reed ( 1988 ). *Fear of Crime and Constraining Behavior: Specifying and Estimating a Reciprocal Effects Model.* Social Forces,66.

Liska,Allen E. ,Joseph J. Lawrence and Andrew Sanchirico ( 1982 ). *Fear of Crime as a Social Fact.* Social Forces,60,760 – 71.

Liska,Allen E. ,Joseph J. Lawrence, and Andrew Sanchirico ( 1982 ). *Fear of crime as a social fact.* Social Forces,60,760 – 71.

Lizotte,Alan J. and David Bordua ( 1980 ). *Firearms ownership for sport and protection: two divergent models.* American Sociological review,45,229 – 44.

Lotz,Roy E. ( 1979 ) . *Public Anxiety about Crime.* Pacific Sociological Review,Apr,241 – 254.

Marshall,H. ( 1979 ). *White movement to the suburbs.* American Sociological Review,44,975 – 994.

Matza,David ( 1969 ). *Becoming Deviant*, Dnglewood Cliffs, N. J. : Prentice-Hall.

Meithe,Teranc D. and Gary R. Lee( 1984 ). *Fear of crime among older people: a reassessment of the predictive power of crime-related factors.* The sociological Quarterly,25, 397 – 415.

Merton,Robert ( 1938 ). *Social structure and Anomie.* American Sociological Review,3,672 – 82.

Miethe,Terance D. and Gary R. Lee. ( 1984 ). *Fear of crime among older people: a reassessment of the predicative power of crime-related factors.* The Sociological Quarterly,25,397 – 415.

Miller,Walter ( 1958 ). *Lower-Class Culture as a Generating Milieu of Gang Delinquency.* Journal of Social Issues,14,5 – 19.

Musheno, Michael C. ; Levine, James P. ; Palumbo, Denis J. ( 1978 ). *Television surveillance and Crime Prevention: Evaluating an Attempt to Create Defensible Space in Public Housing.* Social Science Quarterly, 58, 4, Mar, 647 – 656.

Quinney,Richard( 1977 ). *Class,State,and Crime.* Longman.

Rauma,D. ( 1981a ). *Crime and punishment reconsidered: Some comment on Blumstein's stability of punishment hypothesis.* J. Crim. Law Criminol,72,1772 – 98.

Rauma,D. ( 1981b ). *A concluding note on the stability of punishment: Reply to Blumstein,Cohen,Moitra,and Nagin.* J. Crim. Law Criminol,72,1809 – 12.

Rifai,M. A. ( 1976 ). *Older Americans crime Prevention Research Project.*

Portland, OR: Multnomah County Division of Public safety.

Sampson, Robert J. and W. Byron Groves ( 1989 ). *Community Structure and crime: Testing Social-Disorganization Theory.* American Journal of Sociology, 94, 774 – 802.

Sampson, Robert J. and Wooldredge, John ( 1986 ). *Evidence that High Crime Rates Encourage Migration Away from Central cities.* Sociology and Social Research, July, 310 – 314.

Scott, R. A. ( 1976 ). *Deviance, Sanctions and Integration in Small Scale Societies.* Social Forces, 54, 604 – 20.

Shaw, Clifford and Henry Mckay ( 1931 ). *Social Factors in Juvenile delinquency. Vol. 2 of Report of the Causes of Crime. National commission of Law Observance and Enforcement.* Washington, D. C. : Government Printing Office.

Shaw, Clifford and Henry Mckay ( 1942 ). *Juvenile Delinquency and Urban Areas.* Chicago: University of Chicago Press.

Shaw, Clifford and Henry Mckay ( 1969 ). *Juvenile Delinquency and Urban Areas,* rev. ed. Chicago: University of Chicago Press.

Shotland, R. L., and Goodstein, L. I. ( 1984 ). *The role of bystanders in crime control.* Journal of Social Issues, 40, 9 – 26.

Skogan, Wesley G. and Michael G. Maxfield ( 1981 ). *Coping with Crime, Individual and Neighborhood Reactions.* Beverly Hills, Sage.

Smith, Susan J. ( 1987 ). *Fear of Crime: Beyond a geography of deviance.* Progress-in Human Geography, 11, Mar, 1 – 23.

Smith, Susan J. ( 1989 ). *Social relations, neighborhood structure, and the fear of crime in Britain"* In Herbert, D. J Evans and D. T. Herbert( Eds. ). The Geography of Crime. London: Routledge.

Stark, R. ( 1987 ). *Deviant place: a theory of the ecology of crime.* Criminology, 25, 893 – 910.

Stinchcome, A. , C. Heimer, R. A. Iliff, K. Scheppele, T. W. smith and K. G. Taylor( 1978 ). *Crime and Punishment in Public Opinion: 1948 – 1974.* Chicago:

National Opinion Research Center.

Sutherland, Edwin (1939). *Principles of Criminology*. Philadelphia: J. B. Lippincott.

Sutherland, Edwin and Donald Cressey (1970). *Criminology*, 8th ed. Philadelphia: J. B. Lippincott.

Swigert, victoria L. and Ronald A. Farrell (1976). *Murder, Inequality and the Law: Differential Treatment in the Legal Process*. Lexington, Mass. Heath.

Taylor, Ralph and Margaret Hale (1986). *Testing alternative models of fear and crime*. Journal of criminology and criminal Law, 77, 151 – 89.

Taylor, Ralph B. , Stephen D. Gottfredson, and Sidney Brower (1984). *Black crime and fear: defensible space, local social ties, and territorial functioning*. Journal of Research in crime and Delinquency, 21, 303 – 32.

Thornberry, Terence (1979). *Race, socioeconomic status, and sentencing in the juvenile justice system*. Journal of criminal Law and Criminology, 70, 164 – 71.

Tyler, R. B. (1984). *Block crime and fear: defensible space, local social ties, and territorial functioning*. Journal of Research in crime and Delinquency, 21, 303 – 31.

Waller, Irvin and Janet Chan (1974). *Prison use: a Canadian and international comparison*. Canadian Law Quarterly, 47, 47 – 71.

Warr, Mark and Mark Stafford (1982). *Fear of victimization: a look at proximate causes*. Social Forces, 61, 1033 – 43.

Wilson, J. Q. and Kelling, G. (1982). *Broken windows*. The Atlantic Monthly, March, 29 – 38.

Wolfgang, M. E. (1978). *National Survey of Crime Severity*. Report to the National Information and Statistics Service, Law Enforcement Assistance Administration.

Wolfgang, Marvin and Franco Ferracuti (1967). *The Subculture of Violence*. London: Tavistock.

Yin, Peter (1985). *Victimization and the Aged*. Springfield, Ill. : Charles C. Thomas.

责任编辑:李媛媛
装帧设计:王　舒
版式设计:陈　岩
责任校对:吕　飞

**图书在版编目(CIP)数据**

犯罪功能论/刘建宏 著. -北京:人民出版社,2011.7
ISBN 978－7－01－009696－4

Ⅰ.①犯…　Ⅱ.①刘…　Ⅲ.①犯罪-研究　Ⅳ.①D914.04

中国版本图书馆 CIP 数据核字(2011)第 029417 号

**犯罪功能论**

FANZUI GONGNENG LUN

刘建宏　著

人民出版社 出版发行
(100706　北京朝阳门内大街166号)

北京新魏印刷厂印刷　　新华书店经销

2011 年 7 月第 1 版　2011 年 7 月北京第 1 次印刷
开本:710 毫米×1000 毫米 1/16　印张:17.5
字数:280 千字　印数:0,001-3,000 册

ISBN 978－7－01－009696－4　定价:36.00 元

邮购地址 100706　北京朝阳门内大街 166 号
人民东方图书销售中心　电话 (010)65250042　65289539